DANTE'S PARADISO:
THE FLOWERING OF THE SELF

DANTE'S PARADISO: THE FLOWERING OF THE SELF

An Interpretation of the Anagogical Meaning

by

John Saly

Pace University Press
New York

British Cataloging in Publication Information Available

Library of Congress Cataloging–in–Publication Data

Saly, John.
Dante's Paradiso : the flowering of the self : an interpretation
of the anagogical meaning / by John Saly.
p.   cm.
Bibliography: p.
Includes index.
1. Dante Alighieri, 1265–1321. Paradiso. 2. Mysticism in
literature. 3. Self in literature. I. Title.
PQ4444.S24   1988   88–22499 CIP
851'.1– –dc19
ISBN 0–944473–00–8 (alk. paper)

to my wife

Contents

CONTENTS

Acknowledgments

I am grateful to Professor Sherman Raskin of the English Department of Pace University for his constant encouragement and support and Dr. Mark Hussey for his help with the editing of the manuscript. I am also indebted to all my colleagues with whom I discussed the *Comedy* and other works of Dante over the years.

I thank J. M. Dent and Sons/Weidenfeld and Nicolson for permission to quote from the English translation of the *Comedy* and other works of Dante published in the Temple Classics edition, and the Oxford University Press for the use of Paget Toynbee's translation of Dante's letter to Can Grande. I also wish to thank Marjorie Reeves, The Society for Promoting Christian Knowledge, and Harper & Row for permission to quote from *Joachim of Fiore and the Prophetic Future*.

I thank my wife Judith for the devotion with which she prepared the MS for publication and participated in every phase of its long evolution.

Finally, I want to remember Eva Pierrakos who with her inspiration opened my eyes to many fascinating glimpses of the "*dottrina sotto il velame degli versi strani.*"

Textual Note

The interpretation that follows can best be appreciated with a copy of the *Paradiso* in hand. The reader who may need help with the Italian text is advised to use a bilingual edition with a strictly literal prose translation. I have at times used the Temple Classics' translation to formulate my own, but I find the archaizing diction not easily accessible for the contemporary reader. For a more modern version I recommend John D. Sinclair's prose translation, published by Oxford University Press, New York, or Charles Singleton's prose version, published by Princeton University Press in the Bollingen Series.

The Italian text I have used throughout is of the Temple Classics Edition. I have italicized some lines for the sake of emphasis. My choice is perhaps in need of an explanation.

The beginnings of this interpretation of the *Paradiso* go back many years. As a young man, I discovered Dante by reading T. S. Eliot's essay on him. I immediately bought the three volumes of the Temple Classics edition of the *Comedy* and followed the Italian text with the help of the literal English translation. For many years I carried one of the little volumes in my pocket and became very attached to them, making marginal notes on their pages. They became my companions and guides. They were still a source of inspiration later, when my ideas for this book began to take shape. I hope this will explain why, after much hesitation, I decided to stay with the Temple Classics text, which was so much a part of the development of my thoughts, rather than using Petrocchi's more recent critical edition.

Introduction:
The Anagogical Meaning

In presenting an interpretation of Dante's *Paradiso* I have chosen to focus on the third allegorical level, which the theologians interpreting Scripture call spiritual or mystical. Dante calls it the anagogical sense or meaning. The reason I have attempted to explicate this level of the allegory is that I believe no other level of Dante's polysemous structure of meanings is as accessible to the modern reader as the anagogy. It is least affected by the changes of relative values, beliefs, and conditions that have taken us so far from Dante's time, the late Middle Ages. The mystical or spiritual life, however, has not changed that much. When considering it, we are dealing with the great constants of human nature and the human soul. The enduring states of the spirit, whether they are awareness or confusion, understanding or knowing, purgation or illumination, joy, union, or the dark nights of the soul are the same today as they were in Dante's time. So are the laws of spiritual progress, which, working by causes and effects, produce ascent and descent, pain and pleasure, hope and despair, insight and blindness, fulfillment and deprivation. My endeavor here is to define more closely what allegory, and specifically anagogy as a type of allegory, is. I am not proposing a definitive and circumscribed interpretation as the only right one. The fourth level or anagogy is by its nature the most general, but paradoxically also the most personal, because its generalities have to be concretely understood by each reader. Only when this personal meaning is applied to the reader's own consciousness can the lesson

1

Dante intended to convey become a bridge across the historical abyss that separates us from him.

I will try to answer two questions about Dante's specific use of the anagogy in the *Comedy*. First, how it was shaped by Dante's experience; second, how it was shaped by the influence on him of other people's ideas. Then I will present an interpretation of the anagogy in the *Paradiso*.

The explication of the anagogy canto by canto is paralleled with an analysis of the imagery. I would be disregarding the emotional impact of the poem were I to rely completely on an abstract argument. It is the images that supply the poetic equivalent of the intellectual schema. In the process of spiritual understanding—the level on which the anagogy has to be comprehended—to experience the heat of feeling is indispensable. Without it the clear light of the analytical understanding remains lifeless. Only when the reader's awareness includes both and fuses them into one experience, can the true progression in the unfolding of the soul's potential be understood spiritually for what it is: a transformation of a fragmented consciousness into wholeness, of blocked, stagnant energy into the life-flow, and of weakness into the soul's native power.

In my conclusion I will attempt to summarize the argument for a coherent pattern of development on the anagogical level, both conceptually and in terms of the imagery. After this I will try to connect some of my findings with poets and philosophers who might or might not have had direct influence on Dante. My notes and references often point out affinities between Dante and moderns to give the reader a sense of the persistence of some anagogical themes across the centuries.

To start with the definition: the word *anagogical* comes from the Greek and means that which leads upward. In the simplest way this is what Dante means by the anagogical sense. To see what is meant by "leading upward" we have to understand how the anagogical meaning relates to the other meanings of the poem.

In his letter to his friend and patron, Can Grande, ruler of Verona,[1] Dante explained that his poem, just like the Bible, has three additional meanings beyond the plain literal sense. It is true that the literal story is about "the state of souls after death," for, as he goes on to say, "the whole progress of the work hinges on it and about it." But the literal story is merely a cloak, as Dante says in his *Convivio*,[2] a *bella menzogna*, a beautiful lie which hides the truth; it is the outward garment of the allegorical, the moral, and the anagogical meanings, which together constitute the body of the poem's truth as opposed to the "beautiful lie."

The three allegorical meanings in the *Comedy* reveal to us first the state of human society and the way to the realization of the Kingdom of God on earth, secondly the progress of the individual soul *in this life* from sin to purification and to the life of grace and, finally, a series of inner states through which a human being passes from complete isolation to unity with all that *is*. These three meanings Dante calls in turn allegory proper, which reveals the inner truth of history, meaning the universal significance of certain events, followed by the moral allegory, and the anagogy. In his insistence that the truth of his poem has to be found by the interpretation of his verses on three different levels, Dante follows the general medieval tendency to allegorize, that is, to regard any "outer" event, person, or circumstance as symbolically representing an "inner" or higher truth. Given the medieval focus on the human soul, its relationship to God and to the entire invisible supersensible reality of the spiritual universe, it was inevitable that the entire visible world of nature and human history was interpreted as a storehouse of symbols revealing the invisible world of the soul and the spirit.

The origin of this approach to poetic exegesis is pre-medieval, going back as far as interpretations of Homer by pious commentators in the sixth century B.C. With the coming of Christianity, the allegorizing method became widely used in Scriptural interpretation and also in didactic poetry with a moral purpose, such as Prudentius' *Psychomachia* in the fourth century, depicting the invisible battle between Christian virtues and pagan vices in the human soul.

In the early Christian centuries Scriptural interpretation was developed with great subtlety by theologians, expecially Origen, who combined neoplatonic mysticism with deep Christian faith. He distinguishes a threefold sense of Scripture, a grammatico-historical, a moral, and a pneumatic—Greek for spiritual—which had the highest and most fundamental meaning. Later theologians, like Cassian, further elaborated these distinctions which became commonplace, down to mnemonic devices like this:

> "Littera gesta docet, quid credes allegoria
>   Moralis quod agas, quo tendas anagogia."
> (The literal sense teaches historic deeds,
> allegory what you should believe;
> the moral how you must act,
> and anagogy what you should strive for.)

Explaining his own use of allegory in the letter to Can Grande, Dante calls his work "polysemous, that is to say of more senses than one." In his first exposition of the allegorical method in the *Convivio*, Dante distinguishes two kinds of allegories. One is the allegory of the poets who presented inner truths hidden by the cloak of poetic fables on the literal level, and he calls it the truth that is underneath a beautiful lie. He then refers to the theologians who use allegory differently from the poets as they interpet Scripture to demonstrate articles of faith. In addition to allegory proper, they postulate two other levels, namely the moral and the anagogical, the latter concerned with truths that are above the reach of the senses. The theologians, he says, deal differently with the allegory of the Scriptural text than the poets with the allegory of their fables. But, he says modestly, my intention is to follow the method of the poets, because I take the meaning of the allegory proper according to the usage of the poets.

Many years later, in his letter to Can Grande, Dante no longer distinguishes between the allegory of the poets and the theologians, and makes it clear that his poem has to be read on all four levels, including the levels so far reserved to the theologians, just like the poem of the Holy Spirit, the Bible. Now he does not speak as a mere poet, but as the author of a "poema sacro," a poet and prophet, whose creation is as full of divine truth as the Bible itself. This attitude foreshadows both Luther's claim that any believer can interpret the Bible if he be inspired by the Holy Spirit, and also that of Romantics like Blake and Shelley who consider the sum of all inspired poetry the Bible of the Imagination, a storehouse of eternal truths for those who have "cultivated their understandings."[3]

Throughout the *Comedy* Dante expects the reader to understand all four levels if he or she wants to fully experience his "polysemous" creation. He was unhappy that people were paying attention only to the literal level and often totally ignored the inner truth of the communication which had been his primary purpose. If they could not penetrate the veil of the allegory, how could they gain the liberation that Dante called "the end of the whole and of the part of the work, which is to remove those living in this life from the state of misery and lead them to the state of felicity."[4]

This goal is reached only when all levels are comprehended, including the anagogical. The multilayered structure of the allegory is not just a brilliant rhetorico-poetical device, but, more fundamentally, a deep understanding of the physical, social, ethical, and spiritual reality we live in. Dante stresses explicitly in the *Convivio* that in understanding this reality of levels within levels we must start with the literal sense because we know the physical best and, he says, Aristotle in the first book of his *Physics* advises us to follow the order of nature and progress from what we know better to that which we know less well. We have to comprehend fully what is stated on the literal level, before we can proceed to the three allegorical levels, because they are all indicated by the literal. Nonetheless, when it comes to importance and value, the physical comes last, because it is most remote from the immutable truth of the First Cause. Social and historical reality is the product of higher causes than imagined stories, moral behavior is guided by eternal laws, and spiritual perception belongs to the super-sensible level where the operative causes are of the highest order, symbolized throughout the poem by the stars, *stelle*, the word on which each *Cantica* ends.

The progression of the reader from the literal to the allegorical levels becomes at every step the exploration of this fourfold structure. The four levels of meaning have to be understood as four concentric circles through which the conscious reader of the *Comedy* proceeds in a shuttling movement from the periphery to the central, spiritual, com-prehension and then back again to the physical-literal, the most changeable and contingent reality. From the immutable center the basic spiritual laws spread out through the more contingent and cor-ruptible spheres, like a series of emanations, and the reader gradually is drawn into the marvellous interdependency of Dante's universe created by Justice and Love. The anagogy is at the very center, because, as Dante says in the *Convivio*, that sense reveals to us the highest realities of eternal glory, meaning that the soul, as it leaves sin behind, becomes holy and free and assumes its full power.

As an illustration of how the fourfold structure works let us take, for example, the three animals which confront Dante at the beginning of the poem as he is trying to leave the obscure forest where he had gone astray. A beautiful hillside lies before him invitingly in the morning light, but a leopard first, and then a lion and a wolf drive him back "to where the sun is silent." Now in the literal story these animals are simply what they seem to be, wild beasts, preventing Dante from leaving the wood where he finds himself lost halfway through this mortal life. But in the social-political allegory that teaches the inner truth of history they are emblems of the Florentine city-state, the Kingdom of France, and the worldly power of the Papacy, all of which prevent the unification of Italy and the establishment of a juster social-political order. For Dante this level is the allegory proper.

In the moral allegory they represent the habitual vices of lust, anger, and greed, which stand in the way of the individual Christian's moral improvement and salvation.

Finally, in the anagogical interpretation we see in them permanent states of mind and soul, such as self-will, pride, and fear, which prevent any human being from reaching the lasting happiness that comes from living with the full power generated by leaving all crippling habits, pretenses, false beliefs, sins—or to use a psychological term, neuroses—fully behind.

The goal of the journey, too, can be distinctly stated for each level. On the literal it is union with God by beholding Him directly. On the social-historical it is the perfect community of the just; morally it is the attainment of the supreme good. The goal of the anagogy is the state of Being beyond duality, arrived at by the contemplation of the Source of all being, the One, Who is both Principle and Person, without contradiction.

The anagogical meaning is the most abstract, the most general of all and yet, in its application, it is the most concrete and individual. The anagogical meaning is only "objective" in the sense that it describes truths known to many, and laws that have an existence independent of one's keeping, breaking, or ignoring them. But these truths are known to each of us in individual ways, for abstract knowledge of them is not real knowledge; only by experiencing these truths, by uniting with them, can we have any worthwhile awareness of what they are. Therefore the anagogical interpretation of one reader will always differ from that of another, it will always be "subjective," in the sense of reflecting a personal experience.

Dante, too, experienced these truths personally. It is by way of the transmutation of his own experience that these anagogical verities shine in the poem. They speak and move and exert their sway under the personae of his City, Florence, his Country, Italy, his Teacher, Virgil, his Beloved, Beatrice, and his eternally evolving, forever onward struggling self, Dante.

To see clearly the relationship of the anagogical meaning to the three other levels of the fourfold allegory, one must also look at the relationship between the reader and the poet on each distinct allegorical level. On the literal level of the beautiful lie, Dante is, of course Dante, visiting the three kingdoms of the dead, but on the other levels he fulfills figural roles. On the social-political level he is the Italian in search of the just state of Empire of which he longs to be a citizen. In the moral allegory he is the Christian in search of salvation through purification from sin. In all three roles he teaches the reader how "man as by good or ill deserts, in the exercise of the freedom of his choice becomes liable to rewarding and punishing justice."[5] In the anagogy, however, which is the unitive meaning par excellence, Dante and the reader become one by virtue of their common spiritual nature. Both are pilgrims of eternity, both are fellow-travellers on a journey from the depths to the heights, both are eternal spiritual beings, one in their common essence. Both are involved in an endless growth process, in striving, progressing from mental state to mental state as self-actualizers driven by the "concreata e perpetua sete"—the constant thirst that was created with them—to reach complete fulfillment in union with being. Therefore, on the anagogical level which is the focus of the present interpretation, there is no more Dante or reader, there is only *us*, this common essence.

Because the anagogical meaning is the most general, it is least tied to any historical period or theological doctrine. The political allegory of Dante's poem advocates a certain kind of world government which he calls the empire; the moral allegory is worked out in the religious terms of virtue, sin, and salvation. The modern reader finds both meanings somewhat remote when attempting to experience them feelingly. This is not the case with the anagogical meaning. In fact, the rise of the various schools of individual psychology in the twentieth century has given us a new key to the anagogical meaning. This key is the concept of inner development. There is a school of psychologists which speaks of psychological health as a state of "growth toward self-actualization." I have in mind especially the so-called "growth" or humanistic psychology, represented by people like Maslow, Murphy, Rogers, Allport, Fromm, which aims primarily at the development of the human being's latent potentialities. All immature behavior is, in their view, only a series of steps toward the full realization of all the inherent potentialities of the human being. It is interesting to note that one of them—Abraham Maslow—speaks of psychogogy. "If psychotherapy makes sick people not-sick and removes symptoms, then psychogogy takes up where therapy leaves off and tries to make not-sick people healthy," he says.[6]

The similarity between the words "anagogy" and "psychogogy" is not accidental. Both use the Greek word, *agein*, to lead: *anagogy* in the sense of leading upward, to the vision of God, and *psychogogy* in the sense of leading to full psychological health, to self-actualization, wherein all the creative powers of the psyche are unfolded. Both lead through series of inner states which may be quite similar, if not identical.

People striving for self-actualization must, according to growth-psychologists, go through three broad and overlapping stages of development. First of all they have to understand themselves as they are at present. They need to see all the distortions, misconceptions, neurotic patterns in their psyche, which prevent them from growing toward psychological health. They can achieve the state of self-knowledge first in the sense of knowing their own sickness. Next, they must learn to *use* this self-knowledge to gradually correct those neurotic, distorted patterns of behavior which their inner confusions and misconceptions have given rise to. They must, in brief, accept the consequences of their self-knowledge in actual behavior.

This state we might call coming up to one's own standards of psychic health. Once a person has straightened out the distorted concepts in his or her psyche as well as the neurotic patterns of behavior through self-understanding and conscious living, he or she becomes free to enter the third and last stage, which is the state of self-actualization, self-unfoldment. The first two stages might be accomplished in psychotherapy; the final stage is where "psychogogy" takes over.

Dante's journey through the three kingdoms of the spirit parallels this threefold division. He, too, writes about the human self, and the poem can be legitimately interpreted as an exploration of the inner world, not only Dante's but also of the human psyche in general.

The entire *Paradiso* is therefore an itinerary of positive self-unfoldment. With each stage on the journey toward the inmost divine center, greater and greater powers are liberated. Seen in this context, all the figures Dante meets in the *Paradiso* are but reflections of his own yet unrecognized potentialities, and in coming to know them he increases the knowledge of his own higher self. The subject of the last cantica is the empowering of the soul that has left sin, or neurosis, behind.

Dante's way to unity of the self is essentially the same as the modern person's attempt to reach full psychological health. The state of self-knowledge, the knowledge of the soul's sickness, is common to both. So is the state of freeing oneself from distortions in thought and in action until one is able to realize one's original aspiration to the good life. Finally, going beyond those aspirations, Dante anagogically points to the attainment of perfect selfhood. Here modern psychology is much less sure, but it does extend a directionary signal toward a goal vaguely called greater creativity, self-actualization, becoming authentic, a real person. Yet the direction in both instances is upward to a greater image of the human entity.

The *Paradiso* is the last stage of the journey that leads to supreme self-actualization, where the slumbering powers of the self, which we might justly call its intrinsic divine aspect, are fully unfolded. Dante himself points out that "the beatitude of the eternal life (which is the central theme of the *Paradiso*) consists of the fruition of the divine aspect which man is unable to effect by his own powers unless aided by divine light."[7] I have tried to bring out this aspect of the anagogy on the pages that follow. The last cantica of the *Comedy* is also the most significant for us because it maps the stages of an inward growth of which most of us know very little. The *Inferno* is quite well known— though far from conquered; if the annals of crime and politics proved insufficient, the notebooks of any psychoanalyst would provide excellent illustrations. The *Purgatorio*, too, is known somewhat; many people do learn to adjust themselves to the laws of life, they work on themselves to find self-identity and change some of their negative patterns. Through this they attain a measure of inward freedom. But what about the tremendous potentialities hidden in the human spirit? Great self-actualizers, such as Goethe, have shown us part of the way, but only the future can fully answer the question. Dante, in his own fashion, has answered it already. Here psychology leaves us and Dante leads the way.

From him we can learn of the hidden ecstasies of inward bliss that come from questioning the narrow limits we impose on ourselves, and of the as yet undiscovered joys of human relationships which stand in the light of truth and being. Our true self wants to grow with the expanding states of the spirit through which fearless love is eager to guide us. With Dante we can enter the world of the *Paradiso*, a world of undreamed-of fulfillment.

One more question remains to be answered. What influences shaped Dante's formulation of the anagogical meaning?

If the anagogical meaning is the deepest, most personal, yet at the same time the most generally true for all people, it must be that intimations of it come to us in our most exultant or terrifying experiences when the walls of the self are shaken, the everyday stage-set collapses, and we stare into a new revelation.

To Dante this revelation came at the age of nine: "She appeared to me clothed in most noble hue, a subdued and modest crimson, tinctured and adorned after the fashion that was becoming to her most tender age. At that point I verily declare that the heart began to tremble so mightily that it was horribly apparent in the least of my pulses, and trembling, it said these words: *Ecce Deus fortior me, qui veniens dominabitur mihi.*

"At that moment the animal spirit which dwells in the high chamber to which all the spirits of sense carry their perceptions, began to marvel much, and speaking especially to the spirits of sight said these words: *Apparuit jam beatitudo vestra.*

"At that moment the natural spirit which dwells in that part where our nourishment is distributed began to weep, and weeping said these words: *Heu miser! Quia frequenter impeditus ero deinceps.* From thenceforward I say that Love held lordship over my soul, which was so early bounden unto him and he began to hold over me so much assurance and so much mastery through the power which my imagination gave to him, that it behoved me to do all his pleasure perfectly. He commanded to me many times that I should seek to behold this most youthful angel: wherefore in my childhood often did I go seeking her, and I beheld her of so noble and laudable bearing that assuredly of her might be said those words of the poet Homer: 'She seemed not the daughter of a mortal man but of God.' And although her image that continually abode with me was an exultation of Love to subdue me, it was yet of so perfect a quality that it never allowed me to be overruled by Love without the faithful counsel of reason, whensoever such counsel was useful to be heard."[8]

His overwhelming visionary experience on meeting Beatrice and being overcome by the spirit of Love repeated through the years of adolescence, set Dante's feet on the path toward being. He had come to feel early the indelible impact of the state of being in love so completely, that whenever Beatrice made him feel blessed by granting him her salutation, he came to a more articulate awareness of love's transforming power.

Even though the experience of being saved by her salutation totally overwhelmed him, yet the domination of Love over him was not a tyranny, as Love would never overrule him without the faithful counsel of reason. The state in which Dante became fully receptive to the gift of Beatrice's salutations was the balance of Love's power with reason's counsel. Lover though he was, he never lost sight of the other great need of his soul: understanding. It was not quite enough for him to be in love; he also needed to understand, like the angels of the Heaven of Love whom he addressed in the First Canzone of the *Convivio*:

> You, who with your understanding move the third heaven
> > [i.e., the Heaven of Venus]
> Listen to the reasoning that goes on in my heart,
> I cannot tell it to anyone else, so new it seems to me.

Between his youthful yearning for understanding and its fulfillment, bitter experience had to be gathered from political strife, exile, and endless labor on the sacred poem that had "made him lean" for many years.

But when, on the threshold of the ultimate vision he emerges into the Empyrean Heaven with Beatrice who has become his teacher and guide through paradise, both his need for understanding and his yearning for love is finally gratified. The light that first breaks on the pages of the *Vita Nuova* now engulfs Dante. Beatrice instructs him:

> "Noi semo usciti fuore
> del maggior corpo al ciel, ch' è pura luce;
>
> luce intellettual piena d'amore
> amore di vero ben pien di letizia
> letizia che trascende ogni dolzore."
> > [*Paradiso* XXX. 38–42]

(We have emerged from the greatest heavenly body [i.e., the Primum Mobile] into the heaven of pure light, intellectual light full of love, love of true good overfilled with joy, the joy that transcends every other sweetness.)

In her triumphant affirmation light answers to light, love responds to love, and joy ringing out echoes joy. Here the clarity of understanding and the fervor of love have become one light that is nothing but fullness of understanding and fullness of love, a complete unfolding of the original spark of intuitive knowledge and burning love that sprang up in that childhood meeting on the now so distant earth. This living light reveals what is ultimately real and destroys all falsehoods. It is the anagogical meaning itself that this light reveals, because it renders the Creator and His workings visible to the creature.

Here, having briefly indicated the one decisive experience of Dante's early life, we need to consider another, less concentrated and dramatic, but equally decisive influence. This is the combined Franciscan-Joachimist movement for radical reform of the Roman Church in the thirteenth and fourteenth centuries. In relating some of the origin and history of this influence on Dante, I have to ask the informed reader's patience because the explanation has to be of some length to allow me to fully make my point.

In Dante's time, hardly any prominent person in the Church could remain outside the prolonged and often violent controversy in which the so-called Spiritual Franciscans agitated for a thorough reform of the Church many of them saw as hopelessly corrupt, and the boldest did not hesitate to call the Babylonian Whore. Wasn't Saint Francis, their founder, sent by Christ to restore and renovate the ruined Church and rebuild it on more spiritual foundations? He married the Lady Poverty and practiced true Christian love, but there was great resistance within the Church to his convictions, especially among the hierarchy. In spite of the resistance, the Spirituals of the Franciscan order continued to believe that their order was divinely elected to lead the Church back to its original purity. Their reformist zeal was fed by the genuine writings of Joachim of Fiore, abbot of the small Cistercian monastery of Fiore in Calabria who, about fifty years before, had preached and prophesized the coming of the third *status* under the Holy Spirit, to supersede the previous dispensations of the Father and of the Son—represented by the Old and New Testaments respectively. Under this new *status* an outpouring of the Holy Spirit was supposed to take place to purge the corrupt Church and establish the authority of the Spirituals and visionaries in its rejuvenated body. The ambitions of these utopian idealists were generally honorable. They were harking back to the time of St. Francis when miracles rained from heaven, and the order produced one saint after another. What they did not see, however, was that the irruption of the spirit into the world of time which took place during Francis's lifetime was an extraordinary event impossible to replicate when the charisma of the founder and of his immediate followers had weakened and, after the initial shock, the rest of the Church tended to go back to business as usual.

They had their hour, however, when Peter of Morrone, a saintly hermit, was elected pope in 1294 as Celestine V. With such a spiritual man on St. Peter's throne, the Spiritual faction was sure of taking over the leadership of the Church. How great was their disappointment when Cardinal Gaetani, a shrewd power politician, persuaded Celestine V to take an unheard of step and resign the papal office, allowing Gaetani to become pope himself as Boniface VIII.

Dante sided completely with the Spirituals, and his indignation at Celestine's betrayal of the Spirituals' cause can be clearly heard when, in the third canto of the *Inferno*, he picks him out from the crowd of the trimmers and brands him as "the one who out of cowardice has made the great refusal." Celestine's place in the allegory becomes a very dishonorable one: he is the type of a well-intentioned weakling who has been given authority to carry out reforms, but in the hour of need refuses to undertake the defense of truth. His vacillation allows unscrupulous power brokers to take over and open the floodgates of corruption and the reign of injustice that oppresses God's faithful and rewards His enemies. Such an attitude is justly placed right by the Gate of Hell, since the road to hell is proverbially paved with good but ineffectual intentions.[9]

Boniface, who took the papal crown from Celestine, was Dante's *bête noire*. The poet believed he was tricked and betrayed by the pope when Boniface detained Dante who was on diplomatic mission in Rome just at the time his political foes, the Blacks, staged a coup in Florence and expelled Dante's party, the Whites. He believed that his exile from his native city was in part the consequence of Boniface's machinations. It is enough to read St. Peter's scathing denunciation of Boniface in the twenty-seventh canto of the *Paradiso* to know full well what Dante's feelings were concerning this pope. He calls Boniface in *Inferno* XXVII "lo principe de' novi Farisei," literally translating this epithet from the *"princeps nuovum Phariseorum"* in the pseudo-Joachimite prophecies *Super Hieremiam* and *Super Isaiam*. Boniface was regarded by the Spirituals as their greatest enemy and, by some of the extremists, as the Antichrist himself.

Dante, on his part, became a student of Joachim's ideas probably through his contacts with the Spiritual Franciscans. He received the Joachimist tracts circulated among them, and listened to the lectures of their leaders, John Peter Olivi and his pupil Ubertino da Casale in the Santa Croce Monastery, a stronghold of the Spirituals in Florence. The coming of the third *"status,"* which many conceived of as a cataclysmic revolution in history inevitably separating the good from the wicked, rewarding the former and punishing the latter, seemed imminent to them. Those who remained steadfast in the face of persecution would endure to the end, while a vast outpouring of the Holy Spirit, renewing the Church and all the earth, ushering in an age of peace and harmony, would begin. The various prophecies of Dante throughout the *Comedy*, like the DXV [*Purg.* XXXIII. 37–45] or the Veltro [*Inf.* I. 100–111] have a lot in common with Joachimist expectations.[10] He, too, had his utopian leanings and looked upon the venal clergy with great disapproval. He also cherished St. Francis, whose life he apotheosized as the perfect expression of the way of love to God [*Par.* XI. 39–123], recognizing in him the same central core of love that had awakened within him in his encounter with Beatrice.

Dante's deep interest in the prophecies of Joachim and in the

writings of the Franciscan Spirituals which expound and amplify the
Calabrian abbot's ideas on universal history often goes without full
recognition by his commentators.[11] Yet when one comes to reflect on
the anagogical meaning of the *Comedy*, it is impossible not to pay
attention to this influence, which is basically twofold. The first strain
of the Spiritual-Joachimist influence which we can call the prophetic,
announces retribution to the greedy she-wolf for her depradations—
obviously identified on the social-political level with Boniface's papacy—and anagogically with the world's endless craving for money
and power that makes any just order impossible [*Inf.* I. 91–111].
Another warning related to the corrupt church and her allies occurs in
Purgatorio, XXXIII, 40–45 in the so-called DXV prophecy, uttered by
Beatrice. Finally, at the end of St. Peter's denunciation of Boniface
and his successor popes in the strongest terms in *Paradiso* XXVII,
Beatrice forecasts speedy help to end the desperate situation, which
was to culminate soon in the Avignonian captivity of the Papacy. Dante
here puts on the mantle of the prophet, following the Spirituals who
believe themselves divinely chosen to restore the Church to her original purity.

In Dante's Heaven of the Sun Joachim himself takes his honored
place among the learned doctors of the Church, and is called "endowed
with the prophetic spirit." The images of his prophetic books, especially from the *Liber Figurarum*, reappear in the *Paradiso* as the eagle
in the Heaven of Jupiter and in the most intense final vision of the
triune God represented by three interlocking circles of three different
colors.[12] In the Heaven of the Sun the two circles of saints, theologians
and other spirits of deep knowledge are also related to Joachim's
prophetic ideas. They are figures of the two dispensations, meaning
the Old and New Testaments, also interpreted as the two world-ages of
the Father and the Son. After the voice of Solomon, discoursing on
the resurrection of the body, falls silent, a third circle, larger than the
other two, rises on the brightening horizon. Dante greets it ecstatically
with:

> O vero isfavillar del santo spiro,
> come si fece subito e candente
> agli occhi miei che vinti non soffriro!
> [*Par.* XIV. 76–78]

(O truthful sparkling of the holy breath! How sudden it became bright
incandescence before my eyes which could stand it no more!)

There can be little doubt that Dante here speaks of the impending
revelation of the Third Age, that of the Holy Spirit, which will produce

new spiritual men compared to whose radiance the lights of the two previous ages will pale. A part of the prophetic-apocalyptic strain of the Joachimist influence can be seen in the similarity between Joachim's use of number symbolism in the *Liber Figurarum* and elsewhere and Dante's use of the numbers 1,2,3,7,9 in marking the various divisions in the structure of his *Comedy*. Joachim's favorite numbers were two, three, and seven. Two stood for authority, three for the spirit, seven for periods of world history. Dante's system of divisions in the *Comedy* applies to all three cantiche: it is based on three, subdivided into seven, raised by two unlike additions to nine and by a final number on a totally different plane, to ten.[13] I tend to think that this pattern was also, if not borrowed from Joachim, at least worked out under the influence of his ideas. It is now beginning to be widely recognized that the prophetic-apocalyptic influence of Joachim and the Spiritual Franciscans is more than incidental in the *Comedy*. It is definitely a structural element shaping the very substance of the work and indispensable to its full understanding.

However, there is a second strain of the same influence, which tends to be even more overlooked, though it runs deeper than the first, and sometimes even contradicts it. Between Dante and Joachim there seems to be a personal affinity; both reflect, to a striking degree, a mixture of artistic and intellectual qualities in their works. This perhaps explains how Dante seemed to have seized on Joachim's central concept of the *intellectus spiritualis* as the indispensable requisite to the understanding of the anagogy and its interplay with the other levels of the allegory in the Comedy. Joachim, in a conversation with the Cistercian abbot Adam of Persigny, said that he did not really prophesy, conjecture, or use revelation about the future. Instead, he said, ''God Who in times past endowed the prophets with the spirit of prophecy has given to me the *spiritus intelligentiae*, so that I can understand *clarissime* all the mysteries of the Scriptures.''[14]

Joachim believed that this gift was not unique to him, but a foretaste of the coming Spiritual Intelligence to be poured out to all people before the end of history. He believed that just as he had meditated on the Old and New Testaments and from this exercise received the gift of Spiritual Intelligence, others, too, could do the same if the Holy Spirit endowed them with the spiritual understanding,[15] which did not manifest in prophetic visions and utterances, but in discovering repeating patterns in history. This, he thought, was the key to the destiny of all people. In the history of mankind from the work of God the Father

and of God the Son inevitably must proceed the work of God the Holy
Spirit, enlightening all, not only a select few.

Nothing could have been more welcome to Dante as he was floun-
dering in his long drawn-out spiritual crisis after the death of Beatrice
and the collapse of his political ambitions, leaving him hopeless,
homeless, and broke, than Joachim's acknowledgment of the spiritual
understanding as a gift of prime importance to the comprehension of
human destiny and history. He may have lost everything he ever
valued, but he knew what spiritual understanding was. Before the age
of thirty he had written the greatest spiritual autobiography since
Augustine's *Confessions*, which also, like his own, was the record of a
conversion. He had met his Lord, the spirit of Love, was conquered
by him, but through all the ecstasies and pains of this experience he
came to understand the spiritual meaning of his life. That understanding pointed beyond itself. It was not enough to be Love's servant and
to remain faithful to the memory of Beatrice, living the life of the spirit
on earth with many sighs, until he could rejoin her in blessedness.

While Love was the first leading light of Dante's life, desire for
knowledge through rational inquiry was the other. Love never contra-
dicted the faithful counsel of reason in his heart while Beatrice was
alive, but after her death he devoted himself to what Francis Fergusson
calls his "cult of reason"[16] and to the Lady Philosophy, hoping that
the love of learning would fill the place the death of Beatrice had left
in his heart. But the great philosophic project of the *Convivio* was
abandoned and with it the lady who in the *Convivio* became, from "the
lady in the window," Philosophy herself. Dante's goal was to use his
vast knowledge of metaphysics, science, rhetoric and practical affairs,
the art of government and politics to impart his knowledge to others
and help them order their lives. His motivation is given in the *Convivio*:
"I am moved by the desire to teach a doctrine, *which in very truth no
other can give*."[17]

But his new career as an itinerant scholar and teacher was only
partially successful. At some point in the early years of his exile his
complete devotion to the calm and disciplined life of reason received a
staggering blow from the onslaught of a new and virulent love.[18] He
suffered terribly from the loss of his freedom and self-esteem. Nevertheless, this, too, was a movement of the spirit, albeit not in the same
direction which had led him to Beatrice. Love, to Dante, is always
spiritual in its energy, but without reason it becomes the love that
leads not to life but to death, not to creation but destruction, as
expressed by Francesca's words in *Inferno*, V. 105: "Amor condusse

noi ad una morte." After a long agony one day, as he records in the *Vita Nuova*, a powerful fantasy arose in him. He seemed to see Beatrice wearing the same crimson dress she did when he met her first. He began to think of her again, repenting grievously of that desire for others which his heart allowed itself to entertain. Thus the spiritual life began to be rekindled in him and he became inspired to write the last poem of the *Vita Nuova*:

> Oltre la spera, che più larga gira
> Passa il sospiro ch' esca del mio core:
> Intelligenza nuova, che l'Amore
> Piangendo mette in lui, pur su lo tira.
>
> Quand' egli è giunto là dov' el desira
> Vede una donna, che riceve onore,
> E luce si, che per lo suo splendore
> Lo peregrino spirito la mira.
>
> [*Vita Nuova* XLII, 47–54]

> (Beyond the sphere that has the widest circuit
> Rises the sigh that issues from my heart:
> Love sends with it a new-born understanding
> Which draws it high above.
>
> When he arrives where he desired to be
> He sees a lady who is praised on high,
> And shines so that the pilgrim spirit
> Gazes at her splendor, marvelling.)

Shortly after writing this sonnet, Dante received a "wondrous vision." "It made me decide"—he says in the *Vita Nuova*—"to speak no more of this blessed lady, until I could treat of her more worthily. And to attain to this, I will study all I possibly can, and this she truly knows. So that it be the pleasure of him by whom all things live, that my life persevere for some few years, I hope to write of her what has never been written of any woman."[19]

From this time on, the study he undertook with the purpose to write the "sacred poem to which both heaven and earth have put a hand," became the very center of Dante's life. It was not an obsession but a noble mission, and all his immense ambition was channeled into it. Everything he had learned became a part of it: his dreams of human-kind living at peace under a just emperor, his hope of a renewed and purified Church, his ardent desire to teach his fellow-humans the way to God by first teaching them how to learn to be happy on this earth, which is their birthright.

In the sonnet "Oltre la spera" Dante speaks of a new understanding given by Love that draws his spirit upward to the Empyrean heaven. It is in response to this sigh's message that he is rewarded with the wondrous vision which evidently contained the germ of the *Comedy* and provided the driving force for the colossal labor of its composition.

That *intelligenza nuova* was not only new but also miraculous just as Beatrice was, accompanied by the number of miracles: nine. It was a spiritual, not an earthly creation. It was akin to the *intellectus spiritualis*, Joachim's gift, and may have led Dante in a flash of intuition to grasp the entire upward striving movement of the poem.

The sonnet clearly indicates that the new understanding is drawn upward beyond the physical universe to the ultimate causes in the Source of all being. Love knew full well that only by taking the anagogical route of spiritual understanding can that sigh, or desire, reach Beatrice. Therefore, Love provided it with the capability which love has, to understand the essence of the beloved. Here Dante resolved, at one stroke, the basic duality of his life—love versus knowledge. Both are harmoniously united in the *nuova intelligenza*. Love for Beatrice is the spiritual component, and understanding is the rational part. Dante, as a man in the world, continued to struggle with adversity, humiliation, hostilities, sudden eruptions of passion, but as an artist he was at peace. He had found the balance of his creative forces, which generated maximum energy for his sacred poem.

With this insight he also found the answer to the question of what to do with his life and mission. He wrote in the *Convivio* about his desire to teach such a doctrine "which in very truth no other can give." Perhaps already then he was beginning to find out from his studies of Joachim's books what the *intellectus spiritualis* was, which in the new spiritual age can become the common property of all human beings, if and when they become ready to undertake the threefold journey the *Comedy* maps out for them.

In the *Convivio* Dante referred to "the allegory of the poets" as his only level of allegory, but by the time he wrote the Epistle to Can Grande he came to look at his poem as a text analogous to Scripture, that had to be understood according to the allegory of the theologians in whose text even the literal level had a truth of its own—the truth of historical fact.[20] This fourfold poem would become the vehicle of his teaching, which "in very truth no other could give." The spiritual understanding, which may also be called an intuitive direct perception of the spirit, was Beatrice's and Love's special gift to him, but he only became conscious of it through Joachim's influence. He will give it only to those of his readers who can comprehend it and who are ready to take in spiritual truth. They will find on his pages the key to the Earthly Paradise in a laborious and arduous way of purification, which can take place in this world. Then they can attain the higher states where new and hitherto unknown virtues and powers are liberated in the soul. Thus true earthly happiness and heavenly blessedness—to which the angelic butterfly in every human being yearns to rise—can be attained through the spiritual understanding of the way that is Dante's *Comedy*, provided they make steady progress from one spiritual state to the next. Unflinchingly facing all the possibilities of evil in the soul through acceptance and understanding, they can purge themselves and finally attain the fruition of the divine aspect implanted in them from the beginning.

Dante had become disillusioned with his former expectations of some savior, whether an angelic pope or a world emperor, by the time he wrote the *Epistle to Can Grande*, between 1319 and the time of his death. He had probably given up on expecting the great authorities of his time to guide humanity either to the earthly paradise in this world or to heavenly bliss in the other. Neither did he hope that violent revolutionaries like Fra Dolcino would usher in the spiritual millennium.[21] Yet he was driven by his sense of mission to do something, even after his own failure of political leadership and of ambitious ecclesiastical reform. All that was left to him was his art, and his hard-won faculty of spiritual understanding with which he wanted to equip his conscious readers, providing them with the best itinerary to the greatest happiness imaginable, both in this life and in the beyond.

Instead of assuming the mantle of the prophet, he assumes in the letter to Can Grande the office of a lecturer and teacher who has an eminently practical goal in sight. "The end of the whole [*Comedy*] and the part [the *Paradiso* which he dedicates to Can Grande] is to remove those living in this life from the state of misery and lead them to the state of felicity." He takes care to emphasize once more that his poem is not a speculation or a fantasy to horrify or delight his readers. He is interested in practical results. Instead of speculating, he believes in the wondrous realities he had seen in the widest heaven and "he demonstrates that it is possible to see them when he says that he will tell of those things which he had power to retain; *and if he had such power, then others shall have it, too.*"[22]

What Dante proposes, then, is that he wants to be a universal teacher, leading people from misery to felicity in this life (and *not* in the life to come) by means of training them in exercising their—still latent—capacity of spiritually understanding the stages of the Way as depicted in his *Comedy*. His readers then will perceive the operation of spiritual laws that regulate by clear cause and effect how every human being, in the exercise of the freedom of his or her choice "becomes liable to rewarding or punishing justice."[23] Having developed their gift of spiritual discernment, those who listen to him carefully and perceive the spiritual meaning will no longer need to entrust themselves to erring leaders, be they temporal or spiritual. Through a purification process guided by the sacred poem they will become their own guides to paradise in this life. He, like his Virgil, will "crown and mitre them" with the true teacher's satisfaction, to follow their perfected will. He will teach them—as Joachim had taught him—spiritual understanding to see their way to salvation.

For this purpose all three allegorical levels of the Comedy have to be understood, because they together constitute the total truth of the poem. Their relationship to each other is very like the relationship of the three states of Joachim, which Dante presents in his final vision. Two circles, God the Father and God the Son, equally breathe forth the Holy Spirit. Of Dante's three allegorical levels the first, what I have called the social-political meaning, best corresponds to the "*status*" of the Father who rules with the power of the law. The second level, which is the moral-ethical meaning, is connected with the Son who brought humanity grace by the example of His life and teaching, and the third level, the anagogy, is the Spirit's who brings the plenitude of understanding to all. The interplay of the three levels is necessary for the full development of the "*intellectus spiritualis*," in the manner in which Joachim pictured the third "*status*" as proceeding equally from the Father and the Son.[24] Although the anagogical meaning sums up in itself the two levels below it, yet it raises them simultaneously to a higher plane. Marjorie Reeves expresses this felicitously when she describes Joachim's diagram of the third development hovering over the two previous dispensations, "a new quality of life rather than a third set of institutions, a quasimystical state rather than a new age."[25] This "quasimystical state" is related to Dante's sense of the anagogy, an upward movement of emergent spirituality which carries with it the meanings of human history and politics as well as the significance of the individual's moral choices, but also puts these into the larger context of the truth of being.

The line-by-line explication of the anagogical meaning and the parallel discussion of the imagery is the central concern of this study. My hope is that it may help to generate an in-depth awareness of the journey from the periphery into the center of the human psyche, which is so much needed today. Whether the terms in which it is described come from the vocabulary of poetry or depth psychology is not as relevant as the direction the journey takes. For me the experience conveyed by Dante's words was charged with emotion and has had a lasting impact. The line-by-line translation of Dante's literal level into the anagogical sense can take the reader from a surface awareness to a deepening realization of what the inner life, with its unfolding potentialities, has to offer. An ever-deepening inner life of integrity and complete self-honesty is perhaps the only way that can save us from the worst misuses of our outer-oriented technological power. Dante's vision is one of the best expressions of such a journey. But without a teacher like Dante, not many of us would find such a path.

Although in this study I have attempted to present an examination of the anagogical meaning in the *Paradiso* only, the reader needs to be aware that the anagogy applies likewise to the *Inferno* and the *Purgatorio*. The anagogy in the *Inferno* should perhaps be called katagogy, or a "leading downward" until the last masks and futile pretenses are ripped away and one gazes, in a state that is suspended between life and death, at the demonic self in its utter isolation. But this horrible vision is the precondition of our turning around, our changing direction, our beginning to heal the ancient wound as we start the ascent toward the stars.

The light of the *plenitudo intellectus*, the *luce intellettuale piena d'amore*, becomes therefore the ultimate guide of humanity's political, social, and moral progress. Dante intended his *Comedy* to carry on its pages the reflection of this light of love and truth, "the true light, that lighteth every one that cometh into this world."[26]

I.

Birth: Awakening

Canto I

As Dante stands with Beatrice in the Earthly Paradise, he sees the whole universe on fire with being. Being shines forth everywhere, brighter in one part, dimmer in another. The poet had been to the realm where all things are bathed in the intensest light:

> La gloria di colui che tutto move
> per l' universo penetra, e risplende
> in une parte più, e meno altrove.
>
> Nel ciel che più della sua luce prende
> fu' io...
>
> [I. 1–5]

(The glory of Him who moves all things penetrates the universe and shines in one part more and in another less. I was in the heaven that most receives His light. . . .)

But this experience, the attainment of humanity's ultimate desire, cannot be reported in words. Our intellect, in an ecstasy of fulfillment, sinks into being so deeply that memory cannot follow it. The final union between the spark of our intellect and the central fire of everything that *is* takes place at a depth where all symbolism, even language itself, fails. Yet the mind retains memories of the way that led to

23

fullness of being and these form the subject matter of the *Paradiso* [I. 5–12].

To talk about this journey to the depths of being, the poet has to allow inspiration to take possession of him, he has to shed his everyday self, however painful this may be, and speak with a voice more authentic than his own:

> O buono Apollo, all' ultimo lavoro
> fammi del tuo valor sì fatto vaso
> come dimandi a dar l' amato alloro.
>
> * * *
>
> Entra nel petto mio, e spira tue
> sì come quando Marsia traesti
> della vagina delle membra sue.
>
> [I. 13–15; 19–21]

(O good Apollo, for the last labor make me such a vessel of thy power as thou requirest for the gift of thy loved laurel. . . . Come into my breast and breathe there as when thou drewest Marsyas from the sheath of his limbs.)

Only when inspired can he represent even the shadow of his experience. This is Dante's invocation. Now we stand with him and Beatrice in the Earthly Paradise, where the journey begins.

The Earthly Paradise on the top of Mount Purgatory is the place where the human will is finally straightened out; it is no longer inclined more to evil than to good. Here we regain the freedom with which Adam was endowed in that garden. But this state is by no means the end of the journey; it is rather its true beginning. For Adam was not created—to continue talking in the terms of the Genesis story—in the full perfection of his powers. Potentially he had in him all the perfections that human nature is capable of. These potentialities would have ripened into actual powers had Adam not fallen almost as soon as he was created. Adam's life therefore in the earthly paradise was innocent but sheltered, like the life of an infant. When he awoke to the fullness of his freedom, he fell. The earthly paradise is thus not the place where we can find perfection of human nature. What we find there is freedom.[1]

But freedom is a beginning as well as an end; it can only be kept by making choices, and if these choices preserve freedom they also involve a growth, an unfolding of our human potentials. The journey through Dante's paradise is the growth of the seed of freedom into the full-blown rose of the tenth heaven. Like Adam at his creation, anyone standing in the garden of the earthly paradise is a spiritual embryo awaiting a birth in freedom. Of course, to most of us the very attainment of inward freedom is already more than we can hope for. But we must not think that because we find it so hard to attain, nothing lies beyond it; what lies beyond is precisely Dante's paradise.

As we stand with Dante at this secluded, sheltered place of birth, where eternal nature, unlike nature in the world of generation which is still fraught with dualities, produces flowers without seed,[2] the sun rises to the meridian above us. The hour of noon, when the power of the sun is at its height, is the hour of birth for the free human being who is no longer enchained in habits that impede development, whose mind is no longer clouded in error. This birth takes place at a particularly auspicious moment. The power of the midday is reinforced by cosmic influences:

> Surge ai mortali per diverse foci
> la lucerna del mondo; ma da quella,
> che quattro cerchi giunge con tre croci
>
> con miglior corso e con migliore stella
> esce congiunta, e la mondana cera
> più a suo modo tempera e suggella.
>
> [I. 37–42]

(The lamp of the world rises on mortals by different entrances; but by that which joins four circles with three crosses it issues on a better course and in conjunction with better stars and tempers and stamps the wax of the world more after its own fashion.)

The symbol of perfection, the circle, and the symbol of the Christian faith, the cross, mark the appropriateness of the time. The conjunction of such specially favorable cirumstances is indeed important, for we are called upon to rise above human nature as we know it in its weakness and confusion. To embark upon this flight, our nature has to be molded and stamped by higher influences.

The first act is to turn our eyes on revelation. Beatrice, whom Dante meets in the Earthly Paradise and who unveils her face to him, standing on her triumphal car, is, of course, the allegorical figure of revelation. Yet she is also Beatrice Portinari of whom Dante once wrote:

> Dico che quando ella apparia da parte alcuna, per la speranza
> dell' ammirabile salute nullo nemico mi remanea, anzi mi giungea
> una fiamma di caritade, la quale mi facea perdonare a chiunque
> m'avesse offeso: e chi allora m'avesse domandato di cosa
> alcuna, la mia risponsione sarebbe stata solamente, *Amore*

con viso vestito d' umiltà.[3]

(I say that when she appeared from any direction, by the hope of her
wondrous salutation no enemy was left to me, but rather a flame of charity
possessed me which made me pardon whomsoever had offended me; and to
him who had then asked of me concerning any matter, my answer would
have been simply: *Love!* with a countenance clothed in humility.)

Beatrice, therefore, is not only an allegorical figure, the masked actress
in an abstract pageant. She is also herself. Consequently the revelation
she symbolizes is not only a system of theology based upon the Bible,
tradition, and the authority of the Church, but is also the personal
revelation (re-velatio, unveiling) Dante experienced when he fell in
love. That nothing matters in life save love is indeed a revelation which
has been given to many of us not by word of mouth but by experience
in rare moments. In the lives of very few did the experience take such
an overpowering and dramatic form as in Dante's. In my reading of the
Paradiso I found this approach to the figure of Beatrice as the embodiment of a personal revelation, given to us in our first and intensest
love, more meaningful than the traditional interpretation of her as the
mouthpiece of doctrine. Revelation as usually understood is a body of
doctrine contained in the Bible or taught by the Church; it is directed
first of all at our intellect. Personal revelation on the other hand is an
experience which affects intellect, emotion, and will in equal measure.
For Dante there was probably no reason to differentiate between the
two; his experience was the personal realization of what theology had
abstractly taught him. But Beatrice the theological commentator has
little power over my mind as I read the poem, whereas Beatrice the
representative of personal revelation, of our first encounter with the
power of being, unfolds new and unsuspected meaning all along the
way. Her eyes give us promises of new truths at every step; her smile
is the fulfillment of the promise, a truth perfectly understood.[4]

It is right, then, for us at this moment of new birth to turn to our
first intimation of love. From this recollection arises the desire to
return where, though perhaps only for a moment if measured in time,
love and the self had dwelt together in the light:

> . . . Beatrice in sul sinistro fianco
> vidi rivolta, e riguardar nel sole.
> Aquila sì non gli s'affisse unquanco.
>
> E sì come secondo raggio suole
> uscir del primo, e risalire in suso,
> pur come peregrin che tornar vuole;

così dell' atto suo, per gli occhi infuso
nell' imagine mia, il mio se fece,
e fissi gli occhi al sole oltre a nostr' uso.
[I. 46–54]

(. . . I saw Beatrice turned round to the left [the side of the heart] and looking at the sun—never eagle so fastened upon it; and as a second ray will issue from the first and mount up again, like a pilgrim that would return home, so from her action, infused by the eyes into my imagination, mine was made, and beyond our wont I fixed my eyes on the sun.)

In the state of perfect freedom, our faculty of vision endures much better the power of being than it did previously. Our youth, the promise of which we have never made fully actual, is now renewed like an eagle's in the freedom that is the human being's proper element—*loco proprio dell' umana spece* [I. 57]. Our new strength is enough to sustain for a moment a vision of the world full of the fire of being, a vision in which each individual entity we perceive seems to us a spark from the central sun [I.58–60]. And as a result of our blinding recognition, suddenly an even greater light floods our consciousness; vision has been added to vision, according to the law of visionary progress [I.61–63]. This is the moment of new birth, or mystic awakening. We are no longer in our familiar world; it has been utterly transformed, because we have been changed in the twinkling of an eye. Falling back from the splendor of being, we turn back from the transfigured world to the personal revelation that had been granted to us [I. 64–66]. And as we gaze with our new sight upon the meaning of this experience, upon Beatrice's face, we feel that we have been changed inwardly. We know with a new knowledge surer than anything else that both she and we belong to eternity:

Nel suo aspetto tal dentro mi fei,
qual si fe' Glauco nel gustar dell' erba,
che il fe' consorto in mar degli altri dei.
[I. 67–69.]

(At her aspect I was changed within, as was Glaucus when he tasted of the herb that made him one among the other gods in the sea.)

Dante's simile captures the feeling more concisely than pages of explanation: we are in a new element like Glaucus in the sea and we have been also admitted to the company of the gods. Beyond this words will not serve; but the experience can be attained by all who reach out in freedom and desire [I. 70–72].

Whether the spark of our new consciousness is the only part of the
self that now begins to grow we do not know. The Love that has
brought about this new birth in us knows [I. 73–75]. But as we look
around for the first time in the eternal state that is revealed to our new
consciousness, we become aware of its two main manifestations: light
and harmony [I. 76–81]. The light of the sun sets the whole of heaven
aflame; we are immersed in a sea of light. The harmony is the eternal
music of the spheres. Harmony accompanies us throughout Dante's
paradise, and the Pythagorean conception of the universe as a scale of
harmonies gives a perfect background for this journey through the
eternal states. Light is even more important: light enables the pilgrim
to see more in each successive heaven. The light of paradise is
intellectual light; it illuminates the mind, nourishes the vision. Without
the continuous growth of our visionary capacity we could not progress
in paradise: seeing more and knowing more awakens in us the desire
to ascend. The wish to understand fully, with the insight that only
visionary experience can give, is the force that raises the pilgrim from
one state to another [I. 83–84]. The states themselves can be characterized by an ever greater intensity of love, but the intensity of love
depends upon intensity of vision. And intensity of vision is the result
of our desire for greater understanding, to which grace responds
provided we are ready and open for new insights. So the light of
paradise, the constant nourishment of our visionary capacity, is what
really lifts us up from the limited, slumbering existence in the garden
of freedom to the fully conscious existence in eternity:

> Amor che il ciel governi,
> tu il sai, che *col tuo lume mi levasti*.
> [I. 74–75.]

(Thou knowest, Love that rulest the heavens, who with Thy light didst raise
me.)

In our desire to understand the meaning of our new vision, the increase
of light, the sudden harmony, we turn again to revelation, to our first
experience of love, in which the meaning of our whole paradisal
journey was contained as the flower sleeps within the seed. The full
meaning of our first love is now unfolding progressively at each stage
of the pilgrimage. She reproaches us right here, telling us that we are
still held captive by the material standards, by the false logic of the
unawakened life we have left behind. We no longer are part of that life,
since we are speeding toward our real home, like the lightning returning

to its proper habitation above the upper air.[5] And as we begin to understand this, the recollection of first love is charged with joy: a quick smile lights up Beatrice's face. The first meaning of many meanings that she holds for us has been uncovered [I. 85–95].

But another question rises in our mind as soon as we have made our first step in understanding: what is the law that governs our progress? Or, to put it another way, what is the force that speeds us on more rapidly than we have ever advanced before? And revelation answers: what we think miraculous is the law of reality. There is universal order among all things; upon the great sea of being—*gran mar dell' essere*—all entities have their specific destination and they reach it by adhering to their own natures and realizing their potentials to the full. Here another of the main themes of the *Paradiso* is introduced: the principle of self-identity as the foundation of universal order [I. 103–117]. To fulfill one's part in the universal scheme and to achieve the fullest development of one's own individuality is really one and the same task. Therefore the law of our progress is the law of our own humanity; the force that shoots us to that paradoxical ultimate heaven where the greatest stillness envelops and makes peaceful the greatest speed of action is the force of universal order. Our newborn self obeys the law of unfallen human nature gladly: it rises like an arrow toward its own perfection [I. 118–126]. We have the free will to turn aside from this goal and, since human nature is weighted with the heaviness of pure potentiality, we sometimes do so in search of what seems pleasure to our self-deceived intellect. Yet such pleasure is only illusory. We may turn toward nothingness, but such deviation is contrary to our real nature. The purified self, the awakened self, free of the encrustations of ignorant habits, of the mists of confusion and error, rises in accordance with the universal law, obeying it just as rivers do when they drop from cliff to valley. In a moment of awakening we enter the states of eternity; the spark of a new life has been liberated in us. There is nothing miraculous about this: the miracle would be if we failed to advance toward our real home now. So revelation assures us and leads us on [I. 127–142].

Canto II

But before we continue the journey with him, Dante warns us to turn back and revisit our own shores, to put our own house in order. Unless we have learned to look upon our past life as a preparation for this pilgrimage, we will not experience the meaning of the poem and, instead of following the path that leads toward being, we shall lose our way. The poet himself is as a ship driven by the wind of reason, guided by inspiration and navigated according to the rules of his art. He is sure to reach his haven, but we can follow him only if we have been nourishing our minds with the knowledge of what abiding reality is, a knowledge which is the bread of angels. If we are thus equipped, then we may embark upon the great sea, keeping in the wake of the poet's keel that divides the smooth surface, and follow him before the water falls back to the level, or before life resumes its everyday, smooth and deceptive appearance, which opens up no approaches to being. But if we keep hard after the poet, we shall witness his amazing transformation. He will show superhuman strength and skill in completing his enterprise [II. 1–18].

Images[6]

Light and fire characterize the experience of mystic awakening. The first canto is suffused with a glow as intense as the incandescence of molten iron pouring out in a shower of sparks from the furnace [I. 59–60]. For the newly born, the light of eternity is inded blinding; the whole heaven seems aflame with the sun [I. 79–80]. But to indicate the nature of the transformation of the self, Dante uses an image that suggests not fire but water: Glaucus the fisherman becoming a sea-god. And from this point on, water images multiply:

> parvemi tanto allor del cielo acceso
> dalla fiamma del sol, che pioggia o fiume
> lago non fece mai tanto disteso.
> [I. 79–81]

(so much of the sky seemed then to be kindled with the sun's flame that rain or river never made a lake so broad.)

Here water and fire are brought together in one terzina. And though the fire imagery continues in the lightning that darts upward to its proper place in lines 92–93, or strikes the earth issuing from a cloud in lines 133–134, the great metaphor for universal order is the ocean of being upon which all things keep to their appointed course [I.109–114]. The theme of sea voyage that dominates the beginning of *Canto II* and is repeated throughout the *Paradiso* until the final image of the ship Argo passing over Neptune in the last canto, is thus introduced already here. Dante's warning to his readers is given completely in the language of seafaring: he and those who can follow him will be the new

Argonauts. In this way a gradual transition to the predominant water imagery of the Heaven of the Moon is established.

Air and earth, the other two elements of the Aristotelian world-picture, are also present in the imagery of the first 166 lines of the *Paradiso*. The mountains of the earth are brought before us in I.16, 36 and 138. A metaphor using the image of the seashore occurs in II.4. Air is alluded to in I.99 and appears as the wind with which Minerva drives the poet's vessel in II.8. Thus the imagery of the four elements, which, I think, reveals many of the characteristics of each heaven during the first leg of our journey, is introduced right at the beginning of the poem.

Two groups of images, plant life and the deities of classical antiquity, both of which are developed later to a great extent, also appear here. Leaves and herbs are named in I.26, 32 and 68; later, in the Heaven of the Sun and in the three highest heavens, root, fruit, and blossom are added to these to form images of a fertile, fruitful and always blossoming eternal nature. The mention of Apollo in I.13–33 and in II.8, together with Minerva, is in the three highest heavens expanded into a real Pantheon of Greco-Roman gods.

Subsidiary images, symbols, and themes that link the first canto with the entire poem are the astronomical determination of the most auspicious moment in lines 37–41, the stamping of an image in wax in lines 41–42, the image of the eagle in line 48, the theme of pilgrimage in line 51, and, structurally most important here, the metaphor of bow and arrow representing the force and unerring directness of the universal order in lines 118 and 125–26.

The determination of time and position along the journey by astronomical means is, of course, characteristic of the whole *Comedy*. The stars—*stelle*, a word on which all three *cantiche* end—dominate the whole poem in which man's wanderings are always measured against eternal and perfect movements. The stamping of form into matter occurs everywhere throughout the *Comedy* and is perhaps Dante's most common image for the creation in time of something conceived in eternity. The eagle as well as the theme of pilgrimage link this canto strongly with the *Purgatorio*; they will also reoccur later in the *Paradiso*. Here the pilgrim's way comes to a turning point. In fact, the awakening alluded to in *Purg.* XXVII has actually taken place and the idea of a return to our original home is again suggested. Here, instead of being carried upward by the eagle as in his dream related in *Purg.* IX, Dante, following Beatrice's example, himself acquires the powers of the eagle as he looks at the sun. The metaphor of archery is one of those taken from the common life of his day which Dante uses so well. We will find it again in II.23–24.

The images of these introductory lines are, as we shall see, organically related to the imagery of the rest of the poem, and there are, indeed, hardly any important images or at least groups of images which are not, in one way or another, foreshadowed either in the first canto or in the beginning of the second.

My main purpose in examining the images here is to call attention to the organic connection between imagery and intellectual content. The images deepen the impact of the meaning; they supply the flesh of emotions to the intellectual bone-structure of the poem. In following the development of images one not only studies the ways of Dante's creative imagination, but also understands the anagogical journey; for instance, the presence of practically all the images of the *Paradiso* suggests that in the momentary flash of awakening we glimpse all the riches that become ours as we progress from state to state in paradise.

II.

Infancy: The World of the Self

The ascent through Dante's paradise is an intellectual flight. Each stage deepens our understanding of reality within us and without. We are driven by the eternal thirst of our humanity—*la concreata e perpetua sete*—toward understanding. The speed of our progress is almost the same as the speed with which our vision penetrates into the eternal states [II. 19–21]. It is the contemplation and increased comprehension of the revelation granted to us in our experience of love that lifts us from one state into the next. Such understanding is essentially outside of time. We are enlightened in the timeless interval between the staying and the flight of the arrow of our desire [II. 22–26].

The state that follows awakening is the infancy of the new human being born in the garden of freedom. The first sphere that opens itself to our understanding is precisely the nature of this new being: it is the unfallen, though undeveloped, human nature. Like an eternal pearl it surrounds us here in a firm and polished cloud, sparkling with the fire of diamonds, resting quietly in the innocence of its own being [II. 29–34]. The self of unfallen man has a fundamental unity that remains unbroken, undisturbed by perception: it absorbs the light quietly and remains whole [II. 35–36]. The wholeness of human nature was not broken even when the divine nature of Christ was united to it at the Incarnation. This is the first truth in the second stage of our journey that becomes comprehensible in an instantaneous flash of vision: what we held by faith before, we see here not as a proposition to be reasoned out, but as a self-explanatory axiom [II. 37–45]. This first truth is the axiom on which the whole of paradise rests: for only those can enter eternity who believe that, once purified, human nature can be united to the divine nature, that we can indeed become gods, for Christ can be born within us. Thus in the first eternal state—which is the sphere of the moon in the literal story—this truth is made evident to us and the gate of eternity is thrown open.

But such union cannot take place without the motherly care of revelation—she brings into being the godhead in us, that divine nature we knew first when we were in love. This is why Dante addresses Beatrice here and only here with the title given to the Mother of God: Madonna [II. 46]. Her help is needed right here to enlighten us. We have left behind the world of change, corruption, decay, and yet there are seeming imperfections in this first state which already belongs to the world of eternity. Flaws are apparent in sinless human nature—for how was Cain, born of Adam whose nature before the fall was this very nature, capable of murder? Though Cain was born after the fall, his extreme wickedness seems hard to explain. Does it show perhaps some weakness in the original nature of man? [II. 48–51]. We see that original human nature, though unified, is not homogenous—there are shadows on the surface of the moon—how can this be reconciled with its supposed perfection?

But revelation assures us that in taking diversity for imperfection we fall back into the mechanical reasoning of our unawakened state. Reasoning that follows the senses cannot help us here:

> retro ai sensi
> vedi che la regione ha corte l' ali.
> [II. 56–57]

(following after the senses thou seest that reason's wings are short.)

Unaided by revelation we explain the apparent defects in sinless human nature by supposing that some of its parts are endowed with more goodness (virtue) than others [II. 59–60]. We proceed from the observation of diversity among people and think that some have more goodness in them than others. But if we behold the great saints, examples of spiritual perfection (symbolized by the stars of the eighth heaven), we will see that they not only differ in the amount, but also in the kind of virtue they possess [II. 64–66]. If we supposed that their diversity was due merely to different quantities of the same virtue, we

would deny their different formal principles, i.e., their individual souls
[II. 67–72].

Yet if in spite of this consideration we assumed that the apparent
imperfections in sinless human nature are due to the complete lack in
certain areas of the one kind of virtue which constitutes the whole, it
would follow that where this virtue is missing there is nothing. The sun
of reason would then, at an eclipse, shine through these lacunae,
showing that original human nature was not perfectly filled with virtue
but lacked power in some of its faculties; though it contained no active
evil, yet it did not have all the parts necessary for its perfection. But,
as revelation points out to us, reason does *not* show us such lacunae in
unfallen nature; though some areas are less bright than others, there is
solid substance everywhere [II. 73–81]. If we maintain the hypothesis
that original human nature consists of one kind of virtue, there still
remains a possibility to account for these apparent imperfections, these
"moonspots." Perhaps the areas of imperfection are due to the uneven
distribution of the "goodness" or basic virtue. If the basic virtue were
to be found at one point closer to the observer and at another point at
a greater depth away from him, the light of reason might show the
darkness of apparent—though not real—evil there. But the truth is that
in the case of such uneven distribution of the one basic goodness,
unfallen human nature would appear perfectly spotless, for the same
virtue shines with equal brightness in the light of reason, however near
or far the spectator may be from it. Thus the second argument to
maintain the hypothesis of one basic virtue in original human nature
breaks down [II. 76–105].

We are at a loss: our attempt to explain why original human nature
seems darker in some places and brighter in others, why Cain could
become a murderer only one generation removed from original innocence, ended in failure. Both our former opinions and the rigidity of
our reasoning melted away in the bright rays of true reason. Our mind
is now stripped bare of preconceived ideas and is ready to receive the
imprint of living light, of deeply felt truth [II. 106–111].

This truth is a universal one and underlies the whole structure of
reality. From being itself, revolving upon its own unity, separate
principles of goodness emanate which are further differentiated into
various powers, all serving distinct and separate ends. The universe,
both physically and spiritually, may be regarded as a huge living body
with organs that have individual existences of their own but also serve
the purpose of further individual differentiation:

Questi organi del mondo così vanno,
come tu vedi omai, di grado in grado,
che di su prendono, e di sotto fanno.
[II. 121–123]

(These organs of the universe proceed thus, as thou seest now, grade by
grade, each receiving from above and operating below.)

The same principle works in the human being, so that from the central
spark within, different powers issue which build up the organs and
limbs of the body as well as the faculties of the psyche [II. 133–135].
In the universe, such different powers, joined to the bodies which they
animate, produce individual entities, according to this fundamental law
of individuation that permeates both the visible and the invisible world.
From this it follows that the goodness embodied in existing beings is
not one kind of virtue, but a mixture of virtues: this is as true of human
nature as of the physical world [II. 127–132, 136–141].

Revelation has enlightened us again. The contemplation of our own
experience of love has yielded another meaning: not only one kind of
virtue shines in the nature of unfallen man. We knew this when we first
loved and obscurely felt the stirring of our unknown powers. Human
nature contains a mixture of virtues which shine with quiet joy. All
people do not have to strive after one kind of excellence: "Let not
your heart be troubled. . . In my Father's house there are many
mansions." What appears, therefore, as imperfect in the original
nature of man is not really so; the difference between what seems
opaque to our reason and what seems clear is only a difference between
light and light, between various kinds of goodness. Human nature as
originally created contains within itself the seeds of endless diversity,
but has no evil whatsoever [II. 142–148].

Canto III

The revelation given to us in our first love—*quel sol, che pria d'amor
mi scaldò il petto* (that sun which once before had scalded my breast
with love)—has enlightened us about the nature of the unfallen state
[III. 1–5]. Equally important is perhaps that we recognize the limitations of our own unaided reason: the truth is not always what we
expect it to be. When a thing appears defective or unclear we do not
have to conclude immediately that goodness is lacking in it; another
kind of goodness, which is unkown to us, might well be the cause of
the apparent defect. This new insight prepares us for further progress

in paradise. We can travel through the states of eternity only when we are open to the unexpected, free of preconceived ideas, and not bound by mechanical reasoning.

The truth that there is nothing evil in human nature as originally created, that it does not even lack goodness in any part, fills us with joy and a new sense of human dignity. We lift up our heads to admit our former error freely [III. 4–6]. But with this movement we already step on the next rung of the intellectual ladder: the new understanding we have gained enables us to see what we have not seen before—it amplifies our vision [III. 7–9]. What we see is the mode of individual existence in this state of paradise, exemplified in human beings in whose nature the wound of the fall had closed and who live in the spiritual infancy of the first eternal state. Their individuality appears faint, for the great virtues that blossom and come to fruition in the higher heavens are here still in the bud. No wonder then that we doubt the reality of their existence. To avoid our former error of taking appearances for truth—a characteristic of self-centered reasoning—we now go to the opposite extreme and take the truth for appearance [III. 10–22]. But by doing this we find emptiness where we expected to see the truth. Thus we are still unprepared to accept that truth often comes in a different form from what we are predisposed to see. Our first intellectual advances in the world of the eternal states are faltering baby-steps. Our idea of truth is very imperfect, our thinking is still childlike, for we turn to emptiness instead of turning to reality. We think truth is a reflection in a mirror-like surface.

What we have not realized is that there is more substance to life in this state than in the unawakened existence to which we are still half-bound. Again, we learn this from our personal revelation, who has first shown us a glimpse of a higher form of existence. Yet this is still a state of spiritual infancy: the development of true humanity has just begun. Individual existence in this state is exemplified by nuns who did not fulfill their vows. The non-fulfillment of vows means an unfulfilled life: people in this state are not yet what they were supposed to become. But in spite of this condition, life here already flows in obedience to the eternal laws of being. Those who are in this state have already attained a degree of vision; the light they enjoy does not allow them to turn away. The insight they possess makes them parts of the eternal order and directs their will toward the freedom they can find in the eternal law [III. 22–23].

Those who live in this state already enjoy that sweetness of eternity which cannot be understood except by those who have experienced it

[III. 37–39]. Here begins the life of charity which makes all those who partake of it grow in beauty and feel perfectly content:

> Li nostri affetti, che solo infiammati
> son nel piacer dello Spirito Santo,
> letizian del su' ordine informati.
>   [III. 52–54]

(Our affections, which are kindled only in the pleasure of the Holy Spirit, rejoice in being conformed to His order.)

Their joy is in the fulfillment of the inward promptings of the Holy Spirit and not in the satisfaction of desires that come from the confusions and errors of the illusion-bound self [III. 43–54]. This is already an existence transmuted by a glow of something divine in our humanity [III. 58–60].

Not even the fact that they are in their spiritual infancy, that they have not yet developed all their powers, not yet realized all their potentialities, can trouble the joy of those in this sphere, which seems the lowest in paradise. Seems, I say (par giù cotanto), because we must not apply our ideas of high and low, implying superiority and inferiority, to the eternal world. In the most important sense all dwellers in paradise are equal: they all enjoy uninterruptedly the vision of being, they all live from the true center of their personality, without ambition, rivalry, or envy. They all burn with the flame of their first and eternal love [III. 64–69].

Their wills are not bent on achieving a different state. No longer do they will anything for themselves: charity seeketh not her own. By direct contemplation of the mode of individual existence in this state we learn how all the states of eternal life are based on the surrender of the individual's will to the power of being. But this surrender, instead of depriving us of willpower, paradoxically integrates our hitherto weak and divided will. To say that this is paradoxical is perhaps an exaggeration: what we surrender is the self-will based on the misconception that we may be happy by ourselves, regardless of, or even in spite of, the rest of the universe. By surrendering our self-will, we in fact liberate our *real* will that is based upon an understanding of reality and *is* part of reality. This real will does not aim at unreal happiness; the joy it is intent on is in accordance with the laws of being, a joy not only for ourselves but for everything that is [III. 70–84]. Once we have understood this we know what it means to live in charity: by following the deeper will, following the laws of our own individuality as given by the power of being which makes us into what we are, we shall abide in charity. Paradise has as many ways of happiness as there are individuals living in its states. This principle of individual differences is again and again stressed on our journey [III. 85–90].

To know the life of the first state of paradise—aside from inner personal experience—we have to know people who live in that state. Piccarda is a personification of spiritual infancy: a nun who was prevented from fulfilling herself according to her vocation. People who could not grow to full humanity, though they have set their feet on the right road, belong in this sphere. Their failure to persevere is a kind of inconstancy, and the symbol of their state is the inconstant moon. Yet the brightest light in this heaven is Constance, mother of Frederick II, and Piccarda herself took the veil under the name of Costanza. The nuns remained constant to their vocation, if not in action, certainly in intention: the paradox of their names and their place in this sphere teaches us to accept all we see, but also to refrain from judging by our puerile standards of superiority and inferiority [III. 97–120].

Piccarda's song, an unaccompanied solo, the first faint prelude of the full choral harmonies in the higher heavens, reminds us of the Incarnation. The first heaven thus teaches us that human nature can indeed be united to the divine nature; we have also learned that there is no imperfection in human nature once the wound of the fall has been fully healed. No imperfection, but infinite individual diversity is the cause of the varied character it presents to us. But as we try to fathom fully the joy that the actual living of these truths gives, our vision loses its hold, and Piccarda vanishes "as a heavy thing sinking through water." We have tried to understand her state as much as we could for new understanding is the prerequisite for further progress, but here we have to turn to the revelation of love in our lives, to gain further enlightenment. In the light of our new knowledge she appears so bright that our power of vision is dazzled at first. Each new meaning adds to the splendor of the experience of love that was once ours. Then we loved half-unconsciously, overwhelmed and uncomprehending, in the grip of a power greater than ourselves,[1] but now, as we begin to understand eternity, we also comprehend more and more the depth and promise of our first love. More understood, that experience shines brighter, so bright, indeed, that it dazzles us [III. 121–130].

Canto IV

Another way of describing our progress in paradise would be to say that it is a constant attacking of paradoxes. Only when we question what perplexes us, and our will is fully bent on greater understanding, can we receive enlightenment from revelation and, with enlightenment, new power of vision. The paradox of the first eternal state which we have encountered may be formulated like this: those living in this state must, since they are in paradise, enjoy the fulfillment of their individual natures and yet they are the very ones who, because of the pressure of circumstances outside themselves, were prevented from fully realizing their potentialities. If they were constant (for, after all, their will remained intent on the religious life), why are they relegated to the state symbolized by the inconstant moon [III. 115–117]? On the other hand, if yielding to necessity must be considered inconstancy, how can they be in a state where defect finds no place?

To solve this seeming contradiction is another intellectual task in the first eternal state. In order to solve it we must fully understand the nature of the will.

Action or inaction due to absolute necessity does not merit either praise or blame [IV. 1–9]. Can it be that people who find their place— and peace—in this state of spiritual infancy are here by force of necessity? And if they are here not of their own free will, must they still be content? Perhaps we are, after all, determined by "the stars," by factors outside our control, so that we cannot realize our potentialities to the full against the force of circumstance [IV. 22–24]? Our revelation, who gave us our first taste of inner freedom, our first intimation of the truth how little outside circumstances can shackle the inner man, tells us now that this idea of spiritual determinism is an error. There is no determining necessity in the eternal world; the supreme law is the law of freedom, and the inhabitants of paradise, in whichever stage of development they may be, share the eternal freedom of the spirit [IV. 25–33, 49–54]:

> Ma tutti fanno bello il primo giro,
> e differentemente han dolce vita,
> per sentir più e men l' eterno spiro.
>   [IV. 34–36]

(but all make fair the first circle and hold sweet life in different measure as they feel more and less the eternal breath.)

When we talk of the states along our journey, we try to picture individual differences by sensible means, using symbols and analogies to help our human power of vision. But, in truth, the world of eternity is *one*; our distinctions are only aids to understanding and must not be taken as the real divisions of paradise [IV. 37–38]. Belief in determinism is an outcome of materialism, the most dangerous error. It separates us from revelation [IV. 65–66] and induces us to worship the forces which are merely the manifestations of the laws of being when we should seek being alone [IV. 61–63].

But if no determining necessity can force the will, and the will is really free, what prevents those in this state from further growth? It cannot be outside circumstance, since this was found to be non-determining. It must be some cause within the person's own self. And here—with the help of revelation—we finally discover why some people must dwell in spiritual infancy. Although their will is free and directed toward being, it is yet divided against itself. Outside force cannot bend the will aside unless there is some part in the will itself that agrees with the outside influence:

> chè volontà, *se non vuol*, non s'ammorza,
> ma fa come natura face in foco,
> se mille volte violenza il torza.
> [IV. 76–78]

(For will, if it will not, is not quenched, but does as nature does in fire though violence wrench it aside a thousand times.)

Perfect will, that returns to its purpose as the flame returns to its upright shape as soon as the wind stops, is not to be found in this state [IV. 73–81]. This moon-world of innocence and limited vision does not understand as yet that the only lasting harm that can happen to the human soul is alienation from being. Those who live here are still concerned with avoiding hurt and harm to the self, but their hurt and harm is considered merely from the temporal point of view, for in eternity it is no hurt and harm at all. The shadow of the earth, of time-bound existence, still falls across this state. Ultimately it is the fear for the safety of the self that divides the will:

> Voglia assoluta non consente al danno,
> ma consentevi in tanto in quanto teme,
> se si ritrae, cadere in più affanno.
> [IV. 109–111]

(The absolute will does not consent to the wrong, but the will consents in so far as it fears, by drawing back, to fall into more trouble.)

This is why the state of spiritual infancy is the first rung on the ladder of paradise. A concern with the self, though no longer a destructive concern, characterizes the inhabitants of this sphere. Though they no longer live in error, they still have fear, because they are not completely awakened to the reality that surrounds them. They live inside the eternal pearl of sinless human nature, their wills turned toward being, resting in the assurance of their own genuine existence. Yet in one way they are too much concerned with the joy of their state and somewhat anxious to retain it. This anxiety, this fear is what impairs their will [IV. 100–111]. (Since this state was Adam's when he was created, it shows what in Adam's will made him liable to fall. It was a tendency to enjoy passively what was his in the Garden.[2]) The tendency to retain a joy as if it were ours exclusively is the root of the primal error, a cloud of which still lingers mysteriously over the human entity's spiritual infancy: the error that the self *can* be considered separate from the rest of reality. Thus we think we may have to hold on to our perception of the eternal world; we may gradually grow anxious to retain our place in it, in order to rest in it. But if we human beings are merely anxious to hold our place, to secure the enjoyment that we have, we are already slipping out of the world of eternity, back into temporal existence, into change and decay. As soon as we aim at securing, or retaining happiness, the walls of the self begin to form, and the vision of eternity is gradually shut out. Only by ceasing to think of oneself as separate, by reaching out constantly into the reality that one's vision reveals can one retain and simultaneously increase joy. For there is no inertia in eternity: the life of the spirit is continuous movement, unceasing creation. Those who wish merely to hold what they have lose their vision. "To every one that hath shall be given, and he shall abound: and from him that hath not, even that which he hath shall be taken from him."[3]

What has to be grasped in the first state to which we have risen is the true nature of the will. To see the division between the deeper or absolute will (*voglia assoluta*) turned toward being and the practical will concerned with the safety of the self [IV. 112–114] is the first step in achieving consciousness of our true or eternal self. It is also the first step toward curing the division of the will and overcoming the passivity that would make us merely rest in the pearl-like radiance of our own being. As our revelation enlightens us and the seeming paradox is resolved, we feel an increase of life: it is the result of greater understanding [IV. 115–120]. Our intellect cannot rest anywhere but in the final truth of being. But the way to reach this truth is the way of constant questioning:

> Nasce per quello, a guisa di rampollo,
> a piè del vero il dubbio: ed è natura,
> che al sommo pinge noi di collo in collo.
> [IV. 130–132]

(Doubt, therefore, like a shoot, springs from the root of the truth, and it is nature that urges us to the summit from height to height.)

Our questioning is rewarded by the ever-increasing splendor of our revelation: we begin to see, as much as our power of vision can support this truth, that our experience of love is an inexhaustible fountain of eternal truths for us.

Canto V

This growth of love's power over us is the result of clearer vision. For in paradise the old rule: *video meliora probaque, deteriora sequor,* is not valid. When we understand the good, our will is immediately drawn to it. We also realize now that whenever our love turned to anything other than the eternal light that nourishes our vision, it was some trace of the same light, shining through the object of our love, that attracted us [V. 1–12]. Estrangement from being is therefore the result of error in the Socratic sense; it is due to an imperfect recognition of the true good, the object of our desires.

One more question remains to be asked here, and our progress depends on the full understanding of the answer: can we compensate for the divided state of our will with merits in other fields, so that further progress may be made even while the will is impaired [V. 13–15]? Here our revelation answers with a definite *no*. Without freeing ourselves from the fear for the self's safety we cannot rise beyond the state of spiritual infancy. Our will must be made entire to overcome the separation between ourselves and the reality that surrounds the self. Only when we make a *full decision* to seek being above all else, can we progress—and thus stay—in the eternal world.

To understand this answer fully we must complete our exploration of the nature of the will. On entering the eternal states of paradise, the human will is already turned toward being. The decision to begin the journey toward being was made in the garden of freedom, i.e., in perfect freedom of will. Now to have free will belongs to the essence of the human entity [V. 19–24] and in order to really become what by one's true nature one should be, the free decision must be as final as possible [V. 79–80]. Otherwise freedom of the will is but imperfectly exercised. Once we have decided to seek being and nothing but being, we must fully implement our decision [V. 25–35]. We may change the way in which we seek being, but we can never lose the single-mindedness with which we fix our will on the ultimate aim [V. 43–54].

But revelation adds a qualification to be kept in mind: since we are here still in the state of spiritual infancy, we need the mother's milk of guidance [V. 82–83] both when it comes to making a decision for a particular way and when it comes to changing our path. Otherwise we might go on struggling [V. 83–84] in ignorance and fail to advance altogether.

We have now understood all of what the first state of paradise had to teach us: we saw that it was no illusion, but a true enjoyment of genuine existence illuminated by being itself. We also realized that a division still existed in the will here, caused by the fear that present joy may be lost. Having examined the nature of the will with the help of our revelation—which means that we have recollected and fully understood the operation of our will in our experience of love—we came to the conclusion that the will must be made entire and the fear for the safety of the self has to be overcome before one can rise into the next state. Only by making a full decision do we really exercise our free will and become true to our essence. Thus we have to break out of the world of the self, even though it is the unfallen self of spiritual infancy, and exercise our will in the world outside.

There is a very good reason for positing the pilgrim's task in the first sphere of Paradise as the understanding of the nature of the will. All progress in the world of eternity depends, in the first place, upon the will. Only when we will the progress toward being fully and completely can we become open to the power that increases our vision; without the desire to understand, our vision cannot be enlarged, and without greater vision we cannot grow in love. And the strengthening of the will for the next step in the ascent depends upon how much we can love.

Images

The sphere of the moon that envelops us like a cloud here [II. 31] is a water-world:

> Quali per vetri trasparenti e tersi,
> o ver per acque nitide e tranquille,
> non sì profonde che i fondi sien persi,
>
> tornan dei nostri visi le postille
> debili sì che perla in bianca fronte
> non vien men tosto alle nostre pupille;
>
> tali vid' io più facce a parlar pronte,
> perch' io dentro all' error contrario corsi
> a quel ch' accese amor tra l' uomo e il fonte.
>
> [III. 10–18]

(As through smooth and transparent glass, or through limpid and still water not so deep that the bottom is lost, the outlines of our faces return so faint that a pearl on a white brow does not come less quickly to our eyes, many such faces I saw, eager to speak; at which I ran into the opposite error to that which kindled love between the man and the spring.)

Many similes and metaphors, such as the melting snow in II. 106–111, and the metaphor of wading across a river to find truth, in II. 124–126, depend on water imagery. The pearl to which the moon is likened in II. 34 is born in the depths of the sea and it receives Dante and Beatrice as water receives a ray of light [II. 35–36].

In the passage quoted above from the beginning of the third canto, both the faces on the surface of glass and water and the pearl on a lady's white forehead express something of the union of the human with the inanimate which is so characteristic of the moon-sphere. Through this juxtaposition of the human and the inanimate, as well as through the faintness of the faces appearing in the moon, the still undeveloped character of man in his spiritual infancy is suggested. That the element of water dominates the imagery in itself indicates pure potentiality: the water-world of the moon is the sphere where most of the human being's higher powers are still in a dormant state. In contrast to water, fire suggests actuality and, in accordance with the progress of the development, fire imagery becomes dominant in the higher heavens.

The reference to Narcissus—made with the perfect simplicity so characteristic of Dante [III. 18]—also helps to establish the character of the heaven of the moon as a realm where self-absorption, though no longer a danger, is not yet very far away. Although Piccarda, when she smiles at Dante, "seems to burn with the first fire of love" [III. 69], she vanishes singing, "like a heavy thing sinking through water" [III. 123]. Her unaccompanied *Ave Maria* is the prelude of later choral harmonies and suggests that although she is surrounded by her sister-nuns, she is still alone and lives half-enclosed in the joy of her own being [III. 53–54]. A fire image is used when the perfect will is likened to a flame in IV. 77–78. But Dante also makes clear that people in the state symbolized by the heaven of the moon do not possess this perfect will which would make the potential actual.

Among the similes which contribute to the anagogical meaning of these cantos are those dealing with animals. In the beginning of the fourth canto the problem of free will is introduced by three similes, all applicable to Dante's inability to choose which question to ask first. Free man would be unable to choose between two dishes of equally appetizing food, just as a lamb would be paralyzed by fear between two fierce wolves and a dog paralyzed by desire between two does. The instinct of self-preservation—working through fear and hunger—is presented here as a force that necessarily paralyzes the will. In the natural world necessity rules, and animals as well as hungry man are subject to it. The spirits in the sphere of the moon are in a similar situation: caught between the desire to serve God and the desire for the safety of the self they cannot move forward. Their helplessness resembles that of the animals because they have not yet realized completely that necessity does not rule in the eternal world, that their will is truly free. They can still be held captive by the opposite pull of conflicting motives because they do not recognize that their fear for their own safety is the result of a misconception: people are not animals, not subject to necessity in following their ultimate aims *because their intellect can always find the truth:*

> Io veggio ben che giammai non si sazia
> nostro intelletto, se il ver non lo illustra,
> di fuor dal qual nessun vero si spazia.

> Posasi in esso, *come fera in lustra,*
> tosto che giunto l' ha: *e giugner puollo;*
> *se non, ciascun disio sarebbe frustra.*
> [IV. 124–129]

(I see well that our intellect is never satisfied unless the truth enlighten it beyond which no truth can range. In that it rests as soon as it gains it, like a beast in its lair; and it can gain it, else every desire were vain.)

Whereas the animals in the first quoted passage were held in immobility by necessity, here the wild beast reaches his den and may rest; the recognition of the truth has resolved the impasse and led us home. Thus for Dante free will is inseparable from the capacity for intellectual understanding: it is the knowledge of truth that really liberates us. "You shall know the truth and the truth shall make you free."[4] Of course, once we know the full truth we naturally follow it, but the freedom of the will is not curtailed here: the service of God is perfect freedom. Animals, and people swayed by what they suppose is necessity, are bound because they do not know; and it is interesting that in V. 80, when condemning those who foolishly put their trust in false indulgences, Dante again makes a distinction between the ignorance of animals and the knowledge of men who are really human and thus capable of finding the truth:

uomini siate e non pecore matte.
(be men, not senseless sheep.)

In the next *terzina* he likens people who have turned from guidance
that leads to truth to lambs running away from their mother's milk,
again emphasizing that man should nourish himself on the understanding of truth and cease to imitate the ignorance of animals.

Knowledge is therefore the food that nourishes spiritual infants:
several metaphors present Beatrice as feeding Dante with the truths of
spiritual understanding. His appetite is great:

Ma sì com' egli avvien, se un cibo sazia,
e d'un altro rimane ancor la gola,
che quel si chiede, e di quel si ringrazia;
[III. 91–93]

(But as it happens, when of one food we have enough
and the craving for another still remains, that we ask
for this and give thanks for that.)

But at times he needs help to digest what he has eaten:

convienti ancor sedere un poco a mensa,
però che il cibo rigido ch' hai preso
richiede ancora aiuto a tua dispensa.
[V. 37–39]

(thou must sit a little longer at the table, for the tough food thou hast taken
requires more help for thy digestion of it.)

Yet, however hard it may be to assimilate some of the knowledge that
unfolds before us, this is the only way to grow in paradise.

III.

Adolescence: The World Outside the Self

The meaning of love's revelation deepens continually as we grow in knowledge of what truly is. When we have learned all that the first state had to teach us, and look at revelation again, the change in her face silences even our eagerness to question. While we gaze at her we rise out of spiritual infancy and, with the swiftness and directness of an arrow, we penetrate into the second state of paradise [V. 88–93]. The transition does not depend on time; once we have really understood the limitations of the first state, our "inborn and perpetual thirst" for completeness has already taken us beyond it.

When the division within the will is healed, we can emerge from the world of the self into the world that lies immediately around us: the world of affairs, of everyday human activity. We see this world not in its temporal form, but in the visionary light given by our revelation. This world is still subject to change [V. 97]; the shadow of temporal existence (earth's shadow) still falls across the lives of those who seek to serve being in the world of affairs. Growing out of infancy into adolescence, one begins to develop latent powers and, as against the faint individuality of infancy, an ever stronger glow of the joy of a more distinct individuality surrounds the inhabitant of this state [V. 107–108]. Encountering another, such a soul rejoices at the new opportunity for loving [V. 105]. This is what makes the second state different from the first: here one encounters others and the isolation of the self is overcome. The will is free and engaged in the service of being, but

the service takes the form of working for the greater temporal welfare
and happiness of humanity.

Those who live in this state already burn with the eternal light of
being and our revelation assures us that we have much to learn from
them [V. 118–123]. They draw their luminousness—which indicates
their growing individuality, their closeness to being—from perfected
vision [V. 124–26]. But it is in action and not in contemplation that
their luminousness increases, in action are they closest to being; then
the mists that for them still cover the world and obstruct their vision
are cleared away.¹ When they can *do* something to further their
dedication to being, then they are most themselves and join their song
to the harmonies of paradise [V. 130–9].

Canto VI

The figure representing the mode of individual existence in this state
is the Emperor Justinian. He had dedicated himself to the service of
being in giving laws to the world and establishing the rule of justice in
the temporal realm:

> per voler del primo amor ch' io sento,
> d' entro le leggi trassi il troppo e il vano;
> [VI. 11–12]

(by will of the Primal Love which moves me, I removed from the laws what
was superfluous and vain.)

But he could not even begin to fulfill his task in the world before he
had been freed of intellectual error. Instead of believing in Christ's
humanity, Justinian held that He had one nature only, the divine.

The truth about the union of divine and human nature, the truth of
the Incarnation, became axiomatically clear to us in the first state of
heaven. Here, in the second state, we learn that service of being in the
temporal world is impossible unless the reality of Christ's twofold
nature is fully accepted. This means that those acting in the world, in
order to bring people justice, peace, or welfare, must at all times
remember that Christ had shown the union of the divine and the human
in Himself. When dealing with human beings they must see in their
subjects, partners, employees, etc., not only what is human but also
what is, however hidden, divine; they must see the Christ in everybody
[VI. 13–21]. Only by *living* this truth can we reach the second eternal
state and receive the grace that enables us to fulfill our potentialities
by action in the world of affairs [VI. 22–24].

Even warfare carried on to secure peace, order, and justice is a form of activity through which being can be served [VI. 25–26]. For the building of a world-order that gives people the greatest possible freedom, peace, justice, and welfare is indeed the service of being.[2] The best world-order is the one which enables the human race to "attain its proper work," the unfolding of all its intellectual powers.[3] Thus the work for a just world-order is actually a means to bringing all people closer to being.

Though the aims of their work in the world may be various, such as peace, material welfare, technical progress, etc., the great principle that the people in this state follow is the principle of justice [VI. 104–105].

Justice is the appropriate virtue in this state of ceaseless—mercurial—activity [VI. 113]. In contrast to the state of spiritual infancy where the outside world was unknown save as it impinged upon the self, here is distinct awareness of the identities of others and of the self's relations with them. The principle regulating these relations is the principle of justice. We are now aware of the reality of the outside world and of our place within it. This is why we become concerned with our honor and fame among people [VI. 113–114]. With a mentality so typical of adolescence—both spiritual and temporal—we wish justice to be done, we wish to enjoy what we justly deserve, neither more nor less [VI. 118–120]. Those who have attained the higher states of paradise we cannot envy: instead we rejoice in the perfect justice that has assigned the right place for all [VI. 121–126].

But the best way of life within this sphere is represented by Romeo (a man who has been to Rome, i.e., to the world of affairs), whose good work was ill repaid by his master. The just [VI. 137] Romeo fulfilled all the duties of his office, but when he was not rewarded according to justice he renounced worldly recognition and found his recompense in the peace of the state he had attained. He chose not to depend upon the praise of the world [VI. 127–142]. To bring justice into the world and not to be concerned if others pay tribute to our honor or if they spread our fame, is already a step toward overcoming the limitations of this state, limitations that still stem from concern with the self. Fear has been overcome already in rising out of the first state, but the desire to be recognized and approved by others is still strong; some division in the will still remains, for though we now seek being in ceaseless activity, we do not devote our entire will to the search. With a part of our will we still strive for recognition from others, for status in the temporal and not in the eternal world. These are good people:

> buoni spirti, che son stati attivi
> perchè onore e fama li succeda;
>
> e quando li disiri poggian quivi
> sì disviando, pur convien che i raggi
> del vero amore in su poggin men vivi.
> [VI. 113–117]

(good spirits whose deeds were done for the honour and glory that should follow them; and when desires mount there thus deviously then the rays of the true love must needs mount upwards with less life.)

That they are not yet completely full of true love—*vero amore*—is because they still, however remotely, think of their selves as in some way separate from the rest, as deserving some special place, special status. Of course they only want what is just, they only want the place they deserve and would certainly refuse whatever is more than their just deserts. But this very insistence on justice—noble as it is—is the obstacle beyond which people in this state cannot rise. The concern for strict justice disguises a clinging to the separateness of the self and prevents the absolute surrender that the *vero amore* requires.

Canto VII

The light of being shines over the realm of temporal affairs as well as over all other states of paradise. If we seek being through action in this sphere, then, in addition to our own life becoming a more faithful expression of our own individual being, we will also receive added light from being itself. And the more we become ourselves, the greater the amount of the power that is shed upon us and becomes ours [VII. 1–6]. This power is the eternal source of energy and enables us to continue in the ceaselessly active service of being. Activity here has the rhythm and sureness of a perfectly executed dance [VII. 7–9].

But our questioning, which is the method of our progress on the intellectual ladder, cannot cease here. We again come upon seeming paradoxes that demand solution. For enlightenment we turn to our revelation again, full of reverence and awe, because we now begin to realize that the epiphany of our first experience of love has far greater power to lift us up than we have been able to imagine [VII. 10–15]. The paradox we have to attack is, of course, a paradox about the nature of justice. How can a just act be justly revenged?

In this state we are supremely concerned with justice or, to put it in terms more appropriate to the world of affairs, with fair dealing. But our temporal conception of justice is defective; we are too apt to accept as just an act if that act serves a just purpose. Yet in eternity not acts but intentions are judged: thus an act just in itself may be justly revenged because of the unjust intentions of the doer [VII. 19–51]. This is the first truth we learn from our revelation in this sphere.

But to see fully the limitations of existence in the second state of paradise we have to work out the implications of this truth. Our guide warns us that full comprehension of the greater truth is inaccessible to those whose "understanding has not been matured in the flame of love":

> il cui ingegno
> nella fiamma d' amor non è adulto.
> [VII. 59–60]

In other words, an increase of love is necessary here to enlarge our intellectual vision and to enable us to rise into the next state.

Eternal justice, our revelation tells us, is not the kind which requires in vengeance a tooth for a tooth and an eye for an eye. If it were, man could never overcome the fall, his alienation from being. For the human entity is free; freedom is of its essence, and it is perfectly just—we would say—for him to enjoy or suffer all the consequences of his free choice. When he chose to turn away from being, he did it in perfect freedom and, making himself the center of the universe, he fell out of the eternal world [VII. 64–87]. According to the "equitable" justice to which those in the second state of paradise still cling, man cannot find his way back to being, because his nature has become much too unlike being itself [VII. 79–81]. His choice against being was made in eternity, and according to our strict justice it must keep him estranged from being throughout eternity. Within his finitude man cannot make good an infinite error: he cannot renounce his own self to the same degree as he had exalted that same self when he set it against being [VII. 87–102]. But the fact that we are in paradise proves that another type of justice operates here. For eternal justice nothing is more just than to lead man back to being, and nothing is more in accordance with the nature of being than to appear in the human form so as to make itself once more accessible to people and thus to restore them to the integrity of their own being [VII. 103–120]. Eternal justice, then, is indistinguishable from love.

But if being is, by its very nature, intent on drawing all that has strayed from it back into the full and undecaying life, then why is the temporal world, within which the inhabitants of the second eternal state center their activity, still decaying and corruptible [VII. 124–129]? Revelation, having once, in our youth, lifted us above the temporal realm, now declares that we must make a careful distinction between the world of nature, which includes the world of affairs and human history as a whole, and the world of pure being. In the former, human purposes and aims change and decay just as much as animals and inanimate objects do in the world of nature. They are subject to the force of circumstances symbolized by the stars. They cannot be re-absorbed into eternity because the world of history and human affairs is a creation of causes which themselves are contingent, derived from powers which express the laws of eternity only indirectly [VII. 130–141]. But though we might be active in the world of affairs, our true life consists in our relationship with being and in *that* life we are free. It is this true life, and not worldly activity in itself, that will lead us back to being and to the recovery of complete integrity, with all our potentialities fulfilled, including those represented by the body [VII. 142–148].

What seemed at first a paradox about justice has now been resolved with the help of our revelation. For in our experience of love we had not been concerned with just dealing in the worldly sense, but with the complete and unreserved giving of ourselves. Now we see the limitations inherent in the service of being in the world. Justice, in the worldly sense of fair dealing, is not enough to restore to us the full integrity of existence we had lost. In other words, according to "strict" justice man cannot be redeemed. But when we understand the justice of eternity which is love, and shape our lives according to our larger intellectual vision, we can rise out of the second state and transcend its limitations.

Images

The spirits flocking to Dante and Beatrice are like glittering fish in still clear water [V. 100–3]. The water imagery of the moon-cantos is continued with this simile, but is gradually replaced by images of earth and fire. Like the moon, the planet Mercury is also called a pearl [in VI. 127], a water-born gem. These images suggest that much of human capacity is still in a potential state in this sphere. However, when the spirits engage in action which constitutes the life of this state, they become bright like the sun when its heat has dissolved the vapors of the atmosphere:

> Sì come il sol, che si cela egli stessi
> per troppa luce, come il caldo ha rose
> le temperanze dei vapori spessi;
> [V. 133–135]

(Like the sun, which itself conceals itself by excess of light when the heat has gnawed away the dense tempering vapours.)

In action the fire of one's actual power breaks out and the individual being becomes more luminous. But water metaphors occur as late as VII. 12 and VII. 90. In VII. 124–125 all four elements, beginning with water, are named:

> Io veggio l'acqua, io veggio il foco,
> l'aer e terra e tutte lor misture.

(I see water, I see fire and air and earth and all their mixtures.)

This suggests the close connection of the sphere of Mercury with the temporal world of nature—and of history—where these spirits were active.

But the clearest connection between the earth as the stage of history and the second state of paradise is made in VI. 57–81, where the conquests of the Imperial Eagle are recounted in largely geographical terms. Such geographic references establish the earth as the element within which some of the human potentials are actualized, but actualized only to a limited extent, as earthly activities subject to fortune. The Roman Eagle—though God's instrument in bringing peace and justice to the earth—is still a bird "ravening through century after century,"[3] a bird within time as we may clearly see if we compare it with the eternal eagle of the just in the heaven of Jupiter. Thus the element of earth may be said to dominate the imagery of the second heaven.

Fire images are numerous. The more important are those used in connection with love, which in the spirits of the second state is still not wholly actualized, and also in connection with the nature of God, the source of all being:

> La divina bontà, che da sè sperne
> ogni livore, *ardendo* in sè scintilla
> si, che dispiega le bellezze eterne.
> . . . .
> *l'ardor* santo, ch'ogni cosa *raggia*,
> nella più simigliante è più vivace.
> [VII. 64–66; 74–75]

(The Divine Goodness, which spurns all envy from itself, burning within itself so sparkles that it displays its eternal beauties.... for the Holy Ardour that irradiates all things is brightest in that which is most like itself.)

To become filled with fire and light is, then, to be fulfilled in our own being and to come closer to being itself.

In the heaven of the moon Piccarda's song is the only sign of the harmonies of paradise. In Mercury as the spirits approach Dante they cry out in unison:

> *Ecco chi crescerà li nostri amori.*
> [V. 105]

(Lo, one who will increase our loves!)

They are no longer singing alone but crying out together. And when Dante comes to relate Justinian's answer, in the sound of the poetry the authentic music of paradise is heard for the first time:

> e così chiusa chiusa mi rispose
> nel modo che il seguente canto canta.
>
> [V. 138–139]

(And so, enclosed [in his own radiance] he responded to me closely in the manner which the next canto chants.)

But the chief means by which these spirits contribute to the harmony of paradise is the one most appropriate to their ceaseless activity: dance. Justinian sings Hosanna, turning to the music of his own song, and then the others join in the dance:

> ed essa e l'altro mossero a sua danza,
> e, quasi velocissime faville,
> mi si velar di subita distanza.
>
> [VII. 7–9]

(and he and the others moved in the dance and like swiftest sparks were veiled to me by sudden distance.)

IV.

Youth: Falling in Love

Canto VIII

When we have really understood that love and not simply fair dealing should be the just rule of our relationships with others, we have already attained the third state of paradise, so swiftly that we did not even notice the transition [VIII. 13]. After the quiet, half-unconscious happiness of infancy and the unceasing activity of adolescence, we come to an encounter different from those of the marketplace, as we become aware of another's being with an immediacy we have experienced only in moments of self-recognition before. Such direct experience of another's individuality is falling in love.

The love that has its place here in paradise is, however, not the same as the ancient idolatry of passion—*il folle amore*—exemplified in the story of Dido [VIII. 1–9]. The third state of paradise is the state of love but not of passion imaged by the dark, buffeting wind of the second circle of the *Inferno*. Being in love does not blind us here, whereas passion did blind Francesca and Paolo. On the contrary, in this state our original love experience, our personal revelation, becomes more beautiful, shines with new meaning [VIII. 13–15]. Our vision is enlarged, we see the flame within the flame, hear the voice within the voice, perceive the real being of a person within his or her appearance [VIII. 16–19]. In this state one is guided by love alone and thus participates in the circular dance which all those in this state, and in all the higher states, weave around being. Our actions now revolve, distantly as yet but nevertheless with a directness not found before, around being [VIII. 19–21; 25–27]. Action issuing from a self not on fire with love cannot be as swift as the action of people in this state [VIII. 22–24]; and the main purpose of their love is to give of themselves so that the other may have joy [VIII. 32–33; 38]. They give themselves generously, without reservations [VIII. 43–44]. They know what it is to "plunge into the labyrinth of another's being," to use Yeats's words [IX. 81]. Love here is based on understanding; without the understanding of being, which comes to us when we love otherness in the beloved, we cannot join in the circular dance of the third heaven, the perfect life of true lovers [VIII. 34–37].

Life in this state is figured by Carlo Martello, a young prince and connoisseur of love poetry. Before we can learn more about this state from him, we turn to revelation again and are reassured by her that our first experience of love was indeed of the kind that Carlo Martello exemplifies [VIII. 40–42]. Carlo is the best type of aristocrat: generous, open-hearted, loving, a man of true friendship [VIII. 55–57]. He was heir to the throne of Naples and titular king of Hungary, but left the world before he could reign. "The world kept me below only for a short time" [VIII. 49–50]. Unlike the people in the second state, he was not active in the world of affairs, for the true lover is not detained in the world for long. He is surrounded by an aura of joy, which suggests the soft and silken quality of the feeling he lives in [VIII. 52–54].

The joy given and received in this state comes from a vision of being that is deeper, more ample, than the vision accorded to the first and second state of paradise [VIII. 85–90, IX. 73]. Yet once we have understood this joy we thirst for further enlightenment to increase our vision, again according to the law of progress. The question that naturally occurs to us is a simple one: how can man's life, which—as we now know—derives directly from being, produce the bitter fruit [VIII. 93] which the misrule of the Angevins in Naples has plainly brought to light?

> Ma vostra vita senza mezzo spira
> la somma beninanza, e la innamora
> di sè . . .
>
> [VII. 142–144]

(but your life the Supreme Beneficence breathes forth without mean, and He enamours it of Himself . . .)

To answer this question fully, we must first understand the nature of human freedom in the temporal realm. How can it be that the human will always has a free choice in turning toward being or turning away from it? Even if heredity and the circumstances of life were to precondition one to a life alienated from being, the influences of the eternal world in the temporal realm would restore one's freedom of choice. For as everyone has his own individual being, every person also has an individual path on which he, too, can arrive to the perfect fulfillment of himself [VIII. 97–105]. The fact that each one has a private destiny which does not belong to the temporal realm is the guarantee that he is not totally subject to determining circumstances:

Natura generata il suo cammino
simil farebbe sempre ai generanti,
se non vincesse il provveder divino.
[VIII. 133–135]

(The begotten nature would always take a like course with its begetters if Divine Providence did not overrule it.)

Indeed, as in human society people have to fulfill different functions, so are they born to follow different ways in life; Solon could best fulfill his individuality by being a lawgiver, Xerxes by being a ruler, Melchisedech by following the priesthood, and Daedalus by exercising his genius for invention [VIII. 115–126]. Human freedom, then, consists in the choice of either walking your own particular path which would— heredity and circumstances notwithstanding—take you closer to being, or of abandoning that path so that "your track runs astray from the road":

la traccia vostra è fuor di strada.
[VIII. 148]

Now that we have understood in what precisely one's freedom consists while one lives upon earth, we are ready to tackle the main question. How can our life on earth turn away from being if our own being draws its life from being itself? We now see that this happens certainly not because of circumstance or heredity. The estrangement takes place because we do not take account of the "foundation provided by our own individual nature," [VIII. 143] when we refuse to follow the particular path which opens to our own approach to being. Or, to put it another way, all of us have the possibility of leading a life that would both develop the inner potentials and bring us closer to being—the two processes are really identical—and the only cause of failure is our rejection of the basis of action given in our own individual nature, which is our true self [VIII. 139–148].

The recognition that this true self exists in people, and that it is the basis for all advance toward union with being, is a lesson most appropriate to the third state, in which we meet the true self of the other directly in the beloved. I doubt if the experience of meeting reality within another can ever be more perfectly and succinctly expressed than in the terzina:

> E come in fiamma favilla si vede,
> e come in voce voce si discerne,
> quando una è ferma e l' altra va e riede;
> [VIII. 16–18]

(And as within a flame a spark is seen, and within a voice a voice is distinguished when one holds the note and the other comes and goes.)

To know that in all otherness we are confronted with this true self—and that it is this true self, however hidden, however undeveloped, that we love—is the knowledge reserved for the inhabitants of the third eternal state. Here we love and intuitively grasp the mystery of individuality in another person by the unitive act of love [IX. 81]. Love thus sets our feet on our own individual way to being.

Canto IX

If we do not turn to being, which can amply satisfy all our desires, we tear our hearts away from where they really belong and direct our minds into emptiness; it is the pursuit of illusions rather than true being that brings evil fruit where good could have grown. [IX. 7–12]. In the third paradisiacal state—symbolized by the sphere of Venus—we approach being through the love of another person.[1] Characteristically, our revelation has nothing to say to us here, because what we learn in this state does not come from the unfolding of our own revelatory experience, but from getting to know those whom we love. Revelation merely serves as a safeguard, a touchstone, to test the genuineness of the experience which the other person offers [IX. 16–18]. Therefore the problem which would bring to light the limitations of this state is not treated here in the form of a verbal paradox explained by revelation, as in the first and second heavens. Here we perceive both the problem and the solution in the lives of those whom we love. Since their wish is to please us [IX. 14] and the greatest pleasure we can receive from them is the intellectual pleasure of understanding, they continue to enlighten us [IX. 2; 15] about the implications of the central truth which must be apprehended in this state. They enlighten us in presenting themselves as they are, so that we may know them fully and be at the same time known by them [IX. 80–81]. Such enlightenment is offered by the representatives of this state, Cunizza and Folco. Like Carlo Martello, who listed the dominions which but for his early death should have been justly his, they describe in great detail the particular corner of the earth they have come from. In this way they stress their individual backgrounds, the fact that they have followed their own way, building on the foundation which their nature has provided. But if they did act in accordance with their own natures, then we are forced to ask the question: did they also follow their true selves when they burned with a love that was perhaps all sexual passion, *folle amore*? As for Cunizza, she admits that she was overcome by the influence of Venus [IX. 33]; Folco tells us himself that in his youth he burned as much as Dido, the example of *folle amore* pointed out to us as we entered this state [IX. 97–99]. Was their amorousness a foundation in their own nature, a trait inherent in their true selves? Were they not impelled by their true natures to give themselves to others without reservation, to find the meaning of their lives in knowing others and being known by them in the way open to most people, that of sexual love? The question, put into the most general terms, is simply this: can the human being, following his or her own particular path—which means acting in accordance with his true self—be led astray from being? He cannot, for these lovers *are* in paradise. But, then, can it be possible that all they did in *folle amore*—in sexual passion—had to be recanted, blotted out, denied as an aberration, before they could knock on the gate of heaven? To think this would be to follow the opinion of the crowd, which always tries to apply a common—and abstract—yardstick to individual behavior.

Cunizza, an aristocrat like Carlo, is in no way ashamed to admit that her place is in this state because the influence of Venus overcame her:

> Cunizza fui chiamata, e qui refulgo,
> perchè mi vinse il lume d' esta stella.
> [IX. 32–33]

(Cunizza I was called, and I shine here because the light of this star overcame me.)

She *shines* in this heaven, because *this* planet ruled her life. The influence of Venus, then, contributed in bringing her into the eternal world. And if we say to this what moralists would be ready to say, that because of this influence she could rise into *only* the third heaven and no higher, then we, too, are included in her definition of the "common herd."

> Ma lietamente a me medesma indulgo
> la cagion di mia sorte, e non mi noia,
> che parria forse forte al vostro vulgo.
> [IX. 34–36]

(but I gladly pardon in myself the reason of my lot, and it does not grieve me, which may seem strange, perhaps, to your crowd.)

We have to learn to swallow this "hard saying," that she gladly accepts her past and is not penitent for her numerous loves. Cunizza teaches us not to judge as the vulgar do, for she was herself when she loved. Her loving nature, her joy in giving herself, is the true Cunizza and we had better not judge too closely where she went wrong.

The lesson, however, does not mean that we should not judge at all. Cunizza's generosity does not prevent her from passing judgment upon various acts [IX. 43–60], but these judgments are not hers, they are eternity's. For the inhabitants of this state are already able to discern some of the workings of eternal justice:

> Su sono specchi, voi dicete Troni,
> onde rifulge a noi Dio giudicante,
> sì che questi parlar ne paion buoni.
> [IX. 61–63]

(Above are mirrors—you call them Thrones—and from them God in judgment shines upon us, so that we think it right to say such things.)

Further enlightenment comes from Folco of Marseilles, the troubadour. About his activities as bishop and fierce hunter of heretics he says nothing. He is here as Folco the poet of love, stamped by the influence of Venus [IX. 94–96]. His radiance is ruby-red, the color of love [IX. 69]. His power of love is such that he can enter into our being to know our thoughts and feelings much more thoroughly than we can know his [IX. 80–81]. He knows others the way they really are, because his vision sinks into being itself. [IX. 73–75]. This capacity of entering into the being of another completely, to satisfy the other's desires to the full, is the achievement of those in the third state of paradise. This is the source of their joy which, though it pervades the whole of the eternal world, is the feeling that fills *them* more than any other [VIII. 52; IX. 24, 34, 67, 70, 103].

Folco thus satisfies our wish to understand fully the implications of the truth which we have discerned in Cunizza's speech. How much of Folco's amorous past was the expression of his true self and how much of it was error? Whatever was error is now forgotten [IX. 104]. But the fact that he remembers himself burning with passion shows that the passion belonged to his true self which now rejoices in paradise. He rejoices in remembering the power of being that drew him in his passion to become more and more himself and to fill his unique place in the eternal order [IX. 103–105]. He now understands some of the infinite art with which this order is built up and he sees that it evermore gains upon chaos, as more and more individuals recognize who they really are. He understands because he has discerned that good within himself and others which will one day blossom into the Kingdom of God on Earth. He knows that part in people which will one day return to the source to complete the redemption of all creation [IX. 106–108].

The way to develop the true self is to satisfy all the desires that arise from it. Before we can ascend into the next state, we should satisfy all the wishes belonging to this sphere, we should love fully—but with an illuminated love belonging to our true self and not with illusion-bound *folle amore*—all those whose reciprocal love we desire [IX. 109–111]. As an example of this truth we meet Rahab who, though she does not speak, contributes to our understanding of the eternal state symbolized by the Heaven of Venus. We cannot help thinking that if she had not been a harlot she would not be in paradise at all, for all the other women of Jericho were put to death and she alone was saved. In fact Rahab *had to be* a harlot to live by herself and let Joshua's spies into her house. She was saved, of course, not because she was a harlot, but because she recognized and loved the truth; yet she could not have opened herself to the truth had she not been what she was. Thus her true nature places her into this state across which still falls the small shadow of temporal existence [IX. 118–119]. Though we must not judge the generous and self-giving lovers in this state, the joy they feel is not yet quite free of the power of change. In loving others they have been also drawn by the power of appearance in physical beauty, physical pleasure. They love in others what is real—or good—but their love is still conditioned by things that are illusory, impermanent. And insofar as they are subject to the power of the unreal, they are still in the shadow of the earth.

The harlotry excluded from the eternal world is not amorous disposition but the harlotry of money. To sell oneself for money instead of giving oneself for love is not the vice of prostitutes alone. It can be seen in those, too, who abstain from sexual love altogether [IX. 127–142].

Images

Apart from two metaphors remotely implying water, there is little indication that water-imagery continues in the Heaven of Venus. The two metaphors are:

> Noi ci volgiam coi Principi celesti
> D' un giro e d' un girare e d'una sete,
> [VIII. 34–35]

(We roll here with those celestial Princes in one circle, in one turning and in one thirst)

and

> l'alta letizia
> Che il tuo parlar m' infonde, signor mio,
> [VIII. 85–86]

(the high rejoicing which your speech pours into me, my lord).

These metaphors might well be called dead but for the possibility that Dante's furnace-like imagination reanimates even those. Yet toward the end of the ninth canto the light of Rahab is described as sparkling like a sunbeam in pure water:

> così scintilla,
> come raggio di sole in acqua mera.
> [IX. 113–114]

(that sparkles so, like a sunbeam in clear water.)

The other references to water are not metaphors, but are found in the geographical descriptions by which Carlo, Cunizza, and Folco identify themselves. In fact, locations are indicated mainly by naming of rivers and the relation of land and sea. To take an example, let us see how the three spirits who address Dante begin to talk about themselves:

> Carlo: Quella sinistra riva che si lava
> di Rodano, poi ch' è misto con Sorga,
> per suo signore a tempo m' aspettava;
> [VIII. 58–60]

(The left bank that is washed by the Rhône after it mingles with the Sorgue awaited me for its lord in due course.)

Cunizza: "In quella parte della terra prava
          Italica, che siede tra Rialto
          e le fontane di Brenta e di Piava,
                                        [IX. 25–27]

(In that part of the depraved Italy that lies between the Rialto and
the springs of the Brenta and the Piave)

Folco: "La maggior valle in che l'acqua si spanda,"
          incominciaro allor le sue parole,
          "Fuor di quel mar che la terra inghirlanda. . . ."
                                        [IX. 82–84]

("The greatest valley into which the water spreads from the sea that
encircles the world," he began then.)

In these references water and land dominate and, as in the Heaven of
Mercury, detailed geography establishes the earth as an element very
much present in the Heaven of Venus still touched by the conical
earth-shadow:

          questo cielo, in cui l' ombra appunta
          che il vostro mondo face,
                    [IX. 118–119]

(this heaven, where the shadow ends that is cast by your world).

And, as if growing out of the union of earth and water, a new group of
metaphors appears here, which involves plant life, seeds, germination,
roots. The connection of sexual love with vegetation is made quite
frequently in poetry. One has to think only of Spenser's Garden of
Adonis, or Blake's World of Generation, which he also calls this
"vegetative" world.[2] And though Dante's metaphors of plant, fruit,
and flower are much more fully developed in the higher heavens, it is
significant that they germinate just here. In an important sense something germinates in the Heaven of Venus that reaches its full flowering
in the empyrean rose. Carlo's saying:

          io ti mostrava
          di mio amor più oltre che le fronde,
                    [VIII. 56–57]

(I would have shown thee much more of my love than the leaves)

makes us aware that here we see the first tender leaves of a love that
grows and develops as we ascend in paradise. The references to *seed*
in VIII. 93, 140, and IX. 3 as well as to *root* in IX. 31 have definite

sexual connotations, appropriate to the third heaven. The metaphor of Florence as the devil's plant bearing florins in IX. 127–130 might be regarded as a transition to the more fully developed images of plant-life that characterize the metaphors in the Heaven of the Sun.

The spirits appear here completely surrounded by their radiance, like silkworms by their cocoons:

> quasi animal di sua seta fasciato.
> [VIII. 54]

(like a creature swathed in its own silk.)

In the Heaven of Mercury, Justinian's features could still be distinguished before he hid himself in the light of his own joy [V. 136–137]. Here the light is too strong to allow Dante to recognize his friend Carlo Martello [VIII. 52–53]. Though the light hides the features, it enables the intellect to discern truth more clearly than ever. Love in this sphere is inseparable from understanding [VIII. 37] and implies continual clarification. Dante's request to Carlo:

> Fatto m'hai lieto, e così mi fa chiaro
> [VIII. 91]

(Thou hast made me glad; so, too, do thou enlighten me)

indicates the stages in the love characteristic of the Heaven of Venus: first comes the giving of joy and then the increase in understanding. Thus the light imagery often indicates clarification, as in VIII. 112, IX. 13–15, and—less explicitly—in IX. 112–114.

The planet Venus itself is a body of light in which other lights move:

> vid' io in essa luce altre lucerne
> [VIII. 19]

(I saw within that light other lights).

In comparison to the pearly shine of the moon and even of Mercury [VI. 127] Venus is brighter and the radiance indicates increase of joy:

> Per letiziar lassù folgor s' acquista,
> [IX. 70]

(there above brightness is gained by joy).

The imagery of water, earth, and fire—which is light—contributes to establish the Heaven of Venus as the sphere where much human potentiality is actualized, but many virtues still remain in the seed.

The connection between this sphere and sexual love is stressed by the diction of the eighth and ninth cantos. Venus is the star that "courts" the sun:

> che il sol vagheggia or da coppa, or da ciglio
> [VIII. 12]

(that woos the sun, now from behind, now in front).

The spirits offer themselves to Dante saying:

> "Tutti sem presti
> al tuo piacer, perchè di noi ti gioi."
> [VIII. 32–33]

(We are all ready at thy pleasure, that thou mayst have joy of us.)

Dante addresses Cunizza like a lover expecting satisfaction of his desire:

> "Deh metti al mio voler tosto compenso,
> beato spirto,". . .
> [IX. 19–20]

(Pray, bring to my wish speedy fulfillment, blest spirit)

and she, like a woman in love, gladly forgives herself for her amorous past:

> Ma lietamente a ma medesma indulgo
> la cagion di mia sorte . . .
> [IX. 34–35]

(But I gladly pardon in myself the reason of my lot . . .)

But the words that suggest the closest union between lovers are in Dante's last question, addressed to Folco:

> Dunque la voce tua. . . .
>
> * * *
>
> perchè non satisface ai miei disii?
> Già non attenderei io tua domanda,
> s' io m' intuassi come tu t' immii."
> [IX. 76, 79–81]

(Why then does thy voice . . . not satisfy my desires? I would not await thy question if I were in thee as thou art in me.")

And as he says this we realize how much he has grown in the understanding of love. Folco himself, in obeying Dante's last, and unexpressed, wish, stresses that all desires born in this sphere should be gratified:

> Ma perchè le tue voglie tutte piene
> ten porti, che son nate in questa spera,
> procedere ancor oltre mi conviene.
> [IX. 109–111]

(But, that thou mayst take with thee all the desires fulfilled that are born in this sphere, I must continue still further.)

That both Cunizza and Folco know what Dante wishes to hear without Dante's asking a question emphasizes the difference between the Heaven of Venus and the two lower spheres. In the Heaven of the Moon and of Mercury only Beatrice understood Dante's wordless questions; both Piccarda and Justinian answered him only at his explicit request. So does Carlo, but to Cunizza and Folco Dante merely indicates that he has a wish and leaves its divination to the spirits themselves. Such divination is most appropriate to the state represented by the Heaven of Venus: lovers who have achieved a close union can often guess one another's thoughts. Another progression may be seen in that here several spirits speak to Dante, whereas in the lower spheres he only talked to one.

The unfolding of harmonies proceeds further in the third heaven: the unaccompanied singing in the Moon and the solo of Justinian which ends with the dance of all the spirits in Mercury do not express the joy of paradise as fully as the dance and *Hosanna* of the spirits in Venus. The dance here is described explicitly as a circling centering directly around God:

> quei lumi divini
> veduti a noi venir, lasciando il giro
> pria cominciato in gli altri Serafini.
> [VIII. 25–27]

(had seen these divine lights come to us, leaving the dance first begun among the high Seraphim.)

The circular motion is stressed again and again:

> Noi ci *volgiam* coi Principi celesti
> d' un *giro*, e d' un *girare*, e d' una sete
> [VIII. 34–35]

(We turn in one orbit, at one pace, with one thirst, along with the heavenly Princes) and is an indication of perfection unattained before. Justinian turns around in one place (i.e., spins on his own center) [VII. 4–5] to the music of his own singing, but here the spirits dance around the cosmic center, unless they rest from their dance to satisfy the desire of another:

> sem si pien d' amor che per piacerti,
> non fia men dolce un poco di quiete.
> [VIII. 38–39]

(we are so full of love that, to do thee pleasure, a little quiet will be not less sweet to us.)

In the sun's heaven the circling is further developed, into more intricate patterns.

An indication of the way in which the imagery changes in the higher heavens is also found in a description of Folco:

> L'altra letizia, che m' era già nota
> preclara cosa, mi si fece in vista
> qual fin balascio in che lo sol percota.
> [IX. 67–69]

(The other joy, which was already known to me as precious, became in my sight like a fine ruby on which the sun is striking.)

In contrast to the pearl which is entirely a product of nature, the ruby is polished by human hands, and its beauty is the result of the cutter's art. Thus it indicates a state going beyond the natural perfection of the pearl, a state where beauty and power are added to nature's work by conscious design. Together with the development of plant imagery, metaphors and similes involving human art become more and more frequent in the next heavens, indicating the higher and more complex forms of happiness as we proceed on the ladder of development.

Two metaphors suggestive of spiritual voyage or pilgrimage occur in VIII. 106 and 148, carrying this general theme through this heaven. The metaphor taken from archery occurs again in VIII. 103–104, and the Platonic metaphor of the seal stamping an image into wax—which recurs again and again through the *Purgatorio* and the *Paradiso* is used in VIII. 127–129. Another is taken from a common trade and conjures up a whole picture in one word:

> ma perchè sappi che di te mi giova,
> un corollario voglio che t' ammanti.
> [VIII. 137–138]

(But that thou mayst know the pleasure I have in thee, take a corollary for
a cloak about thee.)

The corollary is a cloak cut by the tailor for a suit of clothes; this is
Dante's way of bringing his reader back to common life even from the
most abstract arguments.

V.

Maturity of the Intellect: Understanding the Order of the Universe

Canto X

Order belongs to the very nature of being; when we become aware of order and take delight in it we taste some of the reality of being itself [X. 1–6]. With the understanding of love, which we have acquired in the state symbolized by the Heaven of Venus, we now turn toward the order manifested in the universe [X. 7–12]. A *loving* contemplation reveals to us that in nature the apparent deviation from perfect regularity is, in fact, the best possible design [X. 13–21]. The first step in the new state into which we have risen is to learn to contemplate the order of being in all that we perceive. We must come to understand the perfection of this order, its excellence and beauty which do not lie in the mechanical regularity that appeals to our simple taste for geometric symmetry. A law of order operates in the seemingly irregular phenomena of nature; when one has learned to see order in these, one has begun to make progress in the fourth state of paradise [X. 22–27].

This state is characterized by intellectual growth, and crowns, as it were, the volitional and emotional growth of the two preceding states. As the sun is the chief mediator between the order of the heavens and life on earth, so reason reveals the universal values in the life of the individual. In an auspicious moment when the power of reason is ascendant in life, one enters the state of intellectual maturity and is united with the Reason that imprints the ideal form on matter. The transition from the state of passionate love into the state of intellectual maturity is unnoticeable; as we are not aware of the rise of our first thought, neither can we pinpoint the change that it has brought about [X. 28–36]. Thinking is an activity of the mind and it arises in eternity; only its deciphering takes time. The state dominated by intellectual activity, as symbolized by the Heaven of the Sun, is the first of the higher states, where illusion, the shadow of earthly existence, no longer intrudes. Without revelation, without the recognition of an ever deepening significance in what we have once experienced of love and eternity, we could never attain such mature understanding [X. 37–39].[1] In this state we reach the natural limits of human reason; fullness of understanding cannot be conveyed with the help of ingenuity, art, or tradition, for it depends on the capacity of vision that must be developed individually. Our undeveloped vision can never transcend the sun: we cannot quite grasp what it is to reach the full development of our intellect before we have actually reached the fourth state of paradise [X. 40–48].

Understanding in this state centers on the ceaseless activity of being in sustaining and continuously creating the universe; the speculative intellect finds its fulfillment in contemplating this process [X. 49–51].[2] To comprehend this state we must first of all turn to being completely, oblivious of all else, even of our personal revelation who now directs our will toward being. Only by turning with all our love toward being can our intellect be united in the One, the center and source of order, and thus strengthened for the highest degree of understanding. This sharpening of the intellect by submergence into the One is like the tempering of a blade. But when our mind is, in a moment out of time, unified in the One, our personal revelation begins to glow with such deep meaning that our mind is turned back from concentration in the One to the perception of the many. But from now on the perceiving power of our mind itself has become sharper and more discerning as a result of its unifying encounter with the One [X. 55–63]. The vision we now contemplate is preeminently of light and harmony. It cannot be adequately represented to those who have not known this state; only by experience can one know the splendor of the universe as it is reflected in the human intellect which has attained maturity. Here whatever we perceive we see as part of the universal order, the cosmic dance, turning around the central, everlasting truth of being [X. 70–78].

We understand, first of all, the very law of progress that lifts us up from state to state. The light of vision, which enables us to love truly and which grows more intense by loving, leads the human entity upward on the spiritual stairway. Once we have come to experience the state of intellectual maturity, we will not fail to return to it, even if we fall from it temporarily [X. 82–87]. Then we understand also that true freedom is maintained by the loving service of others. If we denied love to others, we would be no freer than water that is forced to flow away from the sea; we would be denying our true nature [X. 88–90]. Whatever is made known to us in this state relates to the central experience of personal revelation and can only be grasped if grouped around the experience which is our guide. Personal revelation is the touchstone of genuine progress in the journey through paradise [X. 91–93].

The mental activities through which we may come to know the universal order are various: theology, jurisprudence, government, mystical speculation, history, philosophy, encyclopedic knowledge, and even strict, rationalistic logic. By all these intellectual activities we may acquire the ability to recognize order and reality, which are actually one and the same. True philosophy, for instance, exposes the world of illusion for the attentive pupil and through strict rational inquiry makes him recognize certain truths, which, however unwelcome or unpleasant, are yet necessary to complete the picture [X. 94–138].

As our minds open up to reality we come to see that truths which in temporal existence appeared contradictory are, on this higher plane, resolved into harmony.[3] All truths, however opposed they seemed before we entered this state, are now perceived to be complementary; all contribute to the harmony that makes us turn our love toward being. The intellectual comprehension of the *whole truth* where opposites contribute to a higher unity can be reached only by those who have attained the fourth state of paradise, and the fruit of this comprehension is eternal rejoicing [X. 139–148].

Canto XI

The vanity of temporal cares as well as the defective rationalizations by which people try to cover up their preoccupation with the changing and the illusory, becomes quite clear to us when we reach intellectual maturity. The shadow of temporal life, which still fell across the lower states, no longer intrudes here. We see that no earthly occupation—

not even the priesthood—and no passion can compensate us for inner development. Released from the bondage of illusory pursuits of power, of wealth, of sensual pleasure—and led by our personal revelation—we enjoy the true wisdom which is the vision of universal order [XI. 1–12]. But we cannot stop here: we should develop our understanding of the universal order by the method which has already helped us along the journey, the method of questioning. Every new truth opens the way to further questions and only by questioning can we receive further enlightenment, increase of vision. As we are inclined to question, the truth grows brighter and an answer comes to us even before we have formulated our question in words [XI. 16–24].

The questions we have to ask here are naturally questions concerning wisdom, the achievement of the mature intellect. One has to do with the nourishing effects of wisdom, the other with the different types of wisdom. But in asking these questions we have to know precisely what we are after, otherwise we cannot obtain the correct answer. Intellectual maturity includes the ability to make precise distinctions, for the wisdom of paradise is never vague [XI. 25–27].

We must, however, accept at the outset that the deepest causes of the world order can never be known, not even in this state [XI. 28–30]. Yet the wisdom that we need to advance toward our ultimate aim, union with being, is indeed attainable and it can be reached, broadly speaking, in two ways: through seraphic love exemplified by St. Francis of Assisi or through cherubic knowledge seen in St. Dominic [XI. 31–42]. Our task in this sphere is the proper understanding of these two ways through the illuminated intellect. First we consider the way of love, which begins in utter poverty and humility, as did the life of St. Francis after his conversion. The complete rejection of all worldly goods, the severing of all earthly ties must be the first step. We have to understand fully the worthlessness and illusory nature of possessions and must not let them stand in the way of our progress toward being [XI. 58–77]. We also have to learn to bear cheerfully the contempt of ignorant people for whom the rejection of wealth and of family ties seems foolishness or worse [XI. 88–90]. The way leads through trials where resolution, courage and perseverance are tested, but for those who endure these trials confirmation is not lacking. They are united to being through love and recognize that the temporal world is not their true home; death to them is a welcome return to their own proper realm, for they depart leaving their bodies to the earth, having renounced everything earthly long before [XI. 91–117].

It was Knowledge, in the person of St. Thomas Aquinas, who

expounded to us the nature of the way of love. Now, instead of showing us the ideal way of knowledge, St. Thomas points out the dangers that beset that road. It is fitting that he should refrain from praising the way he himself had followed. Here we become aware of the several ways in which the one end can be reached—and to see the virtues of another's way and the dangers of one's own is not the smallest part of wisdom. It is a measure of perfection to be attained in this state of paradise that talking of others we discuss their excellences and talking of ourselves we reveal where we fall short.

The way of knowledge is indeed fruitful, provided we do not stray from the straight road, driven by hunger for novelty. We must beware of useless, oversubtle distinctions, sterile scholastic vagaries [XI. 121–129]. When people no longer seek the truth but are intent on novelty for novelty's sake, they whittle away the plant of wisdom and lose their direction, never profiting from the way of knowledge [XI. 137–139].

Canto XII

Understanding of the way of love and of the pitfalls on the way of knowledge brings increased power of vision. Grace always adds its measure to our efforts. And the proof of our progress is that we perceive more harmony around us than before [XII. 1–6]. The greater order and increasingly harmonious movement proves that we are proceeding in the right direction. And the harmony is growing more complex; movement answers movement, music answers music in a measure that surpasses all harmonies of human art, just as the source of light is more dazzling than light reflected [XII. 7–9]. Such harmony gives us hope that whatever of beauty we recognize on earth will not be lost, but, on the contrary, will be fulfilled in eternity [XII. 10–18].

The lives of those in this state are harmoniously coordinated. The pleasure that their *vision* of order gives them keeps their movements in mutual accord.

Our enlarged vision leads us now to the understanding of the way of knowledge. It is right that the two ways should be understood together, because both are necessary if one is to reach one's ultimate destination by means of acts (love) as well as of words (knowledge) [XII. 28–45].

The way of knowledge, symbolized here by the life of St. Dominic, requires a vigorous mind [XII. 58–60]. The starting point here, too, is poverty [XII. 73–75], though the motives for embracing poverty—the first counsel of Christ—are different. The rejection of worldly goods,

the understanding of the illusory nature of material possessions is the
necessary prerequisite for true growth in knowledge. The second step
is to become conscious of one's mission in this world, to recognize:
"It was for this that I came" [XII. 76–78]. We must study, not for
worldly gain, but for the love of truth alone if we are to advance on
this way [XII. 82–85]. To put our knowledge to use for acquiring
worldly position or riches is wrong; once we have recognized truth,
our duty becomes to fight against error with all our strength, to make
other minds fertile with our teaching so that the truth we have come to
know may give us and others more abundant life [XII. 88–105].

The way of knowledge and the way of love have a common goal:
wisdom manifested in teaching and in action, the wisdom of the fourth
state of paradise.

But the way of love has its dangers too. It is fitting that the
representative of the way of love, St. Bonaventura, should, after
praising the way of knowledge, warn us that on the way of love we
must avoid extremes both of laxity and asceticism. He also reminds us
that those on the way of love are more involved with temporal concerns
because they have to act more; therefore they must be careful to keep
temporal concerns in the second place where they properly belong
[XII. 112–129].

In following either of the two ways, the human being can arrive at
the intellectual maturity of the Heaven of the Sun and become a
teacher of the truth in word and example. Simple preachers, men of
perfect life but little education, can attain this state just as much as
scholars, logicians, grammarians. To proclaim the truth unafraid of
temporal power, to search for it with the help of both reason and
revelation, to observe it in the universe, are the attitudes characteristic
of this state. Out of search for and love of truth comes finally the spirit
of prophecy which promises a reconciliation of all truths that now
appear contradictory [XII. 130–141].

Canto XIII

Existence in this state is harmonious and ordered as the movement
of the stars, because it is guided by the enlightened intellect. Not only
order and harmony, but, resulting from these, an imperturbable joy
pervades this state of paradise. The mind, having now attained its
maturity, turns naturally toward being itself, toward the nature of being
as expressed in the doctrine of the Trinity and, in particular, toward
the union of man with being, as exemplified by Christ [XIII. 1–30].

Meditation on being and on our relationship to being is necessary before the next illumination will come to us in this state. We have learned about the two ways to wisdom and now we have to understand that, though wisdom seems one, it is nevertheless individual. To understand this we must use discrimination in reasoning. Only by discriminating properly can our intellects arrive at knowledge which may be called real [XIII. 49–51].

Discrimination is inherent in the order of the universe itself. The whole universe is the emanation of the Source of being, at once of the burning that gives light, of the light itself, and of love. Everything that exists reflects the idea of the perfect existence, but, because of the resistance of primal matter or sheer potentiality, the reflection of the perfect form in the actually existing being will be an imperfect copy only. The infinite diversity inherent in being is unfolded in actually existing beings, and we cannot understand ultimate order unless we discriminate between the different attributes of being as they appear in the universe. Only if we possess the power of discrimination can we perceive truth, i.e., the ideal form within a contingent being. And here we must not be misled by appearances which pertain to temporal existence, to the sphere of contingency alone. We must not seek to find a greater or a lesser *amount* of any attribute embodied in contingent beings. For if these beings would perfectly reflect the particular form of being which had brought them into existence, then it would appear that where we supposed more or less of the same ideal attribute to exist, there are, in reality, different qualities. Each individual being thus possesses a different quality of the same attribute, a quality that belongs to the individual alone [XIII. 52–81].

Wisdom, the attribute of being which concerns us here, is no exception. Every type of man, the king, the theologian, the logician, the metaphysician, the geometer, has a wisdom proper to himself, and he must strive to attain perfection in his particular kind of wisdom. The new insight we have received in answer to our questioning is an essential part of intellectual maturity, the fourth state of paradise. We learn that we must not hanker after the wisdom of others; we must seek the knowledge proper to us, an individual, personal knowledge [XIII. 88–108]. Maturity of intellect can never be reached by imitating the intellectual processes of others. We have to find our own vision for only so can we realize the particular form of mental activity which eternally exists in the idea of ourselves by which the Source of being has called us into existence [XIII. 82–87].

But another lesson remains to be drawn, or rather to be stated more precisely. Reasoning is the activity proper to the intellect and therefore the art of reasoning must be acquired at this stage. We have already understood the importance of making accurate distinctions; we must never forget this. We must not say yes or no before we see exactly what it is we are affirming or denying. If we do not proceed cautiously in our argument, we might rashly adopt a false opinion and stick to it afterwards because of an emotional commitment to the false position [XIII. 112–120].

It is particularly foolish to apply speculation to temporal concerns. Events in the temporal sphere cannot be predicted by man; his judgment is particularly liable to error when it comes to estimating the result of a particular action, or the moral worth of people. For what seems harsh and unpromising may yet blossom into loveliness and what appears almost fulfilled may come to grief. People of the common run are apt to pass quick moral judgments on others, but their judgments do not reflect eternal truth [XIII. 130–142].

Canto XIV

Revelation and the wisdom derived from universal order in the fourth state of paradise suggest the same truths; the internal and the external, intuition and mature reasoning upon phenomena speak the same language here. What is received from the "outside" spreads abroad again from within by the same harmonious waves [XIV. 1–8].

The last question which we can ask in this sphere of paradise is this: what will be the function of the wisdom that we have acquired here, in the fullness of our development? Here our intellect reaches maturity; when we reach the fullness of life, where intellect, desire, and will are joined together as the soul is joined to the body, can we keep in undiminished brilliance that perception of universal order which we attain in this state? Or, to put it into slightly different words, in that integrated state, can we keep the sharpness of vision which our intellect enjoys here [XIV. 13–18]?

Those who are afraid to die to themselves cannot imagine the joy and harmony which every new questioning, every new advance toward increased vision brings in paradise. This question, too, brings a new awareness of joy and harmony and a new perception of the threefold nature of being. Infinite and all-encompassing, being is the source of all life and all power [XIV. 19–33].

The answer to the last question is already inherent in the measure of wisdom received in this state; in itself, this wisdom is a promise of the fully integrated life, for its voice is as the voice of the angel announcing the Incarnation of the Godhead [XIV. 34–37]. In paradise our brightness or power—the first attribute of being—increases with our ardor, our burning love—the second attribute of being—which in turn depends upon our scope of vision or understanding—the third attribute of being. Vision depends upon our willingness to receive it, a willingness which is encountered by an equal measure of grace [XIV. 37–42]. When we attain the complete form of personality in a union of intellect, desire, and will—the state described in the last four lines of the *Comedy*—we will receive the light that nourishes our power of vision in even greater abundance. The intensified vision will, in turn, nourish our burning love, and the greater burning will brighten the intellectual light we radiate [XIV. 43–51]. Then the full personality, which in our temporal existence is almost eclipsed and covered over, will shine with the light of the intellect whose radiance envelops us in the fourth state of paradise. The outlines of the completely developed personality will shine with a glow brighter than the light of understanding which surrounds man while he has attained maturity of intellect alone. When the final integration is achieved, our whole being will be glorified, and we will comprehend not only with our intellect but also with our desire and our will the glorified selves of others, whose radiance will then not eclipse or dazzle our new vision [XIV. 52–60].

The state of intellectual maturity which one reaches at this point leads to the desire of emotional fulfillment. One wishes to enjoy the united action of intellect, desire, and will, and wants to feel toward *all life* what one has felt so far only toward those who are closest [XIV. 61–66].

Our desire to attain to this higher vision, where not only the harmonious order of the universe and its eternally perfect laws are grasped by the admiring intellect, but the true substance of each being is also revealed to the unified perception of intellect, desire, and will together, leads us to a prophetic glimpse into the future. Prophecy is the highest form of the wisdom attainable in this state, the deepest insight into the order of the universe and into the working of its laws. The brightening horizon of the future shows a new way to wisdom beyond those already revealed to us in this state. This new way is perhaps a combination of the way of knowledge and the way of love to be attained by humanity in the dawn of a new age directly inspired by the third attribute of being, love [XIV. 67–78].[4]

This hint of the abundance of life that we shall ultimately attain is enough to make us turn inward and see the revelation once granted to

us grow brighter, more meaningful, than ever before. Having understood in terms of our personal revelation what this promise of a fully
integrated existence means for *us*, we become able to receive a larger
vision. As we direct our strengthened power of vision outward, we find
ourselves in the next state, where a purely intellectual contemplation
of universal order is superseded by complete personal and emotional
involvement in the service of that order [XIV. 79–84].

Images

Of all objects of nature the sun carries the greatest weight of
meanings in the entire *Divine Comedy*. Besides being the source of all
light in Dante's physical universe, the sun is also the image of divine
reason, which is the source of intellectual light in the poem. This light
does not penetrate into hell: those who live there "have lost the good
of the intellect." In the first canto of the *Inferno* Dante is driven by
the beasts into a wilderness "where the sun is silent" and no sunlight
falls over his path until the sun rises over the island of Mount Purgatory. It is not divine reason itself, but merely its human shadow in the
shape of Virgil which leads Dante through hell and shows him the inner
landscape of evil and error. But on the winding terraces of Mount
Purgatory the position of the sun is always carefully noted: the pilgrims
have to follow the sun.[5]

Here, in the Heaven of the Sun, the sun's light is surpassed by the
brightness of the spirits:

> Quant' esser convenia da sè lucente
> quel ch'era dentro al sol dov' io entra' mi,
> non per color, ma per lume parvente!
> [X. 40–42]

(How shining in itself must have been that which was within the Sun as I
entered it, showing not by color but by light!)

The spirits are suns themselves: *quegli ardenti soli* Dante calls them
[X. 76]. St. Francis, whose life is narrated here by St. Thomas
Aquinas, was born into our world like a rising sun: *nacque al mondo
un sole* [XI. 50]. As in the Heaven of Venus, the spirits here, too, are
shown as lights: *quei santi lumi* [XIII. 29]. Their being blossoms with
light [XIV. 13–14].

Not only the spirits, but the entire universe is presented in images of
light:

> Ciò che non more e ciò che può morire
> non è se non splendor di quella idea
> che partorisce, amando, il nostro sire;
> [XIII. 52–54]

(That which dies not and that which can die are nothing but the splendor of that Idea which our Sire, in loving, begets.)

In this heaven of pure intellectual light we contemplate the world in philosophical terms: the universe is the reflection of the divine Idea. The light that makes such contemplation possible is given freely by the supreme Good [XIV. 47]; such light enables us to understand until understanding becomes ardor and we ourselves begin to radiate the same intellectual light in proportion to our understanding and joy. This light is, above all, clear: the third circle of lights that brightens around Dante suggests the fullness of an understanding which is yet to come; it has a clarity that is too glowing for eyes not grown strong enough to support it.

> Ed ecco intorno, di chiarezza pari,
> nascere un lustro sopra quel che v'era,
> a guisa d 'orizzonte che rischiari.
>
>   *   *   *
>
> O vero isfavillar del santo spiro,
> come si fece subito e candente
> agli occhi miei che vinti non soffriro!
> [XIV. 67–69; 76–78]

(And lo, all round and all of equal brightness, rose a lustre surpassing what was there, like a brightening horizon. . . . Ah, very sparkling of the Holy Spirit! How suddenly glowing it became to my eyes, which were overcome and could not bear it!)

But light and, to a much lesser extent, fire imagery is not the dominant one in the Heaven of the Sun. The sun is the father of all mortal life—*padre d'ogni mortal vita*—and the Heaven of the Sun is governed by images and metaphors of the life the sun calls forth: plants, fruit, and flowers. The water-world of the moon and the earth-world of Mercury in themselves were incapable of bringing forth life. But the union of water and earth in Venus produced the seed, as shown in the images of germination. The light of the Sun-heaven ripens this seed into an abundant harvest.

The truth of St. Dominic's wisdom which the erring Dominicans whittle away is likened to a plant in XI. 137:

la pianta onde si scheggia.

St. Dominic's birthplace is described as

> quella parte, ove surge ad aprire
> Zefiro dolce le novelle fronde
> di che si vede Europa rivestire,
> [XII. 46–48]

(a part from which the leaf-opening west wind rises to dress Europe in new foliage again).

The spirits themselves are flowering plants in the garland that circles around Beatrice. St. Thomas says to Dante:

> Tu vuoi saper di quai piante s'infiora
> questa ghirlanda, che interno vagheggia
> la bella donna ch'al ciel t'avvalora.
> [X. 91–93]

(Thou wouldst know what plants are these that bloom in this garland which surrounds with looks of love the fair lady who strengthens thee for heaven.)

They form a blessed wreath—*beato serto* [X. 102]. Later they are called eternal roses:

> così di quelle sempiterne rose
> volgeansi circa noi le due ghirlande.
> [XII. 19–20]

(These eternal roses were weaving around us the two garlands.)

Their very being blossoms with light [XIV. 13–14]. They all sprang from the same seed, as St. Bonaventura says to Dante:

> lo seme,
> del qual ti fascian ventiquattro piante.
> [XII. 95–96]

(the seed wherefrom twenty-four plants encircle thee.)

The warning against rash judgments in Canto XIII is also given in two similes taken from plant life:

> Non sien le genti ancor troppo sicure
> a giudicar, sì come quei che stima
> le biade in campo pria che sien mature:
>
> ch'io ho veduto tutto il verno prima
> il prun mostrarsi rigido e feroce,
> poscia portar la rosa in su la cima.
> [XIII. 130–135]

(So also let not the people be too sure in judging, like those that reckon the corn in the field before it is ripe. For I have seen the briar first show harsh and rigid all through the winter and later bear the rose upon its top.)

The growth and harvesting of fruit and ear suggest a natural parallel with the growth and gathering in of wisdom. The whole career of the *"gran dottor"* [XII. 85] St. Dominic is described in terms of cultivation:

> ed io ne parlo
> sì come dell' agricola, che Cristo
> elesse all' orto suo per aiutarlo.
> [XII. 70–72]

(and I speak of him as of the labourer whom Christ chose to help Him in His orchard.)

The work of Dominic and his disciples brought a marvellous fruit which his godmother foresaw in a dream: *il mirabile frutto / ch'uscir dovea di lui e delle rede* (the marvellous fruit that should spring from him and from his heirs) [XII. 65–66]. When Dominic completed his studies, he began to care for the vineyard of the Church:

> si mise a circuir la vigna,
> che tosto imbianca, se il vignaio è reo;
> [XII. 86–87]

(he began to go round the vineyard, which soon withers if the keeper is at fault).

His activities against heresy were like those of a torrent, both destructive and life-giving: destroying diseased stumps and watering the orchard.

> si mosse,
> quasi torrente ch'alta vena preme;
>
> e negli sterpi eretici percosse
> l 'impeto suo, più vivamente quivi
> dove le resistenze eran più grosse.
>
> Di lui si fecer poi diversi rivi
> onde l 'orto cattolico si riga,
> sì che i suoi arbuscelli stan più vivi.
> [XII. 98–105]

(he went forth like a torrent driven from a high spring, and on the heretic thickets his force struck with most vigour where the resistance was stubbornest. From him there sprang then various streams by which the Catholic garden is watered, so that its saplings have new life.)

But harvests are not always good; the straying of the Franciscans from
the example of their founder will bring an evil harvest:

> e tosto si vedrà della ricolta
> della mala coltura, quando il loglio
> si lagnerà che l' arca gli sia tolta.
>   [XII. 118–120]

(and soon will be seen some harvest of the bad tillage, when the tares shall
complain that the bin is refused to them.)

How these images of cultivation, fertility, and plant life are linked with
the concept of understanding in this heaven is shown by St. Thomas'
words. He says in one place that having answered Dante's first question he will now proceed to resolve the poet's perplexity about the
second problem:

> "Quando l' una paglia è trita,
> quando la sua semenza è già riposta,
> a batter l' altra dolce amor m'invita.
>   [XIII. 34–36]

(Since the one sheaf is threshed and its grain now garnered, sweet charity
bids me beat out the other.)

This metaphor likens understanding to the ripe seed to be threshed out
and stored in the mind. A few remaining metaphors of leaf [XII. 121],
fruit [XIII. 70–71], seed [XIII. 66], root [XIV. 12], and fertility [XIV.
27] complete this group of images which represents the particular
virtue of this heaven as *fruitful* wisdom.

But the water and earth images dominating the lower heavens are
not completely absent. The accurate description of both St. Francis'
and St. Dominic's birthplace brings into this heaven the streams,
rivers, hills and cities of the earth and even the waves of the ocean:

> Intra Tupino e l' acqua che discende
> del colle eletto del beato Ubaldo
> fertile costa d'alto monte pende,
>   [XI. 43–45]

(Between the Topino and the water that falls from the hill chosen by the
blessed Ubaldo hangs a fertile slope of the lofty mountain).

and

> non molto lungi al percoter dell' onde,
> retro alle quali, per la lunga foga,

lo sol talvolta ad ogni uom si nasconde,

siede la fortunata Calaroga
[XII. 49–52]

(not far from the beating of the waves behind which the sun, after his long flight, sometimes hides himself from all men, lies favoured Calahorra).

The image of rippling water in a round vessel that comes to Dante's mind when Beatrice begins to talk after St. Thomas Aquinas has finished his discourse, reminds us, perhaps, that much of our capacity is here still dormant in the potential state and that his thought moves on this larger potentiality as ripples do on water [XIV. 1–9].

The difference between the imagery of the Heaven of the Sun and that of the lower heavens does not consist solely in the less frequent use of earth and water images and in the greater emphasis on vegetation and light. There is a greater degree of harmony here than in any of the lower heavens. Here the spirits circle around Dante and Beatrice, singing:

> Poi, sì cantando, quegli ardenti soli
> si fur girati intorno a noi tre volte,
> come stelle vicine ai fermi poli,
>
> donne mi parver, non da ballo sciolte,
> ma che s' arrestin tacite ascoltando
> fin che le nuove note hanno ricolte.
> [X. 76–81]

(When, singing thus, these burning suns had circled round us three times, like stars near the steadfast poles, they appeared to be like ladies not freed from the dance, but pausing in silence and listening till they have caught the new strain.)

Voice joins voice in a harmony that surpasses in sweetness and intricacy the choir of the spirits in the Heaven of Venus:

> così vid' io la gloriosa rota
> moversi, e render voce a voce in tempra
> ed in dolcezza ch' esser non può nota,
> se non colà dove gioir s' insempra.
> [X. 145–148]

(so I saw the glorious wheel move and render voice to voice with harmony and sweetness that cannot be known but there where joy becomes eternal.)

As the order of this heaven unfolds, the harmonies of dance and song grow more and more intricate: another circle of spirits joins the first

and answers its movement with harmonious movement and its song
with corresponding song.

> a rotar cominciò la santa mola;
>
> e nel suo giro tutta non si volse
> prima ch' un' altra di cerchio la chiuse,
> e moto a moto, e canto a canto colse.
>
> [XII. 3–6]

(the holy millstone began to turn, and it had not made a full circle before
another enclosed it round and matched motion with motion and song with
song.)

The metaphor of the two millstones implies, of course, the grinding of
the garnered seeds of wisdom into nourishing flour, from which the
bread of the angels is made. Finally, a third circle embraces the other
two and they form a triple crown, the first of the light emblems which
the spirits form in the higher heavens. There are no such emblems in
the lower heavens; but in the Heaven of the Sun, of Mars, of Jupiter,
and of Saturn the spirits form figures of light which also contribute to
the increasing harmony and integration as we ascend from sphere to
sphere.

Here the spirits dance in circles. Though in the Heaven of Venus
their dance was already circular, it did by no means attain the intricacy
of the circular dances of the Sun-heaven. Images of the circle and of
circular movement occur abundantly in this heaven. The order of the
universe, whose recognition is the first task of the mature intelligence,
is presented, right at the outset, in terms of circular motion:

> lo primo ed ineffabile valore
>
> quanto per mente o per loco si gira
> con tanto ordine fe', ch' esser non puote
> senza gustar di lui chi ciò rimira.
>
> [X. 3–6]

(the primal and ineffable Power made with such order all that revolves in
mind or space that he who contemplates it cannot but taste of Him.)

I have already quoted examples of the circular dance of the spirits, but
I give one more, which shows the intricacy and variety of their
movement. Take twenty-four of the brightest stars, Dante says, and
arrange them in two circles so that one embraces the other,

e l' un nell' altro aver li raggi suoi
ed ambedue girarsi per maniera,
ch l'uno andasse al prima e l'altro al poi:

ed avrà quasi l'ombra della vera
costellazion e della doppia danza,
che circulava il punto dov' io era.
[XIII. 16–21]

(and the one to have its beams within the other, and both to revolve in such
a manner that the one goes first and the other after. Then he will have as it
were a shadow of the real constellation and of the double dance that circled
round the point where I was.)

In the same canto the center of the circle is used to give us a metaphor
about truth:

vedrai il tuo credere e il mio dire
nel vero farsi come centro in tondo.
[XIII. 50–51]

(thou shalt see that thy belief and my words meet in the truth as the centre
of the circle.)

The circle is one of Dante's most powerful images, standing, in
accordance with the philosophy of his time, for order, perfection, and
unity. At the end of the journey the circle becomes part of his final
vision of God. But in this heaven the most effective use of circular
movement is shown in the great simile of the horologue:

Indi come orologio, che ne chiami
nell' ora che la sposa di Dio surge
a mattinar lo sposo perchè l' ami,

che l' una parte l' altra tira ed urge,
tin tin sonando con sì dolce nota,
che il ben disposto spirto d' amor turge;

cosi vid' io la gloriosa rota
moversi. . . .
[X. 139–146]

(Then, like a clock that calls us at the hour when the bride of God rises to
sing matins to the Bridegroom that he may love her, when one part draws
or drives another, sounding the chime with notes so sweet that the well-
ordered spirit swells with love, so I saw the glorious wheel move.)

Here the circular movements in opposite directions give out a greater
harmony: Siger, the "syllogiser of odious truths" turns in the opposite

direction from Aquinas, the official philosopher of the Church, and yet out of these opposite movements a sweet chime is born.

The horologue also indicates the transition between the singing in the Heaven of the Sun and the later, instrumental harmonies of the higher heavens. Its chimes are a prelude of the sounds of the higher heavens: sounds of the viol, the harp, the lyre, and the organ. In another way the horologue, being an artefact, a man-made instrument, indicates a transition toward the jewelry and artefact images of the higher heavens. Plants and flowers, the dominating images in the Heaven of the Sun, are there superseded by images that have less of earthly nature in them.

To the theme of spiritual voyage which is here suggested by two similes taken from sea journeys [XI. 119–120 and XIII. 136–138], the theme of spiritual warfare is added, especially in the representation in XII. 34–45 of the Christian Church as an army on the march under the leadership of St. Francis and St. Dominic. Here Dante seems to remind us that the journey through paradise is not only a pilgrimage toward being and perfect selfhood, but simultaneously a fight against the erring world, *contro al mondo errante* [XII. 94]. In the heaven of wisdom the world of temporal concerns and all that the world stands for are appropriately characterized as erring.

The images of sealing and stamping occur here too and come to a culmination in the great philosophical passage of XIII. 52–78 that breathes a neoplatonic dualism of matter and spirit. The wax of generated things, the things of nature, produced from seed and without seed by the moving heavens

> non sta d' un modo, e però sotto il segno
> ideale poi più e men traluce:
>
> ond' egli avvien ch' un medesimo legno,
> secondo specie, meglio e peggio frutta;
> e voi nascete con diverso ingegno.
>
> Se fosse a punto la cera dedutta,
> e fosse il cielo in sua virtù suprema,
> la luce del suggel parebbe tutta;
>
> ma la natura la dà sempre scema,
> similemente operando all' artista,
> ch' ha l' abito dell' arte e man che trema.[6]
>
> [XIII. 68–78]

(is not always in the same state, and therefore beneath the stamp of the idea the light shines through more and less; hence it comes that trees of one and the same species bear better and worse fruit and you are born with different talents. If the wax were moulded perfectly and the heavens were at the height of their power, all the brightness of the seal would be seen; but nature always gives it defectively, working like the artist who has the skill of his art but a hand that trembles.)

The images in the Heaven of the Sun not only help to place this heaven between the higher and the lower states of paradise, but embody a certain progression within that state itself. The fourteenth canto, which is almost equally divided between the Heaven of the Sun and that of Mars, shows this progression best. The plant and flower images fade out in the beginning of the canto—the last one occurs in line thirteen—and are replaced by images representing perfection and dominated by the number three, the number of the Trinity. The light becomes stronger, but it is surpassed by the incandescence of the glorified flesh in lines 52–57:

> Ma sì come carbon che la fiamma rende,
> e per vivo candor quella soperchia
> sì che la sua parvenza si difende,
>
> così questo fulgor, che già ne cerchia,
> fia vinto in apparenza dalla carne
> che tutto dì la terra ricoperchia;

(But like a coal that gives out a flame and with its white glow outshines it so that its own appearance is preserved, so this effulgence that now surrounds us will be surpassed in brightness by the flesh which the earth still covers).

The human essence, symbolized here by the glorified body, rises out of the earth and surpasses in brightness the light of the Sun-heaven. Such incandescence, together with the appearance of the third circle of lights that completes the emblem of the triple crown, suggests the human entity's rising above the state of intellectual maturity into a state of fuller humanity. This is, of course, a higher state of paradise, but might also be interpreted as Joachim's third *status* toward which humanity is advancing in the corridors of history.

VI.

Maturity of the Emotions: Self-Sacrifice

From intellectual maturity we rise into a higher state, where to the clear light of the intellect the ardor of self-sacrifice is added. The sacrificial dedication of the heart, the first step in the new state, is immediately rewarded by an increase of radiance, a greater vision. Such vision reveals the new state to be clearly superior to the state of intellectual wisdom attained before [XIV.85–93]. But the greater intensity in the new state is the result of the transforming power of the previous state; it is the sunlike wisdom acquired there that adorns the inhabitants of this state [XIV. 94–96].

Looking back, we perceive another characteristic of the state of intellectual maturity which we have just transcended. That state, the first one untouched by the shadow of the earth, has the power of transmuting the states below it into the states above. The fire of understanding changes the incomplete vision characteristic of spiritual infancy that is the Heaven of the Moon into the complete vision of reality in the Heaven of Saturn. The state of honorable worldly ambition that is the Heaven of Mercury is transmuted into the search for perfect justice not motivated by worldly recognition in the Heaven of Jupiter. The still-earthly love of the soul's first meeting with otherness in the Heaven of Venus becomes, transmuted by the wisdom of the Heaven of the Sun, the heavenly love of service and self-sacrifice in the Heaven of Mars.

The sign of burning self-sacrifice is the cross of Christ. Taking up our own cross and following Christ gives us the power to see Him in the fifth state of paradise. Here knowledge is inseparable from action and action is the crucifixion of the ego. In the previous state knowledge came from the contemplation of universal order; it was an intellectual knowledge of the eternal law that governs the universe. Here knowledge is a personal knowledge of the power of being in the human form: not a rapture of the mind only, but, in addition to it, a fire of emotions kindled by our active following of this power. To see the power of being in human form means more than to see the harmony and the order in the world: it is to know it in human relatedness, know it more fully than can be communicated in words. But this felt knowledge is encircled by the purely intellectual understanding, in the way the geometrical figure of the cross is contained within a circle [XIV 97–108].

The virtue of self-sacrifice is manifested in the intercourse between human beings [XIV. 109–111] and its manifestations are completely individual, as individual as are the human beings themselves. The light of self-sacrifice cuts into the protective darkness with which people try to shield themselves with so much ingenuity and skill. But their true personalities can only become evident when they are picked out by this light like motes dancing in a shaft of light [XIV. 112–117].

The harmonies unfolding in this state make a sweet music we do not understand as yet. The idea of self-sacrifice certainly baffles reason, but it carries emotional conviction [XIV. 118–123]. We feel that this is the way to resurrection and victory but we cannot yet see why. But the call heard in this state, exhorting us to "arise and conquer" inspires greater love in the soul than anything encountered before on our journey [XIV. 124–129]. This new love is more intense than any we have known before, more ardent even than the personal experience of love which we have called our personal revelation. The call to self-sacrifice, even without a direct personal content, is enough to set the soul on fire. But in this state we have not yet attempted to see into the meaning of our personal revelation; when we shall turn to her we shall find new understanding. The sacred pleasure of beholding her will give a new intensity to life in this state, an intensity which surpasses our first impersonal ardor for self-sacrifice [XIV. 130–139].

Canto XV

What is necessary to self-sacrifice? Goodwill, that produces the right kind of love and is opposed to the self-will that brings forth greed. It is goodwill and the love born of it which are the foundations of a life of self-sacrifice [XV. 1–3]. Such goodwill produces concord among people; it is also an anticipation of the wishes of others, a constant readiness to "fall silent" to hear the needs of another [XV. 4–9]. But the love of transient things, of the illusions of the visible world, deprives us of the right love necessary to reach this state of development [XV. 10–12]. The fire of self-sacrifice seems short-lived and even futile in the temporal realm, but in eternity it is never extinguished [XV. 13–21]. Living in this state means never to depart from the example of the cross, the emblem of self-sacrifice [XV. 22–23].

At this point of the journey an encounter takes place which indicates that human development here reaches an entirely new phase. We meet a hitherto unknown, yet strangely familiar figure,[1] at whose greeting the memory of our own experience of love begins to glow so intensely that we think we have reached the utmost limit of happiness. Our personal revelation reassures us that the figure, who behaves as if there were a strong bond between him and ourselves, will further increase our insight into the meaning of paradise [XV. 25–36]. But at the beginning we are unable to understand this new experience: its comprehension seems to lie beyond the capacity of our intellect. We know that the figure we meet offers a more intense love than we have known before, but we do not yet see where this feeling comes from [XV. 37–42]. We cannot identify this figure who greets us with so much affection, telling us how much he had expected our coming and calling us his "seed" and his "son" [XV. 49–52]. We are known by him much more intimately than we can know him, because his vision is immersed into being where past, future, and the most hidden thoughts—even those we hide from ourselves—are known. Although he knows what we want to know, he lets us ask our question, for in the secure, bold, and joyous manifestation of our desire to know he sees the fulfillment of the law of love [XV. 55–69].

> Ma perchè il sacro amore, in che io veglio
> con perpetua vista e che m' asseta
> di dolce disiar, s' adempia meglio,
>
> la voce tua sicura, balda e lieta
> suoni la volontà, suoni il disio,
> a che la mia risposta è già decreta.
>
> [XV. 64–69]

(But, that the holy love in which I keep watch with constant vision and which makes me thirst with sweet desire may be better satisfied, let thy voice, confident, bold and joyful, sound forth the will and the longing to which already my answer is decreed.)

He is as eager to fulfill our desire to know him as the people in the third state of paradise—the Heaven of Venus—were to reveal to us their true natures. But there is a difference between our situation here and in the former state of meeting with the true self of another in sexual love. The figure we meet here is not a stranger; he does not symbolize a meeting with otherness. Our personal revelation guiding us anticipates a profounder insight here than that received in the third heaven about meeting another being in sexual love. She assures us that our question is indeed worth asking. And so, once again strengthening the desire which calls for an answer as well as for an increase in the depth of our vision according to the law of progress, we ask our question so that we may *understand* what we have hitherto only *felt*.

The question itself shows already that we have learned something about this new state; the very formulation of a question brings new insight. We feel deep affection toward this unknown figure but cannot as yet say why. Our will is drawing us to him but our reason is unsatisfied. In his case, however, will and reason are in perfect balance, for he is illuminated and warmed equally by the sun of being to which he constantly turns. Unlike the inhabitants of the Sun-heaven, who live in a state of intellectual maturity manifested in philosophical or theological speculation, he has achieved an equal measure of emotion and intellect—following the example of being itself manifesting in human form—and thus reached an emotional maturity, a more integrated existence, which manifests in *action*.

In the people below this state will and reason are not in balance and, in spite of the check of intellect, they are in their actions often carried away by uncontrolled emotions. Though in speculation they are mature, in action they are often prompted by their hearts alone. This new state—symbolized by the Heaven of Mars—is, then, another step toward that fully integrated life which was promised to us pilgrims of paradise by the appearance of the third circle of lights just before we left the Heaven of the Sun [XV. 73–84].

Once we have put our question to him there is no delay in the answer.[2] We are his leaf, he tells us, and he is our root:

> "O fronda mia, in cu' io compiacemmi
> pure aspettando, io fui la tua radice;"
> [XV. 88–89]

(O my leaf, in whom I rejoiced even as I expected thee, I was thy root).

The rest of his answer is, as far as its anagogical content is concerned, only an amplification of this fundamental truth. He is not another, he is our own root, a deeper—or higher—self from which our present this-worldly self had sprung. This self had been waiting for us throughout our long and hard journey. And though he is us in a deeper sense, there are layers upon layers of our personality that separate us from him. He mentions only one of these layers, one of these interposing "selves," but it is, significantly, a "self" of pride that still has to be redeemed from its prison [XV. 91–96].

His first teaching to us is a lesson in simplicity. If we want to keep in touch with our deeper self, the root from which our individuality springs, we should concentrate on the essentials of life, avoid distractions of ornament and luxury and live in continence, peace, and sobriety, as the citizens of a well-ordered city do. A life filled with such traditional virtues is also a life of warfare against the errors of the world. This warfare culminates in the martyrdom of self-sacrifice, which rends the veil of illusion that the visible or temporal world presents to us and restores man to his proper place in eternity [XV. 97–148].

Canto XVI

The nobility of our deeper self, whom we discover when we enter the state that attains the right balance between love and wisdom, emotion and intellect, fills us with joy and even inclines us to be proud of ourselves. Can it be that we—imperfect as we are—have sprung from so noble a root? But this nobility, this simplicity and clarity of purpose, this unwavering self-sacrifice cannot be made to live in us unless day after day we multiply the deeds that correspond to this deeper self. Now that we have encountered it we are apt to glorify it, and since this is, after all, a form of self-glorification, our personal revelation gives us a warning sign that it must not be carried to excess [XVI. 1–15]. It is just such an excessive admiration of the very goodness in ourselves that begins to lead us into pride and alienate us from our deeper self. If we yield to it, then the deeper self becomes overgrown with a far less noble nature until it is completely buried from our sight and forgotten: a root unseen and forgotten by the leaf.

Here we address the root-self in ceremonious terms of respect and love:

> "Voi siete il padre mio,
> voi mi date a parlar tutta baldezza,
> voi mi levate sì ch' io son più ch' io."
> [XVI. 16–18]

(You are my father, you give me all boldness to speak, you uplift me so that I am more than myself.)

Our encounter uplifts us and makes us aware that we are much greater than the little everyday self or ego we had thought we were. There is an original nobility in us which the vicissitudes of living in the deceitful and illusory temporal world could never quite extinguish. Now, on finding nobility again, we are filled with joy almost beyond measure, yet our mind remains clear and conscious, capable of containing this happiness [XVI. 19–21].

We become eager to know all we can about our origins; we wish to know about the conditions in which this noble and simple "root-self" was formed [XVI. 22–24]. Though we cannot, as yet, go beyond it into the remotest depths of the self [XVI. 43–45], we learn much about the world in which this deeper self was molded. As we have heard it said before, it was a world of essential simplicity, of internal unity and harmony, like a well-governed city of virtuous citizens, or like an ancient family proud of its unadorned virtues. The metaphors of city and family are apt here, because it is in the service of these units of society that people usually learn self-sacrifice. The causes of decline in cities and families are pride, greed for expansion, and the resulting mixture of irreconcilable elements, in one word, the abandonment of original purity and simplicity.[3]

Canto XVII

If we spring from so noble a root, if there is deep down within us such harmony of wisdom and feeling, are we not in our present miseries tragic figures like Phaeton, son of the sun, whose divine ancestry could not prevent him from falling [XVII. 1–4]? In spite of the goodness of our deeper self we are subject to evil in the temporal world of bondage; this is, at any rate, how we are shown to be both by the love experience that had first taken us out of the realm of illusion and by the root-self we are encountering in the fifth state of paradise [XVII. 4–6]. Again, it is only by questioning, by showing forth the *heat* of our desire and adding it to the *light* of intellectual curiosity that we can advance toward greater understanding and the wider vision that springs from it. Only if we formulate our desire by asking questions will we receive the answers we need on this journey [XVII. 7–12].

No doubt the deeper self, from which our present personality has sprung, sees our temporal vicissitudes intuitively in the mirror of being, where all things are seen in their true proportion, i.e., in their timeless and not in their time-bound importance [XVII. 13–18]. We ask therefore about the meaning, from the eternal perspective, of those external evils and misfortunes that beset us during our earthly life. How can we reconcile ourselves to evils that to the unilluminated human reason seem evils indeed [XVII. 13–27]?

To understand the answer we have to remember that the infinite ocean of eternity washes the shores of our enisled temporal existence and that in this context even the apparent evils happening to us are seen as parts of a harmonious design. Our free will is not violated by this design, however. This paradoxical truth makes it possible that even the worst outer events of our lives are parts of an eternal music of many notes and of great sweetness.

Outer events which to us seem misfortunes teach us to part with all we have considered most dear; the injunction of leaving our earthly father and mother, our country and our family, is forced upon us by these happenings. Having to give up what we have most clung to, we come to know self-sacrifice. But to lose country, family and friends is only the first step in this hard lesson leading to the wisdom of adversity [XVII. 46–57]. The second step is the abandonment of pride, the hard lesson of humiliation, when even the image of our own strength and self-sufficiency has to be given up [XVII. 58–60]. The third and hardest step we are forced to make is the acceptance of utter solitude among those who betray us [XVII. 61–69].

Yet in the temporal world of hardships we also come across examples of generous self-sacrifice, people who give of themselves in fulfilling the needs of others even before they are asked to do so [XVII. 73–75], and people who care not for gain but engage themselves completely in action that serves a worthy cause [XVII. 83–86]. The hardships we must endure should not make us envious or bitter against our fellow-men; if the undeserving seem unjustly favored by fortune, this is not really so. We shall understand in good time the law of reality that no one ever gets something for nothing [XVII. 97–99].

We have now received the answer to our question; we see the use of adversity in teaching us self-sacrifice. Adversity teaches both by personal deprivation and by the example of others. Yet we have still another doubt and must turn again to this newly-discovered wise father figure, this deeper self, who sees straight and wills straight and, as a result of the right vision and the right will, loves [XVII. 103–105].

How far should we carry self-sacrifice beyond what necessity im-

poses upon us? Must we jeopardize all earthly happiness by being loyal
to truth above everything [XVII. 109–111; 118–120]? The answer of
this treasure we have found in the fifth state of paradise is uncompromising for he draws this truth directly from his vision of being. We
must be faithful to our vision of eternity while we live in the temporal
realm. Uncompromising persistence on our part might appear injurious
to others; but in truth it will ultimately benefit them by making them
aware of their errors, by revealing the bitter truth which can heal them
[XVII. 127–132].

It is only through self-sacrifice learned in adversity that we come to
recognize our true mission in the visible world. By losing all for the
sake of which we might have swerved from fulfilling this mission, we
gain the strength to carry it out to the full. This is the truth our deeper
self affirms, while it reflects with the purity of a golden mirror the fire
of eternal truth [XVII. 121–123].

Canto XVIII.

For the eye of one who sees all in the larger framework of eternity,
even self-sacrifice forced upon us by pressure of circumstances is the
cause of rejoicing. But though we now have met our deeper self, we
have not become identified with it. For this root-self the more complete
the self-sacrifice is the more joy it gives, because it has become a
mirror reflecting the truth of being. But for us it still tastes bitter to be
deprived of what we hold most dear. Here our own experience of love,
our personal revelation which leads us toward the goal of being, comes
to our aid [XVIII. 1–4]. She says that if we can forget about all wrongs
and grievances and cease to be preoccupied with the seeming injustice
of what we have to suffer, we make room for love and she will stand
close to us [XVIII. 5–6]. In this state of self-denial a new truth of love
can come to us, the revelation that self-sacrifice is an essential part of
love. We cannot attain this new intensity of love unless there is another
to guide us, another for whom we are willing to give up our own self.
In doing so we find that all our other wishes are stilled. We are liberated
from any other desire—be it fame, friendship, power, or whatever the
world esteems—for in this intenser love the eternal joy of being
satisfies us completely, as we see it reflected from the face of the
beloved. Thus we discover that not only our deeper self reflects being
continually, but that our experience of love, the revelation made to us
during our temporal existence, also reflects being and thus answers all
our desires [XVIII. 7–18]. This, indeed, is the spiritual content of the

ideal marriage. From the point of falling in love in the third state of paradise—the Heaven of Venus—we have to mature, first intellectually, then emotionally, so as to be able to enter the perfect married state, which is continual self-sacrifice in joy.[4]

Yet we should not remain absorbed in the contemplation of the new depths of our love experience. There is yet more to be learned in this state and we have to turn our attention once more to the deeper self, who, through examples, points out to us the perfection of life as it is lived in his state of self-sacrifice [XVIII. 19–27]. Self-dedication is honored not only in the temporal world, but also in eternity. In fact, self-sacrifice is the way to true greatness, to fame that endures [XVIII. 28–33]. This is a life of action, or warfare, of unceasing struggle to realize the truth of being in the imperfect realm of the temporal. Those who dwell in this state do not put speaking above doing; their words and their actions are inseparable, for they express themselves through the continuous burning of their self-sacrifice [XVIII. 39]. Yet the force that drives them is not a desire of self-annihilation but rather an inexhaustible joy which perfects their deeds [XVIII. 41–42].

The world, however, does not always judge correctly a dedicated life. Some who are condemned by the world as self-seeking are revealed in paradise as leading lives of self-sacrifice. Here, too, as in the state of intellectual maturity, the apparent contradictions of the world of illusion are resolved in a higher order [XVIII. 43–48].

Self-sacrifice is an essential quality of the deeper self. It is, in effect, the crucifixion of the ego. If we acknowledge and recognize this root-self—as we have come to do in the fifth state of paradise—then we shall hear its voice singing within us. And if we dance our lives to the measure of this song, it will acquire the perfection of a work of art [XIII. 49–51].

Images

From the brilliantly clear light-world of the sun we rise into the ruddily glowing fire-world of Mars:

> Ben m' accors' io ch' io era più levato,
> per l' affocato riso della stella,
> che mi parea più roggio che l' usato.
> [XIV. 85–87]

(I was well assured that I had risen higher by the enkindled smile of the star, which seemed to me more ruddy than its wont.)

The planet itself is a fire; Cacciaguida calls it *"questo foco"* [XVI. 38]. Within this fire a burnt sacrifice—*olocausto*—is offered up to God by those living in this heaven. The ruling element in the Heaven of the Sun was also fire, but mainly in the form of light: it illumined the spirits both from without and within, but it did not warm them. Here, however, the heat of emotion is added to brilliance of intellect in equal measure:

> però che il sol, che v' allumò ed arse
> col caldo e con la luce, è sì iguali,
> che tutte simiglianze sono scarse.[5]
> [XV. 76–78]

(because the sun which illuminated and warmed you has such equality in its heat and light that all similes fall short in describing it.)

Dante himself has to put forth the *heat* of his desire—*la vampa del* [suo] *disio* [XVII. 7–8]—to attain the perfect expression of his wish. The spirits are fires here; they dart across the emblem of their unity, the cross, like points of fire across pure and tranquil skies:

> Quale per li seren tranquilli e puri
> discorre ad ora ad or subito foco,
> [XV. 13–14]

(As through the still and cloudless evening sky runs at times a sudden fire.)

Cacciaguida says that the spirits he shall name to Dante will act as the fire of lightning does in the cloud:

> farà l' atto
> che fa in nube il suo foco veloce.
> [XVIII. 35–36]

(will do there as does its swift fire in a cloud.)

Of the other elements, metaphors of flight [XV. 54, 72, 81 and XVIII. 45] and a few uses of the image of the wind [XVI. 28, XVII. 133] remind us of air. There is hardly any use of water imagery, save when the changes of Florence's fortunes are likened to the movement of the tides:

> E come il volger del ciel della luna
> copre ed iscopre i liti senza posa,
> così fa di Fiorenza la fortuna;
> [XVI. 82–84]

(and as the turning of the moon's heaven covers and lays bare the shores unceasingly, so fortune does with Florence).

Flight connotes progress with the help of the equal wings of emotion and intellect; the ebb and flow of water suggests that many potentialities, latent until now, are being realized through action in this sphere.

Earth, whose geography dominated the Heaven of Mercury and was still very much present in Venus and even in the Sun, is not represented here with her mountains and rivers and coastlines; what represents the earth in the Heaven of Mars is the man-made geography of the city of Florence:

> Gli antichi miei ed io nacqui nel loco,
> dove si trova pria l' ultimo sesto
> da quel che corre il vostro annual gioco.
> [XVI. 40–42]

(My ancestors and I were born at the place where the furthest ward is reached by the runner in your yearly games.)

This transformation of the natural features of the earth's surface into man-made landmarks—other cities, castles, villages are also frequently mentioned—has a significance that extends over many images in the Heaven of Mars. The natural is replaced by the man-made—by something that is not the product of unconscious forces but of a conscious mind and thus of a superior order. The plants, fruits, and flowers that grew in the Heaven of the Sun are replaced here by artefacts. The light of the sun had ripened the harvest germinating from the seeds in earth and water, but the fire of Mars would scorch vegetation. This fire belongs in the goldsmith's furnace to produce jewelry more lasting than the fruits and flowers of nature.[6] Gems, jewels, bands of alabaster and golden mirrors adorn this heaven:

> nè si partì la gemma dal suo nastro,
> ma per la lista radial trascorse,
> che parve foco retro ad alabastro.
> [XV. 22–24]

(And the gem did not leave its ribbon, but ran across by the radial strip and seemed fire behind alabaster.)

And:

> vivo topazio,
> che questa gioia preciosa ingemmi
> [XV. 85–86]

(living topaz who art a gem in this rich jewel)

and also:

> La luce in che rideva il mio tesoro,
> ch' io trovai lì, si fe' prima corrusca,
> quale a raggio di sole specchio d' oro.
> [XVII. 121–123]

(The light within which was smiling the treasure I had found there, first became ablaze like a golden mirror in the sun.)

The few metaphors of vegetation left in this heaven illustrate Dante's *natural* connection with Cacciaguida:

> "O fronda mia, in cu' io compiacemmi
> pure aspettando, io fui la tua radice;"
> [XV. 88–89]

(O my leaf, in whom I rejoiced only expecting thee, I was thy root)

he says to Dante in answer to the question asking for his name. And Dante calls him:

> "O cara piota mia, che sì t'insusi."
> [XVII. 13]

(O my dear seed-plot, who art raised so high.)

In Cacciaguida's last speech the whole of paradise with its ten heavens is compared to a tree, but this tree is not like the trees of nature:

> arbore, che vive della cima
> e frutta sempre e mai non perde foglia.
> [XVIII. 29–30]

(the tree which lives from the top and is always in fruit and never sheds its leaves.)

This tree is nourished not from below but from above and never decays; it also belongs to the realm above nature, among the creations of the conscious mind. It is as if the fire of Mars had transmuted the earlier images taken from earthly nature into the image of an undecaying eternal nature.[7] And this transmutation has a spiritual equivalent; though the intellectual maturity which Dante sees in the Heaven of the Sun is the result of a "natural," i.e., unforced, growth, the emotional maturity demonstrated to him in the Heaven of Mars cannot be attained without the conscious effort of the will.

That the imagery here is taken rather from the creations of the mind than from nature is also shown by some references to geometry, the science not of natural but of ideal forms. References to geometrical figures, especially to circles and crosses run through the entire *Paradiso*, from I. 39—*che quattro cerchi giunge con tre croci*—to the final simile of the geometrician's failure to measure the circle in XXXIII. 133–135. But here, in the Heaven of Mars, not only the figures but also the methods of geometry are employed. The chief emblem, the cross, is described in strict geometrical terms:

> il venerabil segno,
> che fan giunture di quadranti in tondo.
> [XIV. 101–102]

(the venerable sign which the meeting of the quadrants makes in a circle.)

The language of geometry is used again when Dante describes Cacciaguida's intuitive perception of what he knows by comparing it to the manner in which we on earth know the axioms of geometry:

> come veggion le terrene menti
> non capere in triangolo due ottusi.
> [XVII. 14–15]

(as earthly minds see that there cannot be two obtuse angles in a triangle.)

Implicit in the concept of the point is the whole Euclidian system[8] and implicit in the concept of number one are all the other numbers. Similarly, knowledge of the principle of all things, the primal One, will necessarily give us a knowledge of all things that derive from It:

> così come raia
> dall' un, se si conosce, il cinque e il sei.
> [XV. 56–57]

(even as from the unit, when it is known, radiate the five and six.)

The transition from "natural" images toward images of man-made objects or ideal forms can also be discovered in the description of the harmonies which pervade this heaven:

> come giga ed àrpa, in tempra tesa
> di molte corde, fa dolce tintinno . . .
> [XIV. 118–119]

(as viol and harp strung with many chords in harmony chime sweetly).

Song and dance, which, in growing intricacy, characterize all the heavens below this, melt here into instrumental harmonies; in the

imagery the "natural" expression of melody and rhythm is replaced
by their more sophisticated embodiment in the sound of man-made
instruments. The image of the chiming horologue in the Heaven of the
Sun provided the transition between the two kinds of music. The sweet
harmony of the organ—*dolce armonia da organo* [XVII. 44]—to which
Cacciaguida likens his vision of Dante's coming troubles, is not only
suggestive of the harmony of life's total design, but is, in its richness
and fullness, also a foreshadowing of the ever more complex music of
the higher heavens. The imagery of artefacts and instrumental music
culminates in the final reference to Cacciaguida, where he is shown
singing like an *artist*:

> mostrommi l' alma che m' avea parlato,
> qual era tra i cantor del cielo artista.
> [XVIII. 50–51]

(the soul that had talked with me showed me what was his artist's skill
among the singers of that heaven.)

The theme of spiritual warfare is continued by Cacciaguida's reference
to his part in the Emperor Conrad's crusade:

> Poi seguitai lo imperador Currado,
> ed ei mi cinse della sua milizia,
> tanto per bene oprar gli venni in grado.
> [XV. 139–141]

(Later, I followed the Emperor Conrad, and he girded me of his knighthood,
so greatly did I win his favour by good service.)

A simile illustrating the freedom of the will with the well-known ship
metaphor provides continuity of the image-theme of ships and sea
voyages, which runs through the *Paradiso* to culminate in the reference
to the Argo in the last canto. The ship simile here illustrates that our
lives in the temporal realm are not determined by the order of eternity
enclosing our earthly existence:

> necessità però quindi non prende,
> se non come dal viso, in che si specchia,
> nave che per corrente giù discende.
> [XVII. 40–42]

(yet does not thence derive necessity, any more than does a ship that drops
down stream from the eyes in which it is mirrored.)

The image of stamping occurs again in XVII. 7–9:

"Manda fuor la vampa
del tuo disio,'' mi disse, ''sì ch' ell' esca
segnata bene della interna stampa;''

(Put forth the flame of thy desire, so that it may issue marked clearly with
the internal stamp;)

and refers again, of course, to imprinting matter with form, but this
time not with a form born in the all-creating Mind but in the mind of
man himself.

In addition to these images, the Heaven of Mars is particularly rich
in familiar pictures of everyday life. These help to characterize the
state of emotional maturity as the one where the individual is fully
involved in direct action. This state brings with it a more complete
acceptance of everyday reality than any of the previous states of
paradise; this is no coincidence, for self-sacrifice always grows out of
the total acceptance of one's condition. The motes dancing in the
streaked sunlight of a sunblind [XIV. 112–117], the mantle that shrinks
as time cuts it around with his shears [XVI. 7–9], the famous picture
of the bitterness of exile: the salt bread and steep stairs of others
[XVII. 58–60], and the entire description of the republican simplicity
of early Florentine life in XV. 97–126 are perhaps the images which
give us the intensest feeling of earthly reality in the whole of the
Paradiso.

VII.

Maturity of the Will: Cooperation

The state of self-sacrifice, too, has to be transcended in the course of our journey. Our personal revelation to whom we turn again suggests that the clarity of joyful vision attained in this state will bring us to new heights. By practicing self-sacrifice and finding delight in it, gradually all preoccupation with the little self ceases, even the urge to deny it constantly. We reach a state—symbolized by the Heaven of Jupiter—where our life moves in a wider sweep [XVIII. 55–63].

In the state we enter now we understand that to live *with* the truth constitutes a higher achievement than to die *for* it. Here every trace of self-consciousness, of shame—which after all was, to some degree, the force that spurred us into self-sacrifice—is overcome by the superior and *more temperate* activity of this state: full cooperation carried out according to ideal justice [XVIII. 64–69].

The joy of this state is a shared emotion: people rejoice together in the common activity that constitutes their nourishment. It also makes their common purpose manifest to all who can read it [XVIII. 73–78]. The essence of this activity is love [XVIII. 70–71]; its mode is alternate movement and rest, both of which are meaningful within a larger design [XVIII. 79–81]. Because this pattern not only expresses harmony, but conveys a meaning directly to the mind just as writing does, it represents fully conscious, fully articulate cooperation—a planned effort. Such cooperation is of a higher order than cooperation in the ambitious, amorous, wisdom-seeking and self-sacrificing states; there it was not a primary aim, but a by-product of other activities. Here cooperation, whose soul is justice, is the main endeavor.

Such common work is the life-blood of human communities: of cities and of kingdoms. Their prosperity and long life may, on the surface, be attributed to economic or political causes, but they fall or survive according to how much search for true justice is carried on by their citizens. The poetic genius knows eternal justice intuitively; in fact, this genius is justice itself and gives long life to the communities and institutions where it is allowed to manifest itself [XVIII. 82–84].

Work achieved by loving and joyful cooperation is, above all, accurate in reflecting eternal justice down to the smallest part of the community [XVIII. 88–94]. From this work, ordered so as to be plainly intelligible to those who have eyes to read it, an even higher, no longer merely intelligible but dynamically living meaning arises. The work becomes an organic unity that speaks for itself. This transformation proceeds from the center of the intellectual meaning of the work[1] and is achieved, after patient accumulation of energy, in a burst of activity that makes foolish people, who do not understand the meaning of such transformations in states and cities, hope for their own material gain [XVIII. 95–102]. In this resurgence of energy that produces a living whole from the idea of justice, each cooperating individual has an exact task to fulfill:

> salir quali assai e quai poco,
> sì come il sol, che l' accende, sortille;
> [XVIII. 104–105]

(to mount, some much, some little, as the sun that kindles them appointed.)

They observe the strictest justice: each is in his just place, moves in the just degree, obeys the order given by the source of his own being. From such work a living embodiment of justice arises, a body of which all are part, yet in which they do not lose their distinct individuality:

> la testa e il collo d' un aquila vidi
> rappresentare a quel distinto foco.
> [XVIII. 107–108]

(I saw the head and neck of an eagle represented in that pricked-out fire.)

What moves us to such highly organized cooperation is our intuition of a just order of being. Our intuition is not guided by others: it guides us. The power within us which inspires and governs the growth of communities is ultimately our intuition of justice:

quella virtù ch' è forma per li nidi;
[XVIII. 111]

(that power which is form for the nests).

But the human being who grasps the just order by intuition obeys this power consciously, with free will, contrary to the nest-building birds who obey instinct. The work raised by cooperative effort progresses beyond the planned patterns to an organic entity and grows in complexity from something like a plant [XVIII. 113] to a higher form, which, in its resemblance to the body of an animal (eagle) fulfills the design of eternal justice [XVIII. 114]. Through such work it appears clearly that whatever justice people possess in the temporal sphere is the effect of eternal justice [XVIII. 115–117].

The cooperative work to embody eternal justice among people in the visible world is threatened by anything that brings disunity, and especially by the corruption of spiritual aims and organizations by money [XVIII. 118–123]. Internecine warfare is the result of disunity; but the worst kind of warfare comes from the abuse, for the sake of material gain, of the spiritual power which was meant to nourish all [XVIII. 127–129].[2] In real cooperation, one dies to the world and to the self that seeks gain, and lives in eternity [XVIII. 131–132].

Opposed to this ideal of cooperation shown in the sixth state of paradise, stands a mistaken concept of the extreme individualist who lives as if no one else existed. It is a concept that seems virtuous on the surface only, for behind the noble-sounding idea of self-sufficiency there hides the principle of "every man for himself" in the scramble for money. The competitive "*bellum omnium contra omnes*" is, of course, at the opposite pole to the truth of cooperation and community lived in the sixth state of paradise [XVIII. 133–136].

Canto XIX

Every individual who cooperates in creating an image of eternal justice in the sixth state of paradise is woven together with others into the fabric of their common work and into the common rejoicing over the sweet fruition of their efforts. Yet at the same time each one is an individual form of love, a distinct ruby whose fire is enkindled by being itself, and who, from the depths of its own self, reflects being without distortion [XIX. 1–6].

Earthly experience cannot attest, time-bound imagination cannot comprehend the perfect selflessness of this state, where *I* and *mine* is

identical with *we* and *ours*. Conceptual reasoning must hold fast to
self-identity and even self-interest, but at this stage of human development there is no distinction whatever between the voice of our own
identity and interest and the voice that proclaims the identity and
interest of a whole community formed to the image of justice [XIX. 7–
12].

Those who live according to justice do not desire a greater glory
than the just place which they occupy within a greater whole [XIX.
13–15], and their example is so powerful that even those who are
bound to the illusions of the temporal world pay lip-service to this
ideal of cooperation, although they refuse to follow it [XIX. 16–18]. A
perfect unity of intention, of love, and of rejoicing characterizes this
fellowship of eternal justice:

> Così un sol calor di molte brage
> si fa sentir, come di molti amori
> usciva solo un suon di quella image.
> [XIX. 19–21]

(As a single glow is felt from many brands, so from that image came forth a
single sound of many loves.)

Having contemplated the image of eternal justice and its workings, we
have fulfilled our first task in the sixth state of paradise. Our increased
vision now again moves us to ask a question. We enter the path to
further enlightenment, in obedience to the law of progress. This
question grows out of a passionate hunger for understanding, which,
at the same time, is a hunger for justice:

> solvetemi, spirando, il gran digiuno
> che lungamente m' ha tenuto in fame,
> non trovandogli in terra cibo alcuno.
> [XIX. 25–27]

(breathe forth and deliver me from the great fast that has long kept me
hungry, finding no food for it on earth.)

In this state of paradise we become more than ever puzzled by apparent
injustices in the lives of others. The love of justice that has now been
kindled within us demands a solution. But before we can understand,
we have to see what kind of understanding it is that we are seeking.
Only by admitting that our capacity to receive light is limited can we
ready ourselves for the answer. In this state of perfect justice we must
realize that even in the desire for knowledge that has ensured our
progress through paradise, there exists a just and an unjust measure.

We have to desire knowledge justly, that is to the degree it befits our inner condition. If we thought we could receive an answer to all our doubts about eternal justice at once, we would fall into the ignorance and distortion of pride by thinking ourselves greater than who we are [XIX. 40–51].

What exactly is our limitation in understanding eternal justice? It is our finitude of being. We are only finite entities whose being is derived from Being itself, and we cannot measure our own source. Being that fills all things fills us, too, and the light of our mind is but one ray of the original light. Perfect understanding is the result of a perfect union between the knower and the known and we, finite as we are both in being and in light, cannot perfectly possess the infinite. Thus we have to admit, before we can receive an answer to our as yet unpronounced question, that though we may perceive the just cause for many apparent injustices in the lives of others, the causes of many other similar injustices lie too deeply hidden in the ocean of being, at depths which are beyond our reach [XIX. 52–63]. Yet we must not forget that as we continue to grow—since our whole journey through the states of paradise is really a growth in being—we will receive illuminations which will clear up more and more of the apparent contradictions between eternal justice and temporal conditions. For all light, all inspiration that comes to us radiates from the untroubled depths of being, and the obscurities and shadows that hide from us the ultimate justice of the universe are not due to the imperfections of that living justice but solely to our own distorted view of things, our own imprisonment in nothingness of which the flesh is the external symbol:

> Lume non è, se non vien dal sereno
> che non si turba mai, anzi è tenebra,
> od ombra della carne, o suo veleno.
>   [XIX. 64–66]

(There is no light but that which comes from the clear sky that is never clouded; else it is darkness, either the shadow of the flesh or its poison.)

We are caught in our own finitude and nothingness as within a labyrinth that hides from us the perfect justice manifest in the whole universe. But acknowledging this, trusting in future illumination and in the full knowledge of our limitations, we may now let justice itself ask the question that has vexed us so long [XIX. 67–70]. "Is it just that different peoples' opportunities to enter the path to being, to draw close to the ultimate aim of all existing things, are so unequal?" "Some people's actions and manner of life seem completely virtuous and yet they spend their lives vainly searching for a meaning, while others, in no way more worthy, receive a direct invitation or even have enlightenment thrust upon them [XIX. 70–78]. This is a crucial question for anyone concerned with the justice of the world-order. But before we can see the answer to it, we must again realize how much we presume when we ask such a question. No one can be the accurate judge of the conditions or the internal justice of another's life; we cannot see what is behind the presence or absence of certain opportunities in the lives of others, for we see their lives only from the outside, never from within and even less from the point of view of eternity [XIX. 79–81].

The first part of the answer we now receive is an explanation about the source of eternal justice:

> la prima volontà, ch' è per sè buona,
> da sè che è sommo ben, mai non si mosse.
>
> Cotanto è giusto, quanto a lei consuona;
> nullo creato bene a sè la tira,
> ma essa, radiando, lui cagiona.
>
> [XIX. 86–90]

(The Primal Will, which in itself is good, the Supreme Good, never was moved from itself; whatever accords with it is in that measure just; no created good draws it to itself, but it, raying forth, creates that good.)

The power of being that gives rise to the rule of justice throughout the universe cannot contradict its own nature. It can only work in ways that are inherently just and is in itself the measure of justice for any situation in the temporal world. To the extent that the life and the actions of a person correspond to the pattern which the power of being, working unobstructedly through him, would produce, to that extent that life and those actions are truly just. We cannot, therefore, compare the workings of eternal justice to some imaginary standard that we construct, or to the imperfect actions of people and then find fault with it. This were to make justice itself subject to a standard that is smaller than itself, its mere distorted echo in the human mind. This would be clearly absurd. We must come to see that whatever is good and right in this world derives its goodness from being. Wherever being truly manifests itself *without obstruction*, there we find perfect justice and nowhere else [XIX. 85–90].

Before we can go on to broader understanding, we are given this truth to absorb. Though we still do not understand the workings of eternal justice, the fact that we begin to see all goodness in people as the result of their conforming to eternal justice prepares us to receive the final answer to our doubts [XIX. 91–99].

No one who does not believe that the fullness of being has appeared among us in human form and thus gave us the possibility to attain the full development of our potentialities, meaning the full growth of our own being, can enter the path to the final union [XIX. 103–105]. But a mere verbal iteration of this doctrine, a mere intellectual conviction, does not amount to belief. Some who have never heard about the Christ attain much greater fullness of being and thus draw closer to being in accordance with eternal justice, than others who have Christ's name always on their lips. Therefore many, who outwardly may not appear to have found the way to being, the way to paradise, are, in reality already on it, since in their actions they reflect eternal justice. Others, on the contrary, may possess the outward signs of abundant life by professing belief in certain doctrines, but by their unjust actions they stand condemned and excluded from paradise. Their verbal profession insists they should be just, but they are not truly so and stand much further removed from being and from its human incarnation than those who do not know the words of doctrine but allow eternal justice to shine through their actions [XIX. 106–148].

Canto XX

Having seen eternal justice appear to us in the perfect cooperation of individuals and having heard how it rules the universe behind the seeming injustices of temporal existence, we can progress from this general truth to the actual contemplation of eternal justice in the dedicated individuals who not only teach us what justice is, but also live it. When we realize what eternal justice is by feeling its power in those who live it, the full glory of our experience becomes impossible to put into words. Such lives are songs of ecstatic delight, which must, of necessity, "slip and fall from our memory" [XX. 1–12]. But such meetings teach us better than the intellect alone could ever have done that eternal justice is joyful love, and that its works are inspired only by thoughts that spring from the contemplation of being [XX. 13–15].

But this is not all. Eternal justice is more abundant than we realize [XX. 19–21], and, as if to respond to our patient waiting, the perfect community of the just that embodies justice now completes the answers to our question, so that we may be fully satisfied. It speaks clearly with one voice now and what it says corresponds to the supreme expectation of the human heart. Justice is indeed what the pure heart expects and ultimately finds in the universe [XX. 22–30].

It is the contemplation of lives devoted to justice that brings us to the final truth. We learn from them that we are best moved to just actions by looking into being itself with an eagle eye which can support the sun undazzled, and then follow the inspiration that comes to us from this vision of being [XX. 31–36]. The supreme ideal of the just man is therefore David, ruler and poet in one, whose poetic inspiration enabled him to show forth perfect justice everywhere in his land.[3] The inspiration upon which the man seeking perfect justice relies becomes clear knowledge ("*ora conosce*") in this state of paradise, because to the original merit of trusting in one's inner voice a corresponding amount of illumination is added that transforms the glimpse of intuition into the full light of conviction [XX. 37–42]. As far as the individual is concerned, it is not the result of his action that makes him just; all depends upon his intention, i.e., his voluntary direction, and not the material consequences. Merely temporal changes can never make the eternal justice unjust [XX. 52–60].

If inspiration moves us to know justice, then inspiration, "the light that shines to every man that comes into this world" is enough to make us just.[4] Our problem, then, that some people have a greater opportunity to discover eternal justice than others, is only appearance, illusion. Regardless of their circumstances, all have the opportunity to draw close to being by embodying eternal justice in their thoughts, feelings, and actions, for eternal justice is the inner voice that talks to all who are willing to listen. This truth is symbolically shown by the presence of the pagan emperor Trajan and of the likewise pagan Ripheus, "*justissimus unus*" among the greatest spirits in this state. Their lives show that all have the capacity to realize their true selves and that they may reach fullness of being through longing for the justice which is

> l' imago della imprenta
> dell' eterno piacere, al cui disio
> ciascuna cosa, quale ell' è, diventa.
> [XX. 76–78]

(that image, the imprint of the Eternal Pleasure by whose desire all things come to have their being.)

To those in lower states, whose understanding did not penetrate deeply enough into the ocean of being where the just causes of everything that happens in the universe are hidden, pleasure and justice seemed opposed. But here, in the sixth state, it becomes clear that in eternity pleasure and justice are one: by longing for eternal pleasure we become what we really (i.e., eternally) are and thus fulfill eternal justice. The fulfillment of our individuality in paradise *is* justice, for though true justice may often contradict the opinion of people in the temporal world of illusion, it always corresponds to the ultimate aspiration of the purified heart [XX. 67–72; 76–78].[5]

The truth that through love of justice all may enter paradise, all may attain these states on the path to being, is the ultimate sweetness that comes from the voice of justice, a sweetness that lingers in the air as the last notes of the song of the lark when she rises higher and higher after becoming silent [XX. 73–75].

One more step remains to complete the understanding of justice. We have seen that justice is realized in perfect cooperation which comes from the self-transcending love of each individual who shares in the common effort [Canto XVIII]. We also understood, as far as our own finitude allowed it, the ultimate justice of the world-order [Cantos XIX and XX]. We have come to realize that justice is both love and pleasure, that it is the fulfillment of our own true self. But what makes justice justice? In other words, what is the quiddity that makes justice be itself and not some other virtue? This is the last question we must ask in this state and we are irresistibly impelled to ask it by our enlarged vision, for not until we have grasped the essence of justice can we see *how* it brings about the results which we have observed in this state [XX. 82–84; 88–93].

To define the quiddity of justice we have to understand how justice is accomplished within ourselves in terms of our own inner world and its familiar forces. (For quiddity is the nut that philosophy cannot crack. Yet it may be cracked by psychology, though not by telling us what the thing is in itself, but what the thing is *within* us.) Thinking about justice in this way we come to see it as dependent on the will. Just as the essence of wisdom was seen in the fourth state of paradise to lie in maturity of intellect, and the essence of self-sacrifice in the fifth state in maturity of emotion, so, in this state, the essence of justice is revealed as the maturity of the will. To be aware of the inspiration or intuition which is the voice of eternal justice within us does not make us just; we have to be able to follow that voice freely. But can we be free in a world order regulated by immutable justice?

The answer is yes, if our will has attained maturity. The mature will is aware of its freedom, for, unlike the immature will that is directed by fear and by the basic desire of self-preservation, the mature will is nourished by hope and love, both of which aim not at the preservation of the self but at its infinite expansion.[6] Thus the mature will "overcomes with violence" eternal justice because eternal justice wants to be overcome by hope and love. In this direction it does not put a limit to human endeavor—in fact, the whole conception of a limit stems from human finiteness and not from infinite being—and responds to the mature will by giving more than we have striven for [XX. 94–99]. To know the essence of justice, to live it—which is the way to know in paradise—is therefore to understand fully the meaning of human freedom, to live it with a mature will, knowing that once we have entered the sixth state of paradise, eternal justice is not a limitation, but an infinite invitation to exercise our will in perfect freedom. There is no greater justice than that which gives us freedom.

The way of justice is a way to being that is perhaps more direct than any other. Whatever his or her condition in life, everyone may attain paradise if he or she desires nothing but justice. Such desire manifests itself in two virtues: in the living hope [XX. 108] which hopes for perfect justice, and even more in the burning love of justice that puts it above all else [XX. 121]. Since justice is the result of direct intuition that sees into the justness of being with an undazzled eagle eye,[7] the voice of our personal revelation, the gradually unfolding meaning of our own experience of love is not heard in this state. A single-minded devotion to justice can take us to paradise even without the profound personal experience of love for another human being which is indispensable to the understanding of all the other paradisal states but this [XX. 106–129].[8]

Unless we see the First Cause in its entirety, unless our vision penetrates to the utmost depths of the Source of being where all the processes of the universe have their origin, we cannot comprehend all the ways in which people, following their own individual vision of justice, may reach this state. What seems to us incredible or scarcely just according to the accepted doctrines or precepts of society, could still be in keeping with eternal justice. Individuals we would never have suspected of attaining paradise are here revealed to us as living in harmony with eternal justice. From this we may learn a last lesson before we can rise higher. Since not even here can we see into the uttermost depths of being, we must refrain from trying to judge people, from trying to determine, with our shortsighted vision, in which state of their development they may be. Instead of judging to what extent others have realized eternal justice in their lives, we should bring about in our own life the harmony of the mature will with justice [XX. 130–

138]. The presence of true justice among people can be recognized by the fact that their wills move according to the guiding inner voice of eternal justice, and their common work shows an outward concord visible to the beholder [XX. 145–148].

Images

The ruddy fire of Mars changes to a white glow in the Heaven of Jupiter. The fire-world of Jupiter is more temperate than Mars in the sense that it seems to burn more evenly, but the white glow shows an intenser burning. The fire of Jupiter has the fierceness of Mars and the luminosity of the Sun. Thus the whiteness of the temperate star—*lo candor della temprata stella* [XVIII. 68]—suggests the union of mature intellect with mature emotion in the movement of the temperate will.

The spirits are both lights:

> sì dentro ai lumi sante creature
> volitando cantavano
> [XVIII. 76–77]

(so within the lights holy creatures were singing as they flew)

and flames:

> quei lucenti incendi
> dello Spirito Santo
> [XIX. 100–101]

(these shining fires of the Holy Spirit).

Air is present here again, as in the Heaven of Mars in a few references to flight [XVIII. 73, 77 and especially XIX. 91–96] and in the impassioned description of the power of love manifested in the songs of those "living lights" [XX. 10], the spirits of the just:

> O dolce amor, che di riso t' ammanti,
> quanto parevi ardente in quei flailli
> ch' avieno spirto sol di pensier santi!
> [XX. 13–15]

(O sweet Love that mantlest thyself in a smile, how glowing didst thou show in those flutes that were filled only with the breath of holy thoughts!)

The air breathed through the flute stops, each of which is a glorified spirit, sounds the music of love.

Birds, the inhabitants of air, supply many images in this sphere. At

Dante's first sight of them the spirits rise up as birds, to form the heavenly writing:

> E come augelli surti di riviera,
> quasi congratulando a lor pasture,
> fanno di sè or tonda or lunga schiera,
>
> sì dentro ai lumi sante creature
> volitando cantavano. . . .
> [XVIII. 73–77]

(and as birds risen from a river-bank, as if rejoicing together over their pasture, make of themselves, now a round, now a long flock, so within the lights holy creatures were singing as they flew. . . .)

The eagle-emblem itself is likened first to a falcon clapping its wings [XIX. 34–37], then to a stork feeding its young and flying in circles [XIX. 91–96], and finally to a lark soaring into the clear of heaven [XX. 73–77]. Such images of birds and of flight have, of course, an obvious appropriateness to the "*benedetto segno*" [XX. 86] of the eagle, but, beyond this, they also remind us of the element of air, more important here than in any previous heaven. Birds, representing—at least to Dante's age—the highest form of animal life,[9] also symbolize a kind of progress beyond the vegetation images of the sun and even beyond the images of artefacts and jewelry in Mars and here in Jupiter. I am reluctant to attribute such significance to bird imagery here, but I feel I have to do so because of its curious recurrence in the next sphere, the Heaven of Saturn [XXI. 34–42], where artefact and jewelry images are almost completely absent.

There are no earth metaphors and almost the only references to the earth are in the list of unjust rulers at the end of Canto XIX. But even here only a few physical features are mentioned: a river, the Seine [XIX. 118], an island, Sicily [XIX. 131–132], and a mountain range, the Pyrenees [XIX. 114]. One more reference to a geographical location is made when Dante's doubts are formulated about "the man who is born on the banks of the Indus" [XIX. 70–71]. The rest of the names are of cities and kingdoms, man-made entities on the surface of the planet.

Water is used in similes that, significantly, refer to the inscrutability and depth of eternal justice:

> Però nella giustizia sempiterna
> la vista che riceve il vostro mondo,
> com' occhio per lo mar, dentro s' interna;

chè, benchè dalla proda veggia il fondo,
in pelago nol vede, e non di meno
è lì, ma cela lui l' esser profondo.
                                        [XIX. 58–63]

(Therefore the sight that is granted to your world penetrates within the
Eternal Justice as the eye into the sea; for though from the shore it sees the
bottom, in the open sea it does not, and yet the bottom is there but the
depth conceals it.)

It is worth noting that the simile recurs twice in connection with the
Trojan Ripheus, whose presence in the Heaven of Jupiter signifies the
possible salvation of all pagans. Thus in XX. 67–72:

Chi crederebbe giù nel mondo errante,
che Rifeo Troiano in questo tondo
fosse la quinta delle luci sante?

ora conosce assai di quel che il mondo
veder non può della divina grazia,
benchè sua vista non discerna il fondo.

(Who in the erring world below would believe that Trojan Ripheus was the
fifth of the holy lights in this round? Now he knows much that the world
cannot see of the Divine Grace, although his sight does not discern the
bottom.)

And in XX. 118–121:

L'altra [i.e., Ripheus], per grazia, che da sì profonda
fontana stilla che mai creatura
non pinse l' occhio infino alla prim' onda,

tutto suo amor laggiù pose a drittura;

(The other, through grace which wells from so deep a fountain that no
creature ever thrust his eye to its primal spring, set all his love below on
righteousness).

The returning simile of the unseen bottom in deep water is a reply in
image language to the problem of an inscrutable eternal justice stated
in the first simile. Though the salvation of Ripheus does not explain
the final origin of eternal justice, it nevertheless assures us that as far
as we can see into the ocean of the First Cause, we find inexhaustible
grace there. The richness of this grace is well conveyed by the image
of the inexhaustible ocean, which is made up of the element of pure
potentiality: water.

When the eagle begins to speak for the fourth time, the sound is first like that of a river:

> udir mi parve un mormorar di fiume,
> che scende chiaro giù di pietra in pietra,
> mostrando l' ubertà del suo cacume.
> [XX. 19–21]

(I seemed to hear the murmur of a stream that fell limpid from rock to rock, showing the abundance of its mountain source.)

This simile, too, shows the inexhaustible quality, the never quite actualized potentiality of eternal justice, which gives always more than we hope for and still has more to give.

But the elevation of the Heaven of Jupiter above the spheres of the lower planets and the sun is conveyed, poetically, not so much by the scarcity of earth imagery as by the further development of the images of artefacts and the presentation of a living emblem. The musical harmonies of the Heaven of Mars are continued here and they culminate in a simile that shows the union between the human voice and the sound of an instrument.

Most similes that present man-made objects come from the workshop of the goldsmith or jeweler who is craftsman and artist in one. His creations convey, beside the shaping power of the human mind, the ideas of value and durability, appropriate to this sphere where eternal justice is manifested. The planet Jupiter itself is a jewel:

> Giove
> pareva argento li, d' oro distinto.
> [XVIII. 95–96]

(Jupiter seemed there silver pricked out with gold.)

On its silver disk the shape of the emblem, the eagle, is pricked out in golden fire:

> la testa e il collo d' un' aquila vidi
> rappresentare a quel distinto foco.
> [XVIII. 107–108]

(I saw the head and neck of an eagle represented in that pricked-out fire.)

The figure is the work of the heavenly Painter [XVIII. 109] or rather mosaic-maker, who uses a profusion of gems:

> O dolce stella, quali e quante gemme
> mi dimostrato che nostra giustizia
> effetto sia del ciel che tu ingemme!
> [XVIII. 115–117]

(O sweet star, how many and how bright were the gems which made it plain to me that our justice is the effect of the heaven thou doest gem!)

Each spirit forming the emblem seems a little ruby, kindled by the sunlight:

> Parea ciascuna rubinetto, in cui
> raggio di sole ardesse sì acceso,
> che nei miei occhi rifrangesse lui.
> [XIX. 4–6]

(Each seemed a little ruby in which the sun's ray burned with such a flame that it was thrown back into my eyes.)

The sixth heaven, thus, is inlaid with precious stones:

> cari e lucidi lapilli,
> ond' io vidi ingemmato il sesto lume,
> [XX. 16–17]

(bright and precious jewels with which I saw the sixth light gemmed).

The work of the goldsmith is alluded to in the metaphor:

> perchè il ben nostro in questo ben' affina,
> [XX. 137]

(because our good in this good is refined,)

which likens the increase in blessedness to the refining of metals. When Dante says how plainly visible his wonder and doubt were on his face as the eagle revealed to him the salvation of the two pagans, Trajan and Ripheus, he takes his metaphor from another art, that of stained-glass making:

> Ed avvegna ch' io fossi al dubbiar mio
> lì quasi vetro allo color che il veste,[10]
> [XX. 79–80]

(And although I was to my perplexity there as glass to the colour that coats it).

In this heaven of jewelry and fire the metaphors taken from plant life are almost completely absent. We have left behind the plant-like unfolding of the human being's powers and have reached the states—already in Mars, but even more emphatically here—where little can be found in the unconsciously growing, blossoming realm of Flora to illustrate a willed and conscious growth that is less and less like the processes of vegetable nature. Only once in this heaven, when address-

ing the blessed spirits here as "perpetual flowers of the eternal gladness" [XIX. 22–23] does Dante use a plant-metaphor, and here, too,
the adjective "perpetual" eternalizes these flowers which breathe a
single sweet scent not for the senses, but for the intellect.

The higher state of development in this heaven is suggested not only
by the elaboration of jewelry images, but also by the emblem, the
figure of the eagle. The earlier emblems, the triple crown in the Sun
and the geometrical cross in Mars, were abstract figures—although the
cross of Mars flashes forth the image of Christ intermittently— but
here the emblem comes to life fully; it moves and speaks and flies:

> Qual il falcon, ch' uscendo del cappello
> move la testa e coll' ali si plaude,
> voglia mostrando e facendosi bello,
>
> vid' io farsi quel segno . . .
> [XIX. 34–37]

(As the falcon released from the hood moves its head and flaps its wings,
showing its eagerness and preening his feathers, so I saw that sign. . .).

Later it flies up and circles, singing, displaying perfection in its
movement as well as in its voice:

> Quale sopr' esso il nido si rigira
> poi che ha pasciuto la cigogna i figli,
>
> *   *   *
>
> Roteando cantava . . .
> [XIX. 91–92; 97]

(As the stork circles over the nest when she has fed her young. . . . Wheeling
it sang . . .).

It might be interesting to consider that the spirits first form a letter, *M*,
then a lily, and finally a bird.[11] Such progression in their activity
suggests to me a change from lifeless abstraction through the growing
unconscious life of plants to animal life, corresponding to the progression from inanimate through vegetative to instinctive—or, to use
Plato's term, passionate—existence in nature. I think that the chain
stopping short of the next, i.e., the rational, or specifically human link
shows symbolically that the Heaven of Jupiter, with all its intrinsic
perfection, does by no means constitute the last stage of paradisal
growth.

The greater harmonies of this sphere also correspond to the great
advance made in rising to this heaven. Whereas in the lower heavens

the spirits greeted the pilgrim with dance and song, here they form the successive letters of the sentence: *Diligite justitiam qui judicatis terram*. Thus their movement goes beyond the beautiful intricacies of geometric patterns; it becomes a distinct communication addressed not only to our sense of proportion and harmony but also to our conscious mind [XVIII. 76–95]. Their movements within the eagle also express a higher unifying principle, for they act in perfect concord to form a living being of a more complex order than themselves. Their voices united become one voice, the voice of the eagle, and in singing they attain a beauty and profundity that passes human understanding:

> "Quali
> son le mie note a te, che non le intendi,
> tal è il giudizio eterno a voi mortali."
> [XIX. 97–99]

(as are my notes to thee who canst not follow them, such is the Eternal Judgment to you mortals.)

The viols, harps, and the organ, which enrich with instrumental music the Heaven of Mars, are answered here by the voice of the flute [XX. 13–15] and the lute (or cittern) [XX. 22; 142–143]. But whereas no images of instrumental music were used in the Heaven of the Sun (unless we think of the horologue as such) and in Mars instruments and Cacciaguida's unaccompanied singing follow each other, here the last image unites the sound of the instrument with the human voice, thus giving the intimation of a more complex, more pleasurable harmony than any heard before:

> E come a buon cantor buon citarista
> fa seguitar lo guizzo della corda,
> in che più di piacer lo canto acquista;
>
> sì, mentre che parlò, sì mi ricorda
> chi' io vidi le due luci benedette,
> pur come batter di' occhi si concorda,
> con le parole mover le fiammette.
> [XX. 142–148]

(And as a good lutanist makes the trembling string accompany a good singer, by which the song gains more sweetness, so, while it spoke, I remember to have seen the two blessed lights, just as winking eyes keep time together, move with the words their little flames.)

This unity of voice and instrument is perfectly paralleled in the second terzina by the simultaneity in the movement of the two eyes and by the flicker of the heavenly flames following the words exactly. The union of vision, words, and action that is attained in this state could hardly be suggested better.

There are slight allusions to two of the continuing image-themes: stamping [XIX. 43–44] and spiritual warfare [XVIII. 123]. Otherwise the Heaven of Jupiter seems to lack these strands which are threaded through the whole of the *Paradiso*. Perhaps the reason for the rather self-contained imagery of this heaven is the same as for Dante's curious neglect of Beatrice here: both may be indications that the way of justice is sufficient unto itself.

VIII.

Old Age: Vision

Canto XXI

By "putting all our love upon justice" [XX. 121] in the sixth state of paradise, we have almost forgotten about our love, the love whose might we have once experienced as a personal revelation. But now we again fix the eye of our soul upon our personal revelation, whose meaning becomes deeper at each new stage of the ascent. To see her we turn inward, with intellect, emotion and will removed from outward objects, and this motion of the spirit which is called contemplation raises us into the next state [XXI. 1–3]. After each expansion of vision we turn inward to contemplate our enlarged understanding of that personal experience which was the manifestation of love in our life. As our innate powers develop we begin to understand that in a past moment of self-forgetting love we really lived an integrated life worthy of our true self. During the heavenly ascent it is by the growing intensity and width of that recollected experience that we measure the gradual liberation of our true self from a bondage "heavy as frost and deep almost as life." In each new stage of our progress a broader field of vision is irradiated by the light that once revealed to us in a momentary glimpse something about our true self and about the true nature of the cosmos.

In the seventh state, which we reach as we turn once again to our personal revelation, this light floods all the inward and outward objects of perception. Here a full illumination is granted to those who have achieved maturity of intellect, emotion, and will. Our personal experience of love is revealed in such brightness that though our intellect may, our emotions cannot yet support its full glory. If we were to *feel* the extreme intensity of that love, all that is mortal in us would be annihilated in the burning [XX. 4–12]. As long as we are, at least partially, bound by temporal existence, our consciousness cannot absorb all that our love contains.

Instead of allowing us to contemplate her full beauty, to explore her full meaning, our personal revelation commands us to perceive the new state into which we have risen with her help [XXI. 16–18]. And we find that to obey the command of the love that speaks within us is an even greater pleasure than to contemplate her perfection [XXI. 19–24]. Here, after we have attained maturity of intellect, emotion, and will, we enter upon the life of vision. We contemplate all things in an inner mirror which reveals their essence. But the mirror of vision is not a cold surface reflecting some distant ideal world. Its crystal clear accuracy does not prevent the vision from being radiantly warm; such vision is not seen in the mirror of merely passive souls. To be able to hold it in ourselves we have had to grow in activity and giving as well as in receptivity. The life of contemplation, which this state essentially is, cannot be lived without the active qualities of courage and alertness; it needs a readiness to act continually upon the truth perceived in contemplation [XXI. 13–15].

The visionary life consists in looking at the world through the eyes of primal innocence, through eyes that have not suffered estrangement from being. The unfallen eye sees no evil in the world [XXI. 25–27].[1] This vision leads, ladder-like, into the world of eternity, toward a fullness of being which, as yet, we are not strong enough to discern [XXI. 28–30].[2]

Those who live a life of contemplation or vision start out in a community, but when they have reached a certain stage of growth [XXI. 42] they can begin to fulfill their individual tasks, since their vision, too, is individual [XXI. 31–42]. Some return to the rules of the community in which they started out, others go their own way and never look back, others again seem to move in circles [XXI. 37–39]. Such apparently irregular movement in a state which is higher than that of cooperation according to eternal justice, prompts us to ask new questions. Throughout paradise new visions always raise doubts, and to ask for clarification of these doubts in a precisely formulated question is the *sine qua non* of progress. We see that the contemplative

life into which we have now risen is a life of love [XXI. 45], but we do
not ask our questions before the love dwelling within us, the personal
revelation which is the touchstone of our utterances in paradise, gives
us the inward sign that we may proceed [XXI. 46–48]. Only when love
prompts us to ask and our desire for knowledge is not mere intellectual
curiosity but is warmed by feeling [XXI. 51], should we formulate our
doubt, because only then are we fully open to the complete answer. Of
course, we do not quite merit an answer, but we will nevertheless
receive it according to our manner of asking [XXI. 52–53].

The actions of those living the contemplative life are individual; they
do not follow a recognizable pattern like the movements of those who
exercised perfect cooperation in the preceding state. Thus our first
question inquires into the cause that directs the actions of the contemplative. The second question, following from the same doubt, asks
why there is no recognizable harmony in this state:

> e di' perchè si tace in questa rota
> la dolce sinfonia di paradiso,
> che giù per l' altre sona sì devota.
> [XXI. 58–60]

(and say why in this wheel the sweet symphony of Paradise is silent which
through the others below sounds so devoutly.)

Our second question is answered before the first. We are reminded
that something of the particular meaning of our personal revelation
which belongs properly in this state must remain hidden, because we
are still not quite free of the bonds of illusory existence. Therefore we
cannot apprehend the harmonies playing around the ladder of contemplation which ascends into the freedom of eternity, into fullness of
being. We have not yet developed the subtle and accurate awareness
which can enjoy and interpret these harmonies. If the music of vision
were to burst upon us in our undeveloped state, our consciousness
could not sustain it [XXI. 61–63].

Now we are ready to receive an answer to our first question, and
that answer leads us further. The power that directs the contemplatives
is, of course, love. They act to give joy to others [XXI. 65] and act in
individual ways not because one has more love than another, but
because each one follows freely the promptings of the power that
governs the universe. Every contemplative understands these directions individually through his loving vision [XXI. 67–72].

This answer has brought us to the first important insight in the seventh state of paradise. We now see clearly that free love here is a sufficient—in fact the only—way to follow the eternal plan:

> libero amore in questa corte
> basta a seguir la provvidenza eterna:
> [XXI. 74–75]

(free love serves in this court for fulfillment of the Eternal Providence).

Whereas individual action appeared still imperfect in the states figured by infancy, adolescence, and first love, and was bound to a pattern in the states of intellectual, emotional, and volitional maturity, here man's behavior is not darkened by earth's shadow, nor does it need an outside pattern to raise it to perfection. Here action, prompted by free love, is freest and, therefore, paradoxically, best fulfills the eternal design. In the life governed completely by vision all constraint is abolished and man is simultaneously freed from every trace of separateness.

But this vision, too, has certain limits. We may see clearly how one contemplative acts following his individual vision, but we still cannot tell why he and not another was granted that particular vision [XIX. 76–78]. To understand this limitation more clearly, we must consider first the nature of contemplation itself. Contemplation is an inward turning, a circling around the ground and center of the self:

> del suo mezzo fece il lume centro,
> girando sè, come veloce mola.
> [XXI. 80–81]

(the light made of its middle a centre and spun like a rapid millstone.)

The center is the point where the sharply focused light of being penetrates into the self; the contemplative turns around this center and with the help of this inward light rises so far above his everyday self that he sees into being, the supreme essence of all that exists [XXI. 82–87]. Such vision fills him with a burning joy [XXI. 88], and the clearness of his vision is shown outwardly in the bright flame of his happiness [XXI. 89–90].

Yet even the most illuminated contemplative cannot answer completely the question we have been moved to ask. For to know why one and not another receives a certain vision and is moved to a certain act as a result, would be to solve the mystery of self-identity: why am I I and not another? No finite being can discern the reason for its identity, not even in the highest state of paradise, much less so in temporal existence [XXI. 91–102]. Awareness of this limit directs our next question toward a possible and even necessary end of contemplation: if I cannot find out *why* a person is himself and not someone else, I can and should find out *who* he really is [XXI. 103–105]. This means that in contemplating our own existence, we should, instead of questioning *the reason* for our identity, be content to *find* our real identity.

Who, then, is the contemplative? In a general answer we can attempt to state some of the attributes of such a person. The contemplative or visionary inhabitants of the seventh state of paradise live on heights far above the turmoils and storms of the world of illusion. They are indifferent to the needs of their bodies and their simplicity enables them to live entirely in their vision of being [XXI. 106–117].

But the contemplative life, as all the eternal states of paradise, has its pitfalls; clinging to the outward marks alone and lacking the essence which is vision, the contemplative first becomes futile [XXI. 118–119] and then degenerates further. The spiritual vacuum is filled by desire for physical gratifications which are perhaps allowed by the letter of the law but which certainly destroy the visionary gift. Through gluttony the contemplative can lapse back into a bestial condition [XXI. 120–134].

The corruption of so great a spiritual gift moves the true contemplative to holy indignation. Such passion does not darken his vision; on the contrary, it makes his love burn even stronger. Fired by his indignation, the visionary sees truth more clearly, but his judgment cannot be understood by us who do not share his vision. His truth overwhelms and stupefies us, but, since we do not know anything to which we may liken it, it defies our powers of expression [XXI. 135–142].

Canto XXII

We cannot understand the holy indignation of the contemplative and must turn to our personal revelation to gain the assurance that in this state, as in all the states of paradise, no trace of error remains, that all actions, words, and feelings are good, since they are prompted by a vision focused upon the Source of being. We feel, as we seek the counsel of our guide who is our own personal experience of love, that no evil thirst for revenge can intrude here. What to us seems anger is rather a justly passionate outburst against the degradation in the temporal life of the world of what is potentially so great: the human being's capacity to live a life of contemplation and vision [XXII. 1–9].

Since we are as yet unable to receive this truth in the right spirit, and still need the guidance of our personal revelation to understand what the indignation of the contemplative really means, we are obviously not ripe to assimilate the full meaning of our experience of love, nor are we ready to participate fully in the harmonious vision of the contemplative [XXII. 10–12]. These harmonies would reveal to us, if only we were able to perceive them, the perfect workings of laws that govern both time and eternity. These laws bring about the necessary consequences of any degradation of spiritual gifts. They operate neither too slowly nor too fast; their working appears too swift or too tardy only to us who fear or desire the results. In order to see with visionary eyes the fulfillment of these eternal laws and to delight in the harmony of such a vision we must liberate ourselves from personal desire for, or fear of, any temporal event [XXII. 16–18].

To discover what else we can learn about the life of vision in this state of paradise, we must again let the love within us guide our sight [XXII. 19–21]. Love shows us that contemplative life is perfect as a sphere—the perfect shape [XXII. 23]—and that, though their vision is individual, the contemplatives increase the light in each other's life by enjoying individual vision [XXII. 22–24]. We fear that our desire to know more about this state may exceed the limit, since our wish to probe the question of identity was checked once before. But beyond accepting our own finitude there are no other limitations to our desire here. To fulfill the desire of another is the joy of the visionary; his burning charity welcomes the unrestrained expression of every wish, since wishes in paradise are the stepping stones toward our final goal, the union with being. His vision enables him to anticipate the wishes of another, even if the wish remains unexpressed [XXII. 25–36].

Our wish to know more of the attributes of the contemplative is speedily satisfied by looking at the ideal of the type exemplified here by St. Benedict. His example shows us that, by keeping to the true way to union revealed on earth by Christ, we can attain this state of fully illuminated vision. The false worship of the ego and the flesh that is leading the world astray must be superseded by the recognition of the principles of true spiritual progress [XXII. 37–45].

The contemplatives, whose meditations bring forth words to guide others right, and actions to serve for examples, are content to live an outwardly restricted life. They do not wish to change the external circumstances into which they have been placed, and thus they keep their simplicity of heart [XXII. 46–51]. A contemplative is able, by the affection he radiates toward all, to make others open up in faith and confidence:

> come il sol fa la rosa, quando aperta
> tanto divien quant' ell' ha di possanza;
> [XXII. 56–57]

(as the sun does the rose when it opens to its fullest bloom).

We are thus emboldened to ask our final question, no longer about the attributes of the contemplative, or about the outward marks of the visionary life, but about its very essence:

> però ti prego, e tu, padre, m' accerta
> s' io posso prender tanta grazia ch' io
> ti veggia con imagine scoperta.
> [XXII. 58–60]

(therefore I pray thee—and tell me, father, if I may gain so great a favour—that I may see thee with thy face unveiled.)

Their essence is the vision they enjoy; the identity of the visionary is revealed by his vision. But here again we come up against the limitations imposed upon us by our own condition which still binds us at this point of our journey to the visible world and to temporal existence. We cannot fulfill our desire to fully share in the vision of another, to enter fully into his identity. Such a wish can be gratified only when all temporal concerns are left behind, and we arrive in the last state of paradise, that abiding eternity where all desires find their fulfillment [XXII. 61–63]. There our desire as well as our self reaches wholeness; there nothing can stand in the way of full satisfaction. That last state, where one comes to live wholly in one's vision and one's vision will be one's true identity, is our true home: there we *are* from the beginning, though to ourselves we seem to stray through time and space, through states of self-knowledge, purgation, and development. We are there always, for there every part is where it ever was:

> in quella sola
> è ogni parte là dove sempr' era.
> [XXII. 65–66]

(In it alone each part is where it always was).

The ladder of contemplation leads to that state [XXII. 68]; but as yet we cannot discern the ultimate vision—which means the ultimate identity of ourselves and others—though contemplation gives us already a promise of fulfillment.

To ascend contemplation's ladder one has to leave all illusory and temporal cares and preoccupations behind. If those attempting to climb it do not sever their feet from the earth [XXII. 73–74] they fall into bestiality, gluttony, sloth, and greed [XXII. 76–81]. Contemplation grows out of inward rest; but if the heart is not detached completely from the illusions of the temporal world, this rest becomes corrupted into love of ease and pleasure. Seduced by the flesh, those who have not detached themselves completely from the illusions of the visible world cannot live the true contemplative life for any length of time. Institutions intended to lead people to true contemplation are similarly corrupted, however perfect their founder may have been [XXII. 85–93]. All human endeavors, institutions especially, are subject to the law of decay that governs all things insofar as they partake of the unreality of temporal existence. Only a miracle, a suspension of the operation of this law, could help these decaying institutions [XXII. 94–96].[3]

Though to our time-bound understanding contemplation may seem a restful state, the last vision in the seventh state of paradise shows us the essence of contemplation as a whirlwind movement. Indeed, among the different methods by which we progress toward union with being, contemplation is the swiftest and can certainly not be called inactivity [XXII. 97–99].[4]

Images

No special group of images distinguishes the Heaven of Saturn. It seems almost that since the essence of contemplation could not be revealed to Dante at this point in the poem, he lacked the central feeling, the atmosphere of the state of contemplation, from which his imagination could have bodied forth dominant images, unless, of course, Dante purposely avoided vivid images and a mention of sounds because he wanted to mute such outer effects to preserve the silence and wakeful emptiness at the heart of all contemplation. There may also be a conscious preparation for the second stage of the journey by a muting of effects. Between the rich harmonies of the Heaven of Jupiter and the splendors of the three highest heavens, Saturn becomes a resting place for the reader's fantasy, a resting place for which the "cold planet" of old age seems particularly suitable. The glories of the vision of eternity cannot be told here; only the *way* of vision is indicated, but the vision itself will be experienced by the traveller once he leaps over the immense void between Saturn and the fixed stars.

This promise, whose fulfillment is delayed, makes the less than two complete cantos in which the Heaven of Saturn is traversed by Dante and his guide intellectually the least weighty, imagewise the most undistinguished of any two cantos in the *Paradiso*.

The role of the images of fire, air, earth, and water has become progressively less important as we ascended. I think that here they have almost ceased to embody the spiritual progress of the poem. The almost complete absence of water imagery—except in XXII. 94–95, where the River Jordan and the Red Sea are mentioned—might nevertheless imply that in the full contemplative vision all potentialities are actualized. The earth appears mainly in the form of mountains where the monasteries of contemplatives are situated [XXI. 106–111 and XXII. 37]. The spirits are described in the usual terms of light and fire imagery, without special emphasis on either aspect (for example, XXI. 32, 69, 80, 88, 90, 136 and XXII. 46, 54). A simile likening the upward movement of the contemplative spirits to the whirlwind in XXII. 99 and two references to thunder [XXI. 12 and 142] remind us of the fourth element, air.

The bird imagery of Jupiter does, however, continue here with the extended simile of the daws' starting out on their morning flight, likened to the movement of the spirits descending the emblematic ladder:

> E come, per lo natural costume,
> le pole insieme, al cominciar del giorno,
> si movono a scaldar le fredde piume;
>
> poi altre vanno via senza ritorno,
> altre rivolgon sè, onde son mosse,
> ed altre roteando fan soggiorno:
>
> tal modo parve a me che quivi fosse
> in quello sfavillar che insieme venne,
> [XXI. 34–41]

(and as by their natural habit the daws rise together at daybreak to warm their cold feathers, then some fly off not to return, some turn back to where they set out, and some stay wheeling about, such movements appeared to me in that sparkling throng that drew together).

In the Heaven of Mars at a sign given by Beatrice the wings of Dante's will began to grow:

> Io mi volsi a Beatrice, e quella udio
> pria ch' io parlassi, ed arrosemi un cenno
> che fece crescer l' ali al voler mio.
> [XV. 70–72]

(I turned to Beatrice, and she heard before I spoke and smiled to me a sign
that made the wings grow on my will.)

Later, in the Heaven of the Fixed Stars, Beatrice is described as

quella pia, che guidò le penne
delle mie ali a così alto volo,
[XXV. 49–50]

(that compassionate one who directed the feathers of my wings to so high a
flight).

Between these two passages, frequent bird images suggest the swiftness and sureness of the flight which the traveller through paradise can
pursue with his now "equally feathered" [cf. XV. 79–81] wings of
intellect and emotion.

The imagery of jewels and artefacts continues from the heavens of
Mars and Jupiter but is far less splendid than in either. In XXI. 7–8,
paradise itself is called the eternal palace whose steps the pilgrim
climbs. The planet Saturn is a mirror [XXI. 18] and a crystal [XXI.
25]. Both mirror and crystal are, of course, aids to vision. Within this
crystal the golden ladder [XXI. 28–29] shines like a piece of jewelry.
The spirits are pearls in XXII. 29 and the greatest of them is St.
Benedict.

Yet images of vegetative nature, reminding us of the Heaven of the
Sun, are also quite frequent. The most outstanding is the simile of the
opening rose in XXII. 52–57:

"L'affetto, che dimostri
meco parlando, e la buona sembianza,
ch'io veggio e noto in tutti gli ardor vostri,

così m'ha dilatata mia fidanza,
come il sol fa la rosa, quando aperta
tanto divien quant' ell' ha di possanza;

(The affection which you show as you speak to me and the promising
goodwill which I perceive and note in all your splendors have enlarged my
confidence as the sun does the rose when it opens to its fullest bloom).

The contemplatives' actions and words are called holy flowers and
fruits in XXII. 48, and the shortness of good beginnings upon earth is
said not even to equal the time from the upspringing of the oak to the
appearance of the first acorn [XXII. 86–87].

Such even distribution of some of the most characteristic image
groups prefigures the treatment of images in the higher heavens where

the four elements, plant life, and artefacts are all drawn upon to suggest the fulfillment of all the gradually developing powers which we saw unfolding one by one on the ascent through the first seven states.

If we look for images that might indicate the progress made in the Heaven of Saturn beyond the lower states of paradise, we have to be satisfied by two references to the gods of classical antiquity right at the beginning of Canto XXI. One is an allusion to Jupiter's burning of Semele who wished to see him without his disguise [XXI. 5–6] and the other is a connection between the Saturn of mythology and the planet,

> che il vocabol porta,
> cerchiando il mondo, del suo chiaro duce,
> sotto cui giacque ogni malizia morta,
> [XXI. 25–27]

(which, circling about the world, bears the name of the world's famous chief under whom all wickedness lay dead).

Dante treats several classical legends and myths—taken mainly from Ovid's *Metamorphoses*—throughout the *Paradiso*. But except for the passage of invocation where he turns to *"buono Apollo"* [I. 13] and where he declares that his ship is driven by Minerva and guided by Apollo [II. 8], the gods themselves seldom appear until this point. There is, however, an allusion to Apollo and Venus, whose sanctuaries at one time were situated close to the future Benedictine monastery of Monte Cassino, in XXII. 37–39. In view of the frequent mention of the gods throughout the next heaven, these references may be regarded as introducing a new group of images, consisting of the deities of Greco-Roman mythology. As the images of jewelry and artefacts suggested a higher state than the images of plant life, so the gods of paganism here stand as high above the creations of the human mind as those did above the creations of nature. The gods, though their nature was misinterpreted by their pagan worshippers, were, according to Dante, heavenly intelligences or Platonic ideas, *"forme e nature universali."*[5] They were not the creations of the human mind whose artefacts existed in time only but of the divine mind, and were thus part of the eternal world.

After the rich music of instruments and accompanied singing in the Heaven of Jupiter, harmonies could hardly be intensified further; in the Heaven of Saturn silence follows music [XXI. 58–60]. Yet we could take this silence for the sign of an even greater harmony. As Keats said:

Heard melodies are sweet but those unheard
Are sweeter; therefore, ye soft pipes, play on;
Not to the sensual ear, but, more endear'd,
Pipe to the spirit ditties of no tone.[6]

Contemplation is spiritual music, too sharp for the sensual ear.

Perfection, often denoted by circular movement, is indicated here,
too, in the circling of St. Peter Damiani's spirit in XXI. 81 and in the
whirling that beautifies the other contemplatives:

vid' io più fiammelle
di grado in grado scendere e girarsi,
ed ogni giro le facea più belle.
[XXI. 136–138]

(I saw more little flames descend from step to step, wheeling, and every
turn made them more beautiful.)

The spherical shape of the hundred spirits surrounding St. Benedict is
another sign of the perfection attained in this state:

e vidi cento sperule, che insieme
più s' abbellivan coi mutui rai.
[XXII. 23–24]

(and I saw a hundred little spheres which beautified each other with their
mutual beams.)

Yet this perfection is not a complete turning away from the temporal
world. In their denunciations of corrupt monks the visionaries of the
seventh heaven use an earthy language which depicts the vices they
castigate in all their repulsive concreteness. Contemplation, Dante
seems to say, is not abstract speculation, but in its vision of anything
it goes straight to the essence, of which the physical is sometimes the
most telling expression. Thus the priests of the poet's own time are so
heavy that they have to be supported on four sides, and when they
ride their mantles cover two beasts:

Copron dei manti loro i palafreni,
sì che due bestie van sott' una pelle:
[XXI. 133–134]

(They cover their palfreys with their cloaks, so that two beasts go under one
skin).

The monasteries have become the habitations of beasts:

Le mura, che soleano esser badia,

fatte sono spelonche, e le cocolle
sacca son piene di farina ria.
[XXII. 76–78]

(The walls that were once an abbey have become dens and the cowls are
sacks full of rotten meal.)

The heavenly ascent never separates us from what happens in the
temporal world; in fact, only through keeping the aberrations of the
world clearly before our eyes do we keep our sharpened awareness of
a greater reality.

IX.

Through Death into Eternity:
Humanity Beyond Illusion

Each state we have traversed so far has unveiled to us more meaning in our experience of love. At last we have come to understand that everything that really mattered in our life was condensed into that single experience. We have come to accept that experience as the guiding light in our journey of unfolding and have surrendered ourselves completely to the knowledge which that experience has revealed about the true nature of both ourselves and the world.

Therefore a single sign from the love within us, a single hint of intuition is enough now to thrust us upward on the ladder of contemplation with a swiftness that is quite contrary to earthbound human nature [XXII. 100–102]. Defying the laws of time-bound existence, we pass the yawning abyss of death between Saturn and the fixed stars in a moment that can hardly be measured in time:

> tu non avresti in tanto tratto e messo
> nel foco il dito, in quanto io vidi il segno
> che segue il Tauro,[1] e fui dentro Ja esso.
> [XXII. 109–111]

(thou hadst not drawn out and thrust thy finger in the fire before I saw the sign that follows the Bull and was within it.)

The equal wings of emotion and intellect we have grown during our journey have lifted us out of the bondage of time, space, and illusion, a bondage which chains everyone in the temporal world [XXII. 103–105]. We can cross the barrier of death even in this life if we fly up the ladder of contemplation and lose the last vestiges of the self which we have constructed in our exile. However much people may dread it, this death is less painful than plunging one's finger in the flame for a second. And it is through the death of the ego which is still temporal in us that we completely gain the true self which has been imperceptibly growing during our ascent through the first seven states of paradise [XII. 109–111].[1]

From this true self spring all human powers, all human genius. It is the perfect humanity inherent in all people [XXII. 112–114]. Our mortal life is lived under its influence and when we finally rise out of the temporal realm altogether, we regain our true identity [XXII. 115–120]. Once we have shed the accretions of the temporal world and have truly become ourselves, the final union with being, the ultimate aim of our journey through paradise, is not far off [XXII. 124]. But before we can undergo such transformation, we must again enlarge our capacity for vision, for without wider vision no progress is possible. Here we have to learn to see even more clearly and precisely than before [XXII. 125–126].

First, to sharpen our vision, we are advised to take a retrospect and see how much, with the help of indwelling love, we have already progressed through the states of paradise.[2] We look back to fill ourselves with joy to the utmost, for unceasing joy is the constant emotion of this state. We exult in the victory over our estrangement from being, in the recovery of our perfect humanity [XXII. 127–132].

From this newly gained height, filled with the understanding that the seven states have given us, we can clearly see the pettiness and insignificance of earthly preoccupations. At last we are able to smile at it all. Those who think least of the fears, ambitions, pleasures of this world of illusion are the wisest; our thoughts should be directed to what is more real [XXII. 133–138].

The states of development, too, appear now clearer than when we were in them. Spiritual infancy, the first state of paradise, no longer seems defective from here; it possesses a perfection of its own [XXII. 139–141]. The relationships between the states we have traversed also appear clearly: the states are eternal themselves and linked in what might be called family ties with one another.[3] Now we can support the light of truth that reveals eternal order; we see how the honorable ambition of the second state and the self-opening love of the third state are influenced and regulated by the wisdom that becomes fully ours in the fourth [XXII. 142–144]. Though the first four states may be known under the names of inconstancy, worldly ambition, sexual desire, and intellectual power in the temporal realm, here we call them by names that signify their stainless innocence and their origin in an unfallen, eternal world.[4] Though the nature of these states may be perverted by those who abuse them to satisfy their self-will, they are all part of eternity and should be used as steps in the ascent to being. In each state certain powers of the soul are developed from potentiality into full activity. The practical sense and inventiveness of the second state may indeed be perverted to serve selfish ambition, but such abuse is against the eternal order. Similarly, the desires for union with another person, as they open in the third state, can degenerate into a lust for possession or domination, although their true function is not to lead one astray but to lead one to unfold the true self.

Observing the three higher states we can now see how the unerring sense of justice in the sixth state tempers possible fanaticism in the fifth and eliminates the danger of frigid detachment from the seventh [XXII. 145–147].

As we now consider their effects upon ourselves, we come to know the seven states through which we have passed better than ever before.

And, last but not least, the earthbound temporal existence, the testing place where the chaff is separated from the grain [XXII. 151], which has caused us so much anxiety and passion, appears now in its true proportions. From the vantage point of perfect humanity [XXII. 152], the origins and ends of all earthly happenings become clear in retrospect. We understand all that we could not account for in our lives [XXII. 153]. But this sight does not detain us too long: the recollected events of earthly life cannot give us new illumination, only the love within can guide our eyes to greater vision [XXII. 154].

Canto XXIII

We now await the great transformation of the self. All the powers we have acquired, all the understanding we have gained, still leaves us in the night compared to the sunrise that will now dawn upon us [XXIII. 1–12]. Our guide awaits almost with impatience the new light which will reveal the likeness of our true self and will enable her to give us more nourishment [XXIII. 4–5]. We are eager to put off mortality and put on immortality, to shed the self that was in bondage to illusion and put on the true self that is free [XXIII]. We follow the prompting of our personal revelation and turn our attention to where love directs it; as soon as we have done so, a new illumination begins to dispel the night of our waiting [XXIII. 16–18].

Love makes us recognize in this new vision the perfect humanity in people who have attained this state through the power of one who has brought the splendor of perfect humanity into the visible world. He has thus opened the way for others to ascend through the states of paradise and regain what He has never lost [XXIII. 19–21]. Thus they gain the light with which they blaze from Him, Who is the Way Himself and points out the right path to our fulfillment [XXIII. 25–30].[5] We cannot yet sustain the manifestation of being apparent in perfect humanity; our visionary power fails before the substance of Christ [XXIII. 31–33]. But the voice of love from within assures us that it is right to be overcome by His irresistible might [XXIII. 34–36]. It is right to be mastered by His power and wisdom because they open to us the way to the lost Eden of eternity. This power and wisdom reveals within our mortal nature the hidden eternal self akin to the Christ and who, in a way we cannot fully understand, is Christ Himself [XXIII. 37–39].

The recognition that, through Christ, we really belong to eternity, blots out our normal consciousness. It is as if the immortal self, having become aware of its true nature, would issue out of its frame like lightning out of a cloud [XXIII. 40–42].[6] It knows itself as infinite, as Christlike, and flashes forth in a way contrary to our nature insofar as we are human and not divine, though our everyday consciousness cannot retain the memory of this transformation [XXIII. 40–45; 49–51].

In this moment of ecstasy the opposition between the mortal and the eternal part in us is overcome. Strengthened by the self-recognition of what is eternal in us, we can now sustain what only the eternal self can understand: the full meaning of our experience of love, of our personal revelation [XXIII. 46–48].

The invitation of love's inner voice to open ourselves and receive the full meaning of our personal revelation brings us back from the ecstasy. With a gratitude never to be forgotten, we follow love's prompting to contemplate what her appearance in our lives really means [XXIII. 49–54]. But as we are unable to recall consciously what passed within us during the experience of ecstasy, so we are powerless to communicate this deep meaning, this "sober certainty of waking bliss"[7] to others. There are experiences on this pilgrimage that cannot be told; each pilgrim has to live through them alone. No petty, timid, self-regarding person can pursue this path, for one has to immerse oneself without reservation in every new experience. We cannot be content with second-hand knowledge [XXIII. 55–69].

It were good to remain forever gazing at the inexhaustible wealth of our personal revelation; but love herself tells us to pay attention again to the landscape through which we pass [XXIII. 70–75]. It is a landscape bathed in the light of being, yet the source of light remains hidden. We see the powers of eternal humanity—powers which were displayed to us in Christ—gather around us [XXIII. 79–87]. Here we recognize, shining with the light of being, the greatest of these powers, who gave birth to perfect humanity and whose help we shall need if we are to reach our journey's end, our own perfect humanity. She is that manifestation of being which is embodied in woman: the receptive principle. On earth she is a flower, in eternity a star [XXIII. 88–93]. Here we see the essence of man's desire for woman as a spiritual movement, a circling of the active male principle around the receptive feminine aspect. Out of this love man's supreme desire, the god-man, is born [XXIII. 94–96].

> "Io sono amore angelico, che giro
> l' alta letizia che spira del ventre
> che fu albergo del nostro disiro;
>
> e girerommi, donna del ciel, mentre
> che seguirai tuo figlio, e farai dia
> più la spera suprema, perchè gli entre."
> [XXIII. 103–108]

(I am the angelic love, who circles around the lofty gladness which breathes from the womb that became the hostelry of our desire; and I shall circle, lady of heaven, until you will follow your son and make the supreme sphere more divine by entering it.)

This interplay of active and receptive energies will last until the sexual polarity characteristic of the dualistic plane of existence will cease to function, because activity and receptivity will be equally balanced in the higher state of perfect humanity. The individual then will not long for a complement in a member of the opposite sex. In the perfection of spiritual powers, both the male active and female receptive principles will be balanced to nourish the ever-abundant life that Christ exemplified. But until that state is reached, man ascends the spiritual stairway with the help of his desire to unite with the feminine aspect of being in woman. It is the eternal feminine which indicates to us the ascent into the next state, though our eyes cannot yet follow her so high [XXIII. 118–120].

But those who have already attained the state of perfect humanity turn to her as infants turn to their mother for nourishment; they all turn to the feminine principle, whose power nurses them into real existence, with grateful love [XXIII. 121–126]. Love and reverence for being in woman makes man creative; he overflows with gifts, he plants the seeds of abundant eternal life in the world of time. Such abundance of life can only come to those who are not greedy for illusory goods which keep one enslaved [XXIII. 130–135]. The abundant life that Christ has opened to humanity is the exaltation and fulfillment of our true nature. Life, in the eighth state of paradise, is a rejoicing in the victory over the fall, over our estrangement from being, because through this victory—won by Christ—the natural impulses of every human being can find their fulfillment here. Everyman,[8] in fact, holds the keys to this life of glory, for human nature once redeemed from the distortions which the fall had inflicted on it, finds here its complete apotheosis [XXIII. 136–139].

Canto XXIV

In this new state symbolized by the Stellar Heaven man turns around his center in a movement that generates the outward radiating fire of love [XXIV. 10–12]. We now understand a truth revealed to us by vision, that the richness of individual differences is never obliterated by spiritual progress.

> E come cerchi in tempra d' oriuoli
> si giran sì che il primo, a chi pon mente,
> quieto pare, e l' ultimo che voli,
>
> così quelle carole differente-
> mente danzando, della sua ricchezza
> mi si facean stimar, veloci e lente.
> [XXIV. 13–18]

(And as wheels in the structure of a clock revolve so that, to one watching them, the first seems at rest and the last to fly, so those choirs, dancing severally fast and slow, made me gauge their wealth.)

All the states we have traversed are parts of a celestial mechanism that we now discover as we look back. Although their movements vary from the almost imperceptible to rapid flight, they all serve a unified purpose like that of a moving staircase to lead us from one state to another of soul-development. As we observe the workings of this cyclotron of transformation, we grasp the polyphonic harmony of the whole.

We communicate with those who are in this state through the love within us; they respond to our desire for enlightenment. To fulfill a loving wish, they readily leave the pleasure of their own harmonious activity [XXIV. 19–23; 28–30].

We now understand that this state can be attained only through the development of the three forces which lift us upward through the states of paradise: faith, hope, and love [XXIV. 40–42]. Until now we have relied upon these forces more or less implicitly, but as they are fully active in this state we must now examine how well we really know them. Have we reached a sufficient measure of faith, hope, and love? Are we able to progress further on our journey? These are the questions that demand answers at this point and these, once answered, will enable us to enlarge our vision. We see, in turn, perfect faith, hope, and love, so that contemplating them we may examine these virtues in ourselves.

The virtue that enables us to rise above the unintelligible chaos of the temporal world, to walk, as it were, its stormy surface, is faith. It provides us with a foundation. Though it may fail us sometimes,[9] faith is a virtue attainable to everyone [XXIV. 34–39]. To see whether we are strong enough in the faith which lifts us to this state [XXIV. 43–44], we must be prepared to define faith rationally [XXIV. 49].

We have arrived at a clear definition of faith and it is accepted as correct contrasted with the erroneous speculations of those living in the temporal realm [XXIV. 79–81]. But the investigation must not end here. More important than the intellectual formulation of what faith consists in is the possession of faith, meaning thereby a profounder knowledge. In having faith we are not looking at it from the outside, in an "objective" fashion, but become one with it. We know it truly when it has become part of our total being, not merely of our intellect [XXIV. 83–85]. We know we have faith when it gives us absolute certainty [XXIV. 86–87].

How did we come to acquire faith? What has prompted us to accept the existence of a reality beyond the sensible world and to make this assumption the master key to the seemingly unanswerable ultimate questions of human life? To make such an assumption really ours, we had to recognize, first of all, the truth of communications, whether old

or new, made from the eternal realm into the temporal through inspiration.[10] The truth of these communications has been pointed up by
events that could not be explained by "natural" causes, events produced by people who lived according to these truths [XXIV. 91–102].
But even if we did not personally witness these events we could see
the working of truth in the victory of some causes in the world which
did not have material wealth or power on their side but with the power
of truth overcame the worldly might of their adversaries [XXIV. 106–
111].

The perfect faith we contemplate here is, of course, no longer an
assumption but direct vision, since here we are no longer guided to
knowledge by the senses but by direct intuitive perception through
spiritual understanding [XXIV. 124–125]. Thus the rightness of our
assumption of a supra-sensual reality which in our state of bondage to
the sense-world had to be upheld constantly against the nagging
criticism of the lower reason and against the attraction to the seeming
goods of material power and pleasure, is completely confirmed by
perfect faith here, in the eighth state of paradise.

All that remains for our inquiry into faith is to state finally the
assumption itself [XXIV. 122]. We have ascertained the form of faith,
examined the way to it, and now must express its content. True faith is
the belief that one eternal being exists, a being who, itself, unmoved,
moves the universe with desire and love [XXIV. 130–132]. Not only
experience and reason, but also inspiration point to the existence of
such a being [XXIV. 133–138]. Further, true faith maintains a threefold
division in the primal being, which, however, does not lose its unity by
such a division. *Is* and *are* are equally applicable to it [XXIV. 139–
142]. Inspiration asserts this threefold division of being [XXIV. 142–
144]. From this basic assumption an unchangeable conviction grows in
us, a faith that shows the way to being with the steadiness of a star
[XXIV. 145–147].

Our examination on faith is concluded; faith is confirmed both in
form and substance: we have based our life on the right assumption.
As we understand that this is the faith which lifts everyone toward the
ultimate experience, we are given a sign [XXIV. 152] to keep firm
especially our belief in the Three in One, which guarantees us oneness
in diversity [XXIV. 148–154].

Canto XXV

We have become strong enough in faith, the first of the forces which
raises us from state to state in paradise; henceforth we will never be

the same as we were in the state of bondage [XXV. 708; 10–12]. Now the voice of love within us bids us turn to perfect hope [XXV. 17–18]. We can hardly support the united light of perfect faith and perfect hope [XXV. 25–27], but it is now our task to examine whether we possess the latter. Hope follows faith; once we believe that ultimate reality exists, we can begin to hope that we shall attain it. Hope is founded upon the bounty of eternity which faith teaches [XXV. 29–31].[11] Thus, however insecure we may feel, however uncertain of our merits we may be, we have to contemplate perfect faith and perfect hope, because only when matured by their influence can we grow ready for a new ascent [XXV. 34–36]. But before we even begin to examine ourselves for a formal definition of hope, our personal revelation speaks to proclaim that we have hope in abundance [XXV. 52–53]. We must have it, or else we could never have left the world of illusion. Faith and hope are eminently the virtues we need in the struggle to overcome the power that binds us to the temporal and dualistic view of reality. We need hope in our warfare [XXV. 52–57] against the bondage of temporal corruption;[12] hope, even in the midst of our struggles, is rewarded by a vision of what we hope for [XXV. 55–57]. But we do not boast of our possession of hope; we accept it humbly and gratefully when the voice of our personal revelation assures us that we indeed possess it [XXV. 49–51; 58–62]. For even when it comes to knowing our own virtues, we prove to be only pupils of the love within us [XXV. 64].

But in giving a formal definition we can display our rational understanding of hope and we do this eagerly: "Hope is a certain expectation that we will attain the ultimate union whose existence we had postulated by faith." Such sureness of expectation is given to us in the measure of our striving [XXV. 67–69]. Hope comes to us from many sources; from the sages who shine like stars in the night of temporal existence[13] and, mainly, from poetic or prophetic inspiration which assures us that those who know the nature of ultimate reality cannot but be hopeful [XXV. 70–74].[14] Since we have faith in the existence of that reality, we must also have hope. Nourished by these sources, our hope will grow so abundant that we can pour it out to others [XXV. 75–78].[15]

Lastly, we have to sum up what exactly do we hope to attain. Our hope is to attain a state in our true home, in eternity—*questa dolce vita*—a state which will be the fulfillment of humanity's natural development on the supernatural plane. Not only do we hope for the eternal life of the inmost unextinguishable spark within us, our ultimate hope includes the perfect development and even enhancement of our individuality in eternity. Thus we hope that not even the part of our personality expressed in and through the body can be lost. On the contrary: *all* our powers will be raised to an undying existence [XXV. 91–93].[16]

Now our hope, too, is recognized to be sufficient for further progress [XXV. 97–99]. Next we are confronted with a vision of perfect love, which banishes all darkness and coldness from the world [XXV. 100–102]. Perfect love acts only out of the purest motives [XXV. 104–105] and moves in complete harmony with perfect faith and perfect hope [XXV. 106–108]. The love within us that had led us so far is now fixed on the harmony of the three perfect virtues. She points out perfect love without averting her attention from the harmonious working of the three [XXV. 112–117].

In contemplating perfect love, we cannot help but look for the form of love we know in the flesh. Faith and hope are virtues which, even in the temporal realm, are clearly supernatural; they contradict the immediate evidence of our senses and enable us to put our trust into a reality not immediately evident to us. But love comes to us human beings so obviously through the senses that it seems at first a power of the temporal realm inseparable from the body, the Venus Genitrix of Lucretius.[17] Thus when confronted with the vision of perfect love we try to discern in vain that form of love within the vision which we have known through the body and through the natural ties that link children, parents, and relatives together [XXV. 118–121]. (Christ, who had brought the order of eternity into the temporal realm, had manifested His love to St. John by drawing him to His breast and acknowledged the tie of blood with His mother when He left her in St. John's care as He was hanging on the cross [XXV. 112–114]. Yet only Christ and His mother, both of whom were never estranged from being, could express perfectly eternal love in the temporal world.) Even the vision of perfect love granted to us here in the eighth state of paradise fails to show the uncorrupted form of love in the body. Not until we have gained the place to which we have been destined from all eternity can this last cleavage between eternity and time, between the supernatural and the natural plane of existence, be healed [XXV. 122–128].[18]

In beholding the three powers of faith, hope, and love working perfectly together, we get a foretaste of the ultimate vision of the Three-in-One. But such a vision must not last too long; if it did we would succumb to weariness or even danger [XXV. 130–135]. Already we have lost our vision by gazing too long into the mystery of perfect love, trying to fit it into our sense-imaginings in vain. Thus, when we turn to our own experience of love to delight in her increased beauty after faith, hope, and love have given us new understanding, we find that our power to perceive anything has gone. To lose the visionary power that has enabled us to progress through paradise is certainly a shock to our mind; we are prevented from discerning the full meaning of our personal revelation, our profoundest intellectual joy in paradise [XXV. 136–139].

Canto XXVI

Excess of love plunges us into blindness, but in the same love we find reassurance. Though we lost the visionary light of direct spiritual discernment when love overpowered us,[19] we can still progress by using our rational understanding. Thus for a stretch of our ascent in the eighth state of paradise we must again grope ahead blindly, using the guiding cane of discursive reason [XXVI. 106]. To examine ourselves in love, we have to declare first what is the chief desire of our soul, for what we most desire is true love.[20] Also, by remembering that we are in paradise, we are reassured that our visionary power will return; the love within, having once opened the doors of vision to us, will restore it. She has the power to give visionary sight because through her eyes truth itself looks at us [XXVI. 7–12].[21]

The good which satisfied the pilgrim in the eighth state of paradise is both the beginning and the end of all the things we love:

> Lo ben, che fa contenta questa corte,
> Alfa ed Omega è di quanta scrittura
> mi legge Amore, o lievemente o forte.
> [XXVI. 16–18]

(The good that satisfies this court is alpha and omega of all the scripture that love reads to me in tones loud and low.)

But we have to inquire more closely into our own love if we are to measure it against perfect love. Why did we turn to the only real good, to being [XXVI. 19–24]? Because by understanding the goodness in all things we came to love them for this very goodness. Once we truly discern the goodness of anything or anyone, i.e., its uniqueness and individuality,[22] we cannot help but love the light that shines out from this manifestation of being [XXVI. 28–30]. Thus above all else, it is this light, the light of being itself that we most desire, once we have learned to see it even in the appearances of the temporal world [XXVI. 31–36].[23] Reasoning leads us to the first understanding of being as the

essence of all good and as the supremely desirable goal. The conclu-
sions of reason are supported by truths revealed to others by inspiration [XXVI. 37–45]. But perfect love is not satisfied by proofs addressed to the intellect only; we must realize that other ties, beside the
intellectual, draw us toward being, that the love of being is not merely
the cold ecstasy of intellectual satisfaction, but also the painful and
pleasurable longings of the heart [XXVI. 46–51]. And so we admit that
our feeling and will also play a part in our love for the supreme essence
[XXVI. 31]. Our feelings and our will are moved by these considerations: recognition of being in the world, the quiddity, what things *are*
in themselves; recognition of our own being, what and who we *are*; the
self-sacrifice of being itself in human form who opened to us the way
to fulfillment by his death in the world of illusion; and, finally, the
possibility of union with being itself [XXVI. 55–60]. The love of being
within us and without, the love of perfect humanity, and the love of a
promised life in the fullness of being, together with intellectual vision,
have liberated us from the confused love with which we once fastened
upon appearances in the disorder of the temporal realm [XXVI. 61–
63]. We have emerged from the confusion of misdirected desires into
the order and freedom of eternity and see that in the garden of eternal
nature everything is worthy of love to the extent to which eternal being
manifests in it [XXVI. 64–66]. Love is blind while understanding is
lacking, but when we understand the love that prevails in the eighth
state of paradise, we cannot remain blind any longer. The voice of the
love within us breaks out in a song of praise to the holiness of being
that shines forth everywhere, and the recognized truth which she has
shown to us restores our vision. Eager to meet this new truth, we
awake from the slumber of ignorance and find that we perceive more
intensely than before; the last motes of error or distortion have been
wiped away from our inward eyes [XXVI. 67–79].

We are now in the garden of eternity, which we have reached
ascending through the seven states of development. Here we recall
that on the way of purification through suffering the garden of eternity
was prefigured in the earthly paradise, which we have reached by
climbing the seven terraces of self-purification. Yet while the climbing
of Mount Purgatory freed the pilgrim from the seven illusions which
hold us in bondage to the temporal world, the planetary ascent in
paradise unfolds our latent spiritual powers. In the earthly paradise
our will was cured of its bias in favor of the seeming as against the real
good. As Virgil said:

Libero, dritto e sano è tuo arbitrio,
e fallo fora non fare a suo senno.
[*Purg*. XXVII. 140–141]

(Free, upright, and whole, is thy will, and it were a fault not to act according
to its prompting.)

Thus in the earthly paradise the will is made perfect, whereas here, in
the eternal garden, our essence, or spirit, reaches its full stature. The
perfection of the will was attained under the constellation of the four
natural virtues: prudence, fortitude, temperance, justice. The perfection of the spirit is shown by the fullness of the three supernatural
virtues of faith, hope, and charity.

What we first see, newly appearing beside the perfection of faith,
hope, and love, is the figure of the full life of the human being, the
result of the harmonious working of the three virtues.[24] This original,
eternal form of humanity, as conceived by the Creator, as close to
being as any creature can be, appears now to our inward sight. Its
state of existence is a perpetual loving dialogue with being [XXVI. 80–
83].

Our understanding of the fullness of human life as conceived from
the beginning reveals new ground for further questioning:

Come la fronda, che flette la cima
nel transito del vento, e poi si leva
per la proprio virtù che la sublima,

fec' io. . .

[XXVI. 85–88]

(As the branch that bends its top in a gust of wind
and then springs up, raised by its own force, so did I).

From this height the fall, humankind's estrangement from being,
appears as a mere bending of a spray which rights itself again by its
own natural elasticity as soon as the wind has passed over it. We now
know the excellence of which our original nature is capable; we have
seen and felt how close we, too, can stand to being. Obviously we find
it hard to understand how the creature, in whom such powers are
inherent, could fall into the chaos and bondage of the life on earth. But
to remember the fall gives us no pain here; on the contrary, we are
eager to understand it, so that we might increase our vision further
[XXVI. 85–96]. The human being who has attained his true self and
unfolded his spiritual powers acts with a vehemence of joy that is as
spontaneous and unrestrained as the movements of animals; yet his

purpose is not directed to self-preservation, but always to giving pleasure to others [XXVI. 97–102]. He sees the truth of all things in the mirror of being, where none of the misleading distortions which come from earthly sense-perception intrude. With the help of such unerring sight we can now look into the question that once appeared so tragic but now merely ruffles our joy: how did we become estranged from being? For greater precision, this problem can be broken down into four exact questions: first, how long was the road from the point where new-created humanity woke up to conscious existence in the earthly paradise of freedom, to perfect humanity? Second, how long did it maintain its unimpaired freedom and its closeness to being, before falling instead of ascending, as its proper nature would have it, the eternal stairway of the states of paradise? Third, what was the true cause of the fall? And, lastly, since it could express its awareness of being only in creating, what were the first creations by which this innocent human nature expressed a vision of being shining forth everywhere in the universe [XXVI. 103–114]?

Since we now understand in what the perfect life consists, the answer to these questions is given to us at once, in the order of their importance. The true cause of the fall was not the pleasure man took in possessing a limited good; we know now that all pleasure derives from being and therefore no pleasure can, in itself, alienate us from being. But man fell into exile because he deliberately disregarded the mark that separates appearance from being, and worshipped appearance instead of giving all his allegiance to being [XXVI. 115–117].[25] Next we look back at the length of man's exile between his first consciousness and his perfection; it can only be measured in time which shows transitoriness and unreality when seen from this garden of eternity where perfect humanity abides [XXVI. 118–123]. Then we turn to the origin and the decline of man's creative power. In the beginning human consciousness created symbols spontaneously to represent the reality of an existence where everything radiated the undimmed light of being. This sheer exuberant activity of the unfallen self was the first language we had. But as a result of the fall, spontaneous creativity decayed and was gradually replaced by a false or mechanized creativity. Man attempted the impossible when he sought to reach by the mechanical action of placing one brick upon the other that world of eternity which lay all around him while his symbols were freely created [XXVI. 124–126]. Symbol-creating belongs intrinsically to our nature; but we can choose whether we want to exercise this urge according to inspiration and imagination, or according to mechanical rules [XXVI. 130–132]. We cannot retain the same symbol language forever because our inclinations and interests are constantly turned into new paths by the changing influences of eternity's great plan, which manifests for us in new eras of history [XXVI. 127–129]. Humanity saw being differently in different periods, called being by many names. This reflects not the changing nature of being but our own diminished condition and our necessary passing through the states of alienation and return [XXVI. 133–138]. Finally, in answer to our second question about the period of existence in the unfallen state, we learn that the time of innocence was very brief. Man, it appears, became estranged from being before he could put his foot on the first rung of the ladder of paradise.

Canto XXVII

The recollection of the fall is no grief here; we see the endlessly joyful life of eternity open up before us like a continuous hymn of praise to the light of being. The truth and the harmony of this vision are intoxicating; we are rapt into a newly integrated life:

> O gioia! o ineffabile allegrezza!
> o vita intera d'amore e di pace!
> o senza brama sicura ricchezza!
> [XXVII. 7–9]

(O joy! O gladness unutterable! O life fulfilled with love and peace! O wealth secure with no craving!)

But this life is no resting place; as our vision is strengthened, new truths are being revealed. We have considered humankind's estrangement from being as it is seen from eternity, but we have not yet faced fully the results of this estrangement as they developed in the temporal world. Though in one sense the fall only serves to manifest the power with which being reclaims the fallen universe and therefore it is a cause for rejoicing in the eternal world, in another sense the consequences of the fall are the scandal of eternity. With the perfect integration of humanity's powers, fierce spiritual energies are released in the eighth state of paradise; we have seen already how vehemently the desire to please another manifests itself [XXVI. 97–102]. Indignation at the perversion of eternal values is equally strong; it unites perfect justice with passionate feeling [XXVII. 10–21]. Such indignation is aroused here by the degeneration of all human institutions; although this is a consequence of the fall, those who promote such decay are not to be excused. Some institutions were founded by people who lived in the spirit of truth and rejected the world of illusion as worth nothing. These organizations—Churches, states, professional bodies, educational institutions, etc.,—were meant to lead us toward the gladness of union with being [XXVII. 43], but they are now leading people into non-being; they serve the spirit of negation and crucify being itself, the Christ, the imagination and spiritual perception in people [XXVII. 26–27; 35–36]. Institutions degenerate because the people leading them fall again into the error of materialism; they care for nothing but material gain [XXVII. 40–42]. As a result, they turn away from unity, foster division [XXVII. 46–48], enter into hatreds, wars, and pretend that they can sell the gifts promised from eternity to all mankind for money and power [XXVII. 49–53].

Perverted by serving such institutions, men of inspiration whose duty would be to lead others to the abundant life of paradise become themselves rapacious animals, blinded by greed [XXVII. 55–56]. Thus good beginnings come to a foul end in the temporal world where so many go astray [XXVII. 59–60].

(The exposure of the weakness of earthly institutions—here symbolized by the Church—has its parallel along the way of self- purification. There, in the earthly paradise, a dumb-show representing the corruption of the Church in history is played out before the pilgrim [*Purg.* XXXII]. But whereas there the hidden meaning of one historical process was revealed to the traveller, who, though purified, had not yet separated himself from temporal concerns, here the root-cause of all such corruption, the greed of illusory riches as a means to power, is laid bare. Here we are beyond history and see directly into the working of the eternal law.)

We can see the magnitude of corruption now because we have experienced the greatness of the state to which we may rise. Therefore it is our duty to denounce such corruption openly: it stands condemned in eternity [XXVII. 64–66]. Perfect charity does not exclude righteous indignation. Other laws operate here than in the world of time; here the power of righteous indignation raises us higher, instead of causing us to fall [XXVII. 67–72]. But we cannot yet see the utmost heights to which we may rise in the fullness of perfection; we still move in the limiting medium of the human ego that dims our visionary sight [XXVII. 73–75]. So, instead of looking onward, we follow the voice of love within us and look back once more to see how much the understanding of this state of perfectly integrated human existence has changed us[/XXVII. 76–78]. We were in this state just as long as primal innocence lasted before the fall [XXVII. 79–81]. Now we can see the black mark [XXVII. 85–87] left by the fall upon humanity's life in the temporal realm. We also see the mistaken and bungling efforts by which mankind is trying to overcome the fall, forever pressing on into the chaos of the material world, instead of letting itself be carried toward a union with being by the power that governs all. Instead of being like Europa, carried by divine power, humankind chooses to try, like Ulysses, to travel on its own, but its mad voyage can only end in disaster [XXVII. 82–84].

Images

In Dante's universe beyond the Heaven of Saturn an immense void separates the planetary heavens from the Heaven of the Fixed Stars. This abyss is not only a physical gap in the plan of the journey; it divides the poem itself on all levels. Though the "sacred poem" can leap [XXIII. 62] as no other, a marked change occurs both in the allegorical meaning and in the imagery. The correspondence between meaning and the use of images is quite close here. On the anagogical level, which I have been following throughout, the successive stages of development liberate various latent powers in the human being. These states grew almost imperceptibly one out of the other. But between the state of contemplation or vision which crowned this gradual ascent and the state of perfect humanity which is the Heaven of the Fixed Stars a leap had to be made from the time-bound into the eternal. The first seven heavens represent a successive development and are thus— though as states they are eternal—still within the limitations of time. They represent one side after another of the complete human life. But what we see in succession through the seven planetary heavens we find unfolded in a single vision among the fixed stars. Here simultaneity and not succession is the law: eternity rules, not time.

Shifts of emphasis to different groups of images in the different heavens indicated that different powers of the human entity are developed in each planetary heaven. The Heaven of Saturn is an exception: there, as I have said, the development of images is arrested, to prepare us for their full flowering in the higher heavens. But, on the whole, the emphasis of images changes at every new step during the first stage of the ascent, whereas in the Heaven of the Fixed Stars almost all the previously used image groups appear together. Yet even among the fully developed potentials of humanity some take precedence to organize and direct the others; so the imagery and diction of the cantos

describing the eighth heaven suggest to the reader through the recurrence and elaboration of certain images and words that in the presentation of the completely integrated human life certain elements must
be stressed above others.

Thus as we search for images and significant words in the Heaven of
Fixed Stars we come upon the verb *spirare*. It is remarkable that the
speech of all four spirits who address Dante in this heaven is at least
once characterized with this verb or with the noun *spiro* derived from
it. St. Peter turns his speaking breath to Beatrice:

> Poscia, fermato il foco benedetto,
> alla mia donna dirizzò lo *spiro*
> che favellò così, com' io ho detto.
> [XXIV. 31–33]

(When it was still the blessed fire breathed forth these words to my Lady as
I have told them.)

Later he approves of Dante's definition of faith and his speech is
described in these words:

> Così *spirò* da quell' amore acceso;
> [XXIV. 82]

(This breathed from that kindled love).

St. James, in exactly the same place in the next canto, begins his
speech on hope thus:

> Indi *spirò*: "L' amore ond' io avvampo
> ancor ver la virtù, che mi seguette
> infin la palma, ed all' uscir del campo,
>
> vuol chi' io *respiri* a te, che ti dilette
> di lei. . . ."
> [XXV. 82–86]

(Then it breathed forth: "The love with which I still burn for the virtue that
followed me even to the palm and the departure from the field bids me
breathe again to thee who delightest in it. . . .)

And St. John, the spokesman of charity, also addresses Dante with a
speaking breath from within his glowing flame:

> Mentr' io dubbiava per lo viso spento,
> della fulgida fiamma che lo spense
> uscì un *spiro* che mi fece attento,
>
> dicendo: . . . .
> [XXVI. 1–4]

(While I was in fear for my lost sight there came forth from the resplendent flame that had quenched it a breathing which held me intent, and it said: . . . .)

The harmonious song of Dante's three examiners is called "suon del... *spiro*" in XXV. 132. And, finally, when Adam turns to Dante after having shown his great desire to please the poet, he begins to speak from within his covering of light:

> Indi *spirò*: "Senz' essermi profferta
> da te, la voglia tua discerno meglio
> che tu qualunque cosa t' è più certa;
> [XXVI. 103–105]

(Then it breathed forth: "Without thy telling of it I discerned thy wish better than thou canst discern whatever is most certain to thee).

Nowhere else in the *Comedy* is the speech of the spirits described as *spirare*, though forms and derivations of the word occur not infrequently, denoting breath, breathing, or spirit. It is perhaps also relevant to note that on rising into this heaven Dante addresses his natal constellation of Gemini in these lines:

> A voi devotamente ora *sospira*
> l' anima mia per acquistar virtute
> al passo forte, che a sè la tira.
> [XXII. 121–123]

(To you my soul now sighs devoutly that it may gain strength for the hard task that draws it to itself.)

The verb *sospirar* does not occur anywhere else in the *Paradiso* and *sospirar* is a sign of the new life that grows out of the harmonious fusion of man's powers.[26] Mature intellect, emotion, and will are all present here, together with the visionary power. Out of all these something larger than the mere aggregate of the parts is created: the life of the spirit in the true sense begins in this state, for where all the powers of the soul have reached complete development, the spirit can at last freely manifest itself.

Except for this new component, images used throughout the earlier heavens return in various forms. Some of the most dazzling are nature images that recall the abundance of fruit, flowers, and foliage in the Heaven of the Sun. Here nature is sempiternal, without even a shade of decay. We are in the garden of the eternal Gardener [XXVI. 64–65]. Beatrice says to Dante:

> Perchè la faccia mia sì t' innamora,
> che tu non ti rivolgi al bel giardino
> che sotto i raggi di Cristo s' infiora?
>   [XXIII. 70–72]

(Why does my face so enamour thee that thou dost not turn to the fair garden that flowers under the rays of Christ?)

And in the vision of Mary and the Archangel Gabriel, flowers and fires and a circling melody, gems and torches and stars sum up the entire imagery of the *Paradiso*:

> Il nome del bel fior, ch' io sempre invoco
> e mane e sera, tutto mi ristrinse
> l'animo ad avvisar lo maggior foco.
>
> E come ambo le luci mi dipinse
> il quale e il quanto della viva stella,
> che lassù vince, come quaggiù vinse,
>
> per entro il cielo scese una facella,
> formata in cerchio a guisa di corona,
> e cinsela, e girossi intorno ad ella.
>
> Qualunque melodia più dolce suona
> quaggiù, e più a sè l' anima tira,
> parrebbe nube che squarciata tuona,
>
> comparata al sonar di quella lira,
> onde si coronava il bel zaffiro,
> del quale il ciel più chiaro s' inzaffira.
>   [XXIII. 88–102]

(The name of the fair flower which I always invoke morning and evening absorbed all my mind as I gazed on the greatest of the fires; and when the quality and magnitude of the living star who surpasses there above as she surpassed here below were pictured in both my eyes, there descended through the sky a torch which, circling, took the likeness of a crown that encircled her and wheeled about her. Whatever melody sounds sweetest here below and draws the soul most to itself would seem a rent cloud thundering, compared to the sound of that lyre which crowned the beauteous sapphire by which the brightest heaven is ensapphired.)

Two great similes continue the bird imagery of the heavens of Jupiter and Saturn. In the first Beatrice is the mother bird, watching for the dawn among the foliage in XXIII. 1–12. This is one of the most suggestive similes in the poem, yielding meaning after meaning to the meditative mind. The second represents St. Peter and St. James meeting as two loving doves in XXV. 19–24. Dante himself now has his wings fully feathered, though he still flies guided by Beatrice:

> quella pia, che guidò le penne
> della mie ali a così alto volo,
> [XXV. 49–50]

(that compassionate one who directed the feathers of my wings to so high a flight).

The allusions to the gods of classical antiquity also continue, especially where Dante looks back on the spheres he has already "put under his feet" [XXII. 139–147]. The more frequent use of classical deities might indicate a rise above nature images or artefacts or even the principles of geometry. The heavenly Intelligences who moved the spheres were variously represented by the people of antiquity, says Dante in the *Convivio* [II. *Cap.* 5]. Plato, Dante says, called them *Ideas*, i.e., universal forms and kinds. "*Li Gentili le chiamavano Dei e Dee, avvegnachè con così filosoficamente intendessero quelle come Plato. . . .*" Thus the names of pagan gods might indicate Platonic ideas, the highest group of images conceivable, for they are the parents of all images, both natural and man-made.

Special emphasis is given in the cantos where Dante undergoes examination to images of warfare and to the terms that describe a feudal society of warriors. St. Peter is called a veteran forefighter—*alto primipilo*—[XXIV. 59], God the Emperor [XXV. 41], and his saints the emperor's Counts [XXV. 42]. Both St. Peter and St. James are termed Barons [XXIV. 115; XXV. 17], and Dante is the child of the Church militant, who is allowed to see Jerusalem before the prescribed limit of his earthly warfare is over [XXV. 52–57]. St. James left the field of battle when he gained the palm of martyrdom [XXV. 84]. To my mind such images of warfare, applied to the saints in this heaven, suggest that the eighth state of paradise, although it is a "*vita intera d'amore e di pace*," is at the same time a state resembling warfare in its passionate intensity and exuberant action.[27] Only in such a state could St. Peter's flaming denunciation of the corrupt papacy be delivered.

Meanwhile the ship of the daring pilgrims continues toward the divine harbor at the end of her journey. Smaller craft, manned by timid souls, would turn back even after having come so far. This voyage is not for everyone:

Non è pileggio da picciola barca
quel che fendendo va l'ardita prora,
nè da nocchier ch' a sè medesmo parca.
                    [XXIII. 67–69]

(It is no passage for a little bark, this which the daring prow goes cleaving,
nor for a pilot that would spare himself.)

X.

Union with the Powers:
The Life of Free Energy

In the perfectly integrated life our mind turns with greater desire than ever to contemplate the revelation vouchsafed to us in our first love. And the truth which we recognize there fills us with a pleasure that no creation of nature or of art has ever given us. The truth about the life of perfect humanity which we have now fully understood with the spiritual intellect—a truth expressed in the smile of our personal revelation—thrusts us upward into the next state. As always on our journey through paradise, the full understanding of the truth of one state means that we have already transcended that state and are ready to receive the wider vision of the next. As we rise, we leave behind all the limiting factors—symbolized here by our natal constellation—which have given us individuality but at the same time have restricted us, made our existence human and therefore contingent. We could not have attained perfect humanity without regaining our natal constellation which contains all the qualities that make us individual human beings. But when we transcend the human state altogether, we must leave behind all the limitations required by an earthly existence. Such limitations as time, place, heredity are no longer necessary; we can retain and even develop our individuality without them. But by this liberation from the unalterable framework of given circumstances surrounding all earthly existence we have transcended any form of life that may be called human; the life we enter here is a life of totally free energies [XXVII. 88–99].

In the abundance of this life it is no longer possible to speak of one's "place" or "position." Where all beings have attained the peak of their development and are overbrimming with life, one cannot "place" oneself as better or worse, higher or lower than others [XXVII. 100–102]. As we pass into this eternal state we still progress in time, but our revelation assures us that we have reached the limit of the phenomenal world and can observe the ultimate causes to which all events in time and space owe their origin. Once we have attained this state we understand completely the nature of our progress and see that from a motionless, slumbering state we have risen through states more and more filled with movement into this new way of life burning with energy [XXVII. 106–108]. The ninth state of paradise is the threshold to that timeless and spaceless existence where the light of the intellect and the energy of love shine and work without diminution. The source of the power that fills the ninth state, and all the others through the ninth, is here [XXVII. 109–114]. This sphere, spinning with the speed of lightning, is itself the measure of all the other states; for all entities who participate in the timeless and spaceless superhuman life of pure energy have attained the fullness of their own being. In the lower states the act of existing (*ipsum esse*), which according to St. Thomas Aquinas is at the core of every being, is still incomplete [XXVII. 115–117]. Here all the energy that once was in a potential state is actualized, and time itself, which is nothing but the diminution of fully actualized existence in a potential state, spreads only downward from here as soon as full activity diminishes [XXVII. 118–120].

Our human failure to attain this state is ultimately due to greed, which is the wish to have something exclusively for one's self. One can indeed wish to live in reality, but the continual preoccupation with appearances—the materialist fallacy—corrupts the will itself. The inability to transcend space, time, and "nature" and emerge into fullness of being comes from the greedy desire for illusory good that keeps us chained to the temporal existence [XXVII. 121–126]. Only the circumscribed state of innocence seems safe from this corruption; as soon as we gain greater freedom we become the prey of every appetite and believe that our own good cannot be accomplished except through harm and diminution of others [XXVII. 130–135].

The fall from innocence has left a black mark upon humanity, as we have observed in the eighth state of paradise [XXVII. 85–87].[1] Now we understand from our revelation, which in this state communicates to us the complete and unerring knowledge that comes from fullness of being, that such corruption is natural to temporal existence. There man lacks guidance and cannot by himself keep his vision fixed on reality, on what truly exists [XXVII. 136–141]. Yet before such corruption could affect the eternal order [XXVII. 142], the error will be put right by those who are in touch with reality and are not slaves to illusion [XXVII. 144]. People bound to the world err little by little so that they hardly notice it until they are quite out of touch with the eternal order and move away from being instead of approaching it [XXVII. 146–147]. Thus their striving brings no fruit though they may show a flower of promise. They have neglected accuracy, forgot about a part of the truth that seemed to them negligible. But to those who have attained fullness of being such error looms large, for unless one wishes to fall out of eternity, truth must be followed down to the smallest detail. In the end the laws of eternity will prevail even in temporal existence and our well-directed striving will bring true fruit [XXVII. 142–148].

Canto XXVIII

Once we have understood what our personal revelation said to us about the nature of the new state into which we have risen as well as about how most people stray from this truth, we are presented with a vision of the new state itself. We glimpse this vision in the mirror of that love-experience whose meaning has become deeper and clearer throughout our journey, until by now it has created a paradise within us corresponding to the reality without. This revelation is no abstract teaching; as we gaze at it we are looking into the same eyes which once have caught us in the noose of love [XXVIII. 1–2].

What revelation shows us accords with reality as harmoniously as the words of a song accord with its music [XXVIII. 8–9]. In this vision we apprehend the truth about the relationship of the One and the many.[2] We see that the One is surrounded by concentric circles of beings which all draw light and movement from It [XXVIII. 13–36]. The greatest intellectual light, (i.e., the clearest understanding) and the greatest energy of movement (i.e., the intensest love) both belong to beings closest to the One. Here, as everywhere in paradise, apprehension of truth and increase of love go together. The deepest insight into the truth produces the clearest flame of love [XXVIII. 37–39]. As the voice of revelation tells us, upon the One depend both the higher reality and the temporal world [XXVIII. 40–42].

The vision, as all the visions of paradise, gives us food for questioning. The physical universe perceived by the senses [XXVIII. 49] to which we are accustomed centers around matter (i.e., around the "nothingness" of pure potentiality) and becomes progressively more spiritualized (i.e., actualized) as we move outward from the center through the concentric circles. But here the order of nature appears reversed. What is closest to the center is of a higher order than what is more removed [XXVIII. 46–51]. How can true reality and its reflection in the world of the senses differ so [XXVIII. 52–57]?

The answer comes immediately from the voice of love within us. In the world of corporeal extension we are used to judge power by its material effects; we infer the presence of great love or great knowledge from the measurable material manifestation which we can observe [XXVIII. 64–73]. But here, in the ninth state of paradise, not the material effect but its *real cause* is shown, and we must again give up judging by appearances [XXVIII. 74]. Here we have to accept the only real standard of measurement [XXVIII. 74], which is the energy [virtù, XXVIII. 73] of perfect beings.[3] If we measure them rightly then we shall see that though this energy produces great material changes, it cannot itself be recognized by mass or extension [XXVIII. 74–77].

What appears smallest—though in truth it has no size—measured by a material yardstick is in reality the most powerful. In the infinitesimal the power of the infinite breaks through [XXVIII. 16–21]. In the ninth state of paradise we must accustom ourselves to this opposite scale of measurement; here all considerations of quantity and size are utterly left behind.[4] All that counts here is fullness of being that comes from spiritual and not spatial proximity to the One. The greater its unity, the higher place the being has on the scale of reality [XXVIII. 22–27; 34–36].

This understanding blows away the last mists of matter-bound reasoning that still clouds our mind. Now the truth is completely visible, shining, unchanging, like a star [XXVIII. 79–87].

As always in paradise, new understanding is again rewarded with the light of intensified vision and this increase of light leads us, in turn, to ask new questions [XXVIII. 88–98]. Our guide, revelation, goes on to explain the relationship of lesser beings to that fixed point which holds them in their eternal existence:

> punto fisso che li tiene all' *ubi*,
> e terrà sempre, nel qual sempre foro;
> [XXVIII. 95–96]

(the fixed point, which holds and shall ever hold them in the place where they have ever been).

Those who are most intense in their perfect activity—symbolized by circling—can come closest to being itself. They circle around the fixed point swifter than thought, as if they wished to touch it from every side always. The point itself is unreachable: no created being can ever become being itself. But their perpetual circling around the fixed point enables these entities to sink their vision constantly into being and from this vision they gain their power:

> Così veloci seguono i suoi vimi,
> per simigliarsi al punto quanto ponno,
> e posson *quanto a veder son sublimi.*
> [XXVIII. 100–102]

(They follow their bonds thus swiftly to gain all they may of likeness to the point, and this they may in so far as they are exalted in vision.)

To make oneself like unto the center and source of all beings depends on vision; and this vision of being in everything fills us with delight because it satisfies the perpetual thirst of our intellect for truth. Only the recognition of the One in the many can give rest to our craving for understanding [XXVIII. 101–108].

Thus the precondition for attaining fullness of being is vision—i.e., knowledge of being itself—and not love. Love follows on understanding and does not precede it. The vision comes to us through grace when we are inwardly ready for it by having set our will on understanding. This is the law of progress which we followed on our pilgrimage through the states of paradise. Now we see that it holds true in eternity as well [XXVIII. 109–114].

The threefold nature of being is reflected in the order and relationship of all the entities that depend on being itself [XXVIII. 105; 115–126]. The joyful activity of those belonging to this state is harmonious like singing and free like play. Here freedom of action, continually increasing through the states of paradise, reaches its peak [XXVIII. 118–120]. Those who turn toward being with their whole intellect and love become, at the same time, magnets to draw those in a less advanced state to the aim of all creation. Thus by their desire to unite with being they acquire the power to draw others toward it [XXVIII. 127–129]. We must remember here that the vision of truth is given to those who strongly desire it, and therefore complete understanding of fullness of being, which is the ninth state of paradise, is also vouch-

safed to those who long for it most [XXVIII. 130–132]. Yet it is a
knowledge difficult to attain for those tied to the temporal world; their
speculations are often mistaken and can be corrected only by genuine
spiritual vision [XXVIII. 133–139].

Canto XXIX

In a moment that cannot be fixed in time [XXIX. 1–7] we understand
fully what the voice of our personal revelation has explained to us
about the relationship of created beings to being itself [XXIX. 7–9].
Then she answers our unspoken question, almost before we could
think of it, for in this state of most profound vision desires are fulfilled
even as they are conceived [XXIX. 10–12].

Once more, and this time on the highest level, we grasp the origin
and history of all that *is*. Here the explanation appears in metaphysical
terms for such are most appropriate to the fully liberated state where
all material, or spatio-temporal, measurements have been finally left
behind.

Being itself would not desire to possess any good outside of itself,
for there is no good which is not already contained within it. Therefore
its aim in bringing other beings into existence is to manifest its own
light reflected in other entities:[5]

> perchè suo splendore
> potesse, risplendendo, dir: *Subsisto*.
> [XXIX. 14–15]

(that His splendor, shining back, might say *I am*.)

To declare *I am* is the eternal act of being; and to repeat this declaration
is the good of all created beings. In giving of itself freely, being takes
pleasure in the self-assertion of created beings; thus being as the
primal love brings new loves into existence. Here again, on the highest
level, the principle of possession and domination, of grabbing for
oneself, is opposed to the true nature of being which is freely outshin-
ing, overflowing, loving:

> In sua eternità di tempo fuore,
> fuor d' ogni altro comprender, come i piacque,
> s'aperse in nuovi amor l' eterno amore.
> [XXIX. 16–18]

(In his eternity, beyond time, beyond every other bound, as it pleased Him,
the Eternal Love revealed Himself in new loves.)

Love and being are inseparable; created beings, insofar as they have not become estranged from being itself, are loves.

When first created, beings were flawless, outside time, and fully manifest:

> Forma e materia congiunte e purette
> usciro ad esser che non avea fallo,
> come d' arco tricorde tre saette;
>
> e come in vetro, in ambra od in cristallo
> raggio risplende sì che dal venire
> all' esser tutto non è intervallo;[6]
>
> così il triforme effetto del suo Sire
> nell' esser suo raggiò insieme tutto,
> senza distinzion nell' esordire.
>
> [XXIX. 22–30]

(Form and matter, united and separate, came into being that had no defect, like three arrows from a three-stringed bow. And as a ray shines into glass or amber or crystal so that from its coming to its completeness there is no interval, so the threefold creation flashed into being from its Lord all at once without distinction in its beginning.)

They carried within themselves the principles of eternal law [XXIX. 31–32]. Created being has three modes of existence: concealed, i.e., pure potentiality; apparent, i.e., matter and form; and fully manifested, i.e., pure act or energy [XXIX. 34–36].

Our vision intensified by personal revelation and by the inspired testimonies of those who have seen the truth [XXIX. 40–41], we come to understand that even those living in the fullness of their own being in the ninth state of paradise may lose their light. We come to grasp how, in fact, such an estrangement from being itself did occur. It was a fall of beings, who had enjoyed the highest state, into pure potentiality, which is the lowest mode of existence and the substratum of the sensible universe.[7] But those who avoided the fall were caught up in the round of the eternal play of energies whose delight keeps them in unceasing activity which they have no wish to leave now [XXIX. 49–54]. The fall into pure potentiality, into "nothingness" is essentially a separation of oneself from the whole, the conceiving of oneself as self-sufficient and self-sustaining. Whoever commits this error will perceive all other entities as aliens, as hostile weights upon the self which is constricted and imprisoned by its own fallen vision of the world [XXIX. 55–57]. But the fall can be avoided by an enlargement of one's vision through grace *after* the first decision was freely made against setting up oneself as the center of the universe. The wider vision obtained in response to the first free decision perfects the will so that it will no longer want to turn away from being. Grace that enlarges vision comes to those who open themselves to it, whose affections are ready to receive grace. Thus the fullness of being manifested in the ninth state of paradise is achieved in three stages: first, by humility, the openness which invites grace—this is an act of the will, an acceptance of our being as it is really, i.e., finite and dependent upon being itself; second, by increased understanding given by vision; third, by the perfected will which grows out of the deeper vision obtained through grace [XXIX. 58–66].

Contrary to some erroneous speculations in the temporal world, beings living in the mode of pure act—which is the ninth state of paradise— exist outside of time in an eternal present [XXIX. 70–81]. Such beings have no need of memory for they enjoy the direct vision of being itself where nothing comes or goes but all that *is* is present [XXIX. 70–81]. But human beings who live in the dream of temporal existence either believe their own delusions or talk as if they took them for the truth [XXIX. 82–84]. In any case they do not walk on the one true path of philosophy, the path that leads to being:

> Voi non andate giù per un sentiero
> filosofando; tanto vi trasporta
> l' amor dell' apparenza e il suo pensiero.[8]
> [XXIX. 85–87]

(You below do not follow a single path in your philosophizing, so much does the love of show and the thought of it carry you away.)

The love of appearance and the thoughts that come from appearance misled them. But their fault is even graver when they distort or disregard the testimony of inspired vision. For in this case not only truth is slighted but also the self-sacrifice of those who brought the truth into the erring world [XXIX. 88–93].

> Per apparer ciascun s' ingegna, e face
> sue invenzioni, e quelle son trascorse
> dai predicanti, e il vangelio si tace.
> [XXIX. 94–96]

(Each tries for display, making his own inventions, and these are discoursed on by the preachers and the Gospel is silent.)

People try to *appear* instead of trying to *be*; thus they endeavor to dazzle others with ingenious trifles, empty sophistries, and the true foundations of the approach to being—the very foundations given by being made manifest in human form—are neglected [XXIX. 109–111]. The search for the foundations from which we might enter the path to being is both philosophical and religious, philosophy and religion being but the two faces of the basic desire. But if we engage in this search— as it is right that we should—we must beware of frivolity, vanity, credulity, sensuality and gluttony, which are the results of our taking appearance for being [XXIX. 115–126].

We should follow the true path without digression now [XXIX. 127] and try to understand further the ninth state of paradise which is the life of free energy deriving from fullness of being. Although the fully manifest beings who inhabit eternity cannot be numbered, yet each of them is unique [XXIX. 130–138]. The light of being is manifested in every one of them in a unique way [XXIX. 136–138]. Since all have their individual visions of being, they all love being in different ways [XXIX. 139–141].

To see this is to understand what to earth-bound minds seems the great paradox of being itself. Being is the One and yet it is also the principle of diversity, of individuation. To have being is to be individual, and yet the being of all that *is* comes from the most universal One [XXIX. 136–145]. (Though being itself is most universal, yet it is the exact opposite to abstraction. Thus to have more being is at the same time to be more universal and more individual.[9] The path to being leads through individuation, through the fullest development of what is most peculiarly ours and not through observance of general rules or through the standardization of the self.)

Images

Metaphysics is the branch of philosophy where images are traditionally avoided. Nothing can be more abstract than a discussion of pure act or pure potentiality. Since in the Heaven of the Primum Mobile, which moves all the others, Dante examines the nature and origin of pure spiritual beings, the cantos are weighted with much abstract argument. The best equivalent to abstract speculation is the strictly geometrical vision in XVIII. 16–39. Yet this abstract argument has at times a rhythm and a splendor of its own. The majestic abstractions following each other in the order of a fugue can throw the mind into an intellectual ecstasy that goes beyond images:

In sua eternità di tempo fuore
fuor d' ogni altro comprender, come i piacque,
s' aperse in nuovi amor l'eterno amore.
                    [XXIX. 16–18]

(In his eternity beyond time, beyond every other bound as was its pleasure,
the eternal love revealed itself in new loves.)

The images we do find belong mostly to groups already familiar from
the lower heavens. If we try to select some that would seem characteristic to the Primum Mobile we will come upon a group of extended
similes that are all describing the sky in one way or another. Four of
them occur in Canto XXVIII in lines 19–21, 22–26, 31–33, and 79–87
respectively. The longest and richest of these compares the clearing of
Dante's mind by Beatrice's instruction to the clearing of the heavens:

Come rimane splendido e sereno
l' emisperio dell' aer, quando soffia
Borea da quella guancia ond' è più leno,

per che si purga e risolve la roffia
che pria turbava, sì che il ciel ne ride
con le bellezze d' ogni sua paroffia,

così fec' io, poi che mi provvide
la donna mia del suo risponder chiaro,
e, come stella in cielo, il ver si vide.
                    [XXVIII. 79–87]

(As the vault of the air is left serene and shining when Boreas blows from
his milder cheek and the obscuring fog is dissolved and driven away so that
heaven smiles on us with all the beauties of its pageantry, so it was with me
when my Lady granted me her clear answer, and, like a star in heaven, the
truth was plain.)

The unveiled beauty of the starry sky is the natural correlative of the
revealed truth about the individual beings burning with the light of the
One. Gazing into the sky is a physical action symbolic of the intellectual act of metaphysical speculation; these similes make us participate
in the appropriate symbolic action. The most splendid of these sky-
similes is the last one in this heaven. It indicates the transition into the
Empyrean:

Forse sei mila miglia di lontano
ci ferve l' ora sesta, e questo mondo
china già l' ombra, quasi al letto piano,

quando il mezzo del cielo, a noi profondo,
comincia a farsi tal, che alcuna stella
perde il parere infino a questo fondo;

e come vien la chiarissima ancella
del sol più oltre, così il ciel si chiude
di vista in vista infino alla più bella.

Non altrimenti il trionfo, che lude
sempre dintorno al punto che mi vinse,
parendo inchiuso da quel ch' egl' inchiude,

a poco a poco al mio veder si estinse;
[XXX. 1–13]

(Some six thousand miles away the sixth hour burns and already this world inclines its shadow almost to a level bed, when the mid-sky, deep above us, begins to change so that a star here and there is lost to sight at this depth; and as the brightest handmaid of the sun advances the sky then shuts off its lights one by one, even to the loveliest. In like manner, the triumph that sports forever round the point which overcame me and which seems enclosed by that which it encloses was extinguished little by little from my sight).

And so metaphysical speculation fades into the light of direct intuitive awareness.

The opening of Canto XXIX is another simile describing the sky:

Quando ambo e due i figli di Latona,
coperti del Montone e della Libra,
fanno dell' orizzonte insieme zona,

quant' è dal punto che il zenit inlibra,
infin che l' uno e l' altro da quel cinto,
cambiando l' emisperio, si dilibra,

tanto, col volto di riso dipinto,
si tacque Beatrice . . .
[XXX. 1–8]

(When the two children of Latona, covered by the Ram and by the Scales, both at once make a belt of the horizon, as long as from the moment when the zenith holds them balanced till the one and the other, changing hemisphere, are unbalanced from that girdle, for so long, her face illumined with a smile, Beatrice kept silence).

In this passage we may notice another characteristic of the imagery of the Ninth Heaven: the continuation of references to classical deities, who, as we have seen, became more frequent from the Heaven of the Sun onwards. Here the sun and the moon are called Latona's children, i.e., Apollo and Diana. In connection with Dante's use of classical mythology another point might be made here. Just before Dante rises out of the Heaven of the Fixed Stars, he calls Phoenicia

> il lito
> nel qual si fece Europa dolce carco
> [XXVII. 83–84]

(the shore where Europa made herself a sweet burden).

As Beatrice's smile thrusts Dante into the ninth heaven, he calls the constellation of Gemini out of which he is "plucked" *bel nido di Leda* (fair nest of Leda) [XXVII. 98]. Lastly, in the simile quoted above he names Latona (Leto). All three were loves of Jupiter and bore him children. These reminders of Jupiter's amours, together with the reference to Semele in XXI. 5–6, indicate the movement toward the complete union between the human and the divine which is the culmination of the *Paradiso*.[10] To Dante there was nothing sacrilegious in this; pagan fables as well as sacred history can be used to mirror forth a divine reality.

In the eternal spring of this heaven [XXVIII. 116] images and metaphors of vegetation unfold again. Light and fire, of course, pervade every part of the Primum Mobile, but the following lines bring out perhaps best the nature of light as the effulgence of being, and the nature of heat as love:

> La prima luce, che tutta la raia,
> per tanti modi in essa si recepe,
> quanti son gli splendori a che s' appaia.

> Onde, però che all' atto che concepe
> segue l' affetto, d' amor la dolcezza
> diversamente in essa ferve e tepe.
> [XXIX. 136–141]

(The primal light that irradiates them all is received by them in as many ways as are the splendours with which it is joined, and therefore, since the affections follow the act of conceiving, love's sweetness glows variously in them, more and less.)

The swiftness, uniformity, and circular movement of this heaven show its harmonious nature [XXVII. 99–101]. The hosanna of the angels who sing in three melodies [XXVIII. 118–119] is another sign of harmony.

A ship metaphor occurs in XXVII. 146–147, continuing this most persistent image-theme in this heaven. Metaphors of warfare are again used in XXIX. 113–114, where Christ's disciples are represented as fighting with the shield and lance of the Gospel to kindle faith in the darkened world.

Finally we might remark that the animal images of XXIX. 106–108, 118, and 124–125 show the grossness of earthly errors compared to the crystalline purity of the truth revealed in this heaven.

XI.

The Eternal Now: Union with Being

> Dentro all' ampiezza di questo reame
> casual punto non puote aver sito,
> se non come tristizia, o sete, o fame;
>
> chè per eterna legge è stabilito
> quantunque vedi, sì che giustamente
> ci si risponde dall' anello al dito.
> [XXXII. 52–57]

(In all the breadth of this kingdom nothing of chance can find a place any more than sorrow or thirst or hunger, for all thou seest is ordained by eternal law, so that here the ring exactly fits the finger.)

Canto XXX

As we contemplate the great paradox that being unites the supremely individual with the supremely universal, we are overtaken by the dawn of ultimate reality. We have so far been looking for being itself in entities which derived the light of their existence from it. We were gazing at the starry sky which reflected the light of the sun,[1] but now the sun itself is rising and the shadow of the earth must leave the sky. Being will no longer appear to us as reflected in its creations; we will stand in the direct light [XXX. 109].

Our vision of the exulting play that constitutes the pure activity of free energy fades away gradually [XXX. 10–13]. When vision leaves us we turn again to our guide, the revelation of the love given to us early in life. As we leave the ninth state of paradise, she appears more harmonious than ever before on our journey. We realize here that we can never grasp the full beauty of the experience which overpowered us so long ago. Only He Who created the beloved and Whose power shines out in every such experience can know its fullness [XXX. 13–21]. But here we see as much of the splendor of our love as the finiteness of our own being permits. Once this love was our only token of the existence of some reality beyond the reach of the senses [XXX. 28]; now total actuality opens up before us with the blinding realization of what our love really *is*:

> Dal primo giorno ch' io vidi il suo viso
> in questa vita, infino a questa vista,
> non m' è il seguire al mio cantar preciso;
>
> ma or convien che mio seguir desista
> più retro a sua bellezza, poetando,
> come all' ultimo suo ciascuno artista.
>
> [XXX. 28–33]

(From the first day I saw her face in this life until this sight the pursuit in my song has not been cut off; but now must my pursuit cease from following longer after her beauty in my verse, as with every artist who has reached his limit.)

When we return to our everyday life we will not be able to remember the full meaning of this experience [XXX. 25–27]. But now the voice of love within continues to guide us and, after our amazement has subsided, tells us where we have arrived [XXX. 37–38].

The last eternal state through which the pilgrims of paradise pass in time has now been left behind [XXX. 39]. We are in the eternal present, in the full light of being; the radiance is complete understanding, the heat the energy of love. Whoever is touched by this light lives in unceasing joy [XXX. 40–42].

For further progress our capacity of vision must be strengthened again by the living light which now surrounds us on every side. But to sharpen our sight we must first lose it; this has happened again and again in paradise. In every new state whose light overpowers our inward eye we have to first accept our inadequacy, admit our blindness. Only when we have consented to lose our sight in order to gain it is our power of vision restored and intensified. This, too, is a general law. No creative vision is possible without a humble acceptance of one's real shortcomings [XXX. 46–51].

Here it is not enough to have keen inward sight; we must go beyond understanding and make ourselves ready to burn with the flame of love, for in this eternal present all entities become eternal candles ceaselessly burning and never consumed [XXX. 52–54]. As we hear this truth revealed to us we surpass our proper powers and our last and deepest inward vision opens within us. A new sight has been kindled in us, strong enough to support the intensest light that reveals whatever truly *is* [XXX. 55–60].

Our first vision here shows us the nature of the overpowering light itself. This light is a river of illuminative power which increases our understanding continually. Now we see sparks rising from the river of light and entering, like bees, the eternal ruby-red flowers on the banks. Then sated with odors, they plunge back into the river again [XXX. 61–69].

By the free flow of illumination, in response to our desire for enlightenment, we were lifted up from state to state in paradise. Now we desire to understand more than ever [XXX. 70–72]. We have to drink of illuminative grace to comprehend the meaning of a vision, to penetrate behind the last symbol-mask that hides the final truth [XXX. 73–78].[2] In spite of our new vision we still see "through a glass, darkly," for we cannot penetrate through the symbols into what they symbolize [XXX. 79–81]. But we follow the motherly command of the voice of love and bathe our eyes in the river of grace with greater eagerness than any child who, awaking late, rushes to his mother's breast for milk [XXX. 82–87].[3]

The last symbol-mask of reality falls off and we become aware of an even greater joy than what the symbols promised [XXX. 91–95]. As grace is added to our already perfected visionary power, we understand the perfection of grace itself [XXX. 88–90]. We see all that truly is in the light of illuminating grace, which, as we now see, is none other than the manifest splendor of being itself.[4] To those who come to realize that they can find no rest and fulfillment except in the contemplation of being, this light makes visible being itself [XXX. 96–102]. Though the light of being is intellectual light because it reveals to our understanding whatever truly exists, we cannot identify it with human reason. It encompasses reason but extends far beyond it on every side [XXX. 103–105]. The life and power of the whole created universe comes from this light [XXX. 107–108], which reveals to us the world of the eternal *now*. Such complete awareness is the actuality underlying all the states of development which we have traversed on our journey so far. Like the sun that calls forth the plant from the seed, it draws and raises the soul from the moment of awakening through all the stages of inner growth.

This eternal present is reflected on the outermost layer of all existence that is still bound in its movement to a determined course.[5] What we see in this reflection is the free order of being and, within it, all those beings who, having once been estranged from being itself, have found their way back to their true home:

> E come clivo in acqua di suo imo
> si specchia, quasi per vedersi adorno,
> quando è nell' erbe e nei fioretti opimo,
>
> sì soprastando al lume intorno intorno
> vidi specchiarsi in più di mille soglie,
> quanto di noi lassù fatto ha ritorno.[6]
> [XXX. 109–114]

(and as a hillside is mirrored in water at its foot as if to see itself adorned when it is rich with grass and flowers, I saw, rising above the light all round in more than a thousand tiers, as many of us as have returned there above.)

As in the chalice of a white rose of innumerable petals, we see perfect order and beauty unfold before us. Our vision can now take it all in without failing. Nothing stands here between the light of being and our intellectual eye; the supreme reality is open to our fully developed understanding, for here no distance is interposed between desire and fulfillment [XXX. 118–123].

While total reality opens up in all its perfection, the voice of love within us points out how leadership is exalted here. All true leadership in history is an attempt to mold the world of temporal human existence into a likeness of this eternal order. But such attempts are foiled by man's greed. By clinging to their greed, people in the temporal world are fighting against their own salvation. Thus our revelation warns us for the last time against greed, the urge to possess illusory goods for ourselves alone. This is the basic error which even those dedicated to the service of the eternal order commit. Insisting on separateness and material possessions, they fall willing victims to illusion and are estranged from the splendor of reality.

Canto XXXI

Having understood the nature of the light which reveals everything as it truly *is*, our vision now takes in the forces that work within total reality [XXXI. 4–15]. Between the source of the light and the beings who are, like flowers, brought into existence and nourished by the light, there is a constant stream of messengers hurrying to and fro. But such a multitude of intermediaries cannot obscure being from the vision of men because the light reaches all who are ready to receive it [XXXI. 19–24]. These messengers of being offer peace and burning energy together, for the two by no means exclude each other here. Both peace and ardor come from free activity [XXXI. 16–18] which is no toil but pure delight [XXXI. 9].

All entities who have attained the ultimate goal turn toward being itself and are secure and joyful in their vision [XXXI. 25–27]. As we stand here at the end of our pilgrimage in silent contemplation, our inquiring intellect is stilled for a while [XXXI. 43–48]. In every face we see charity and joy, in every gesture the full dignity of complete existence [XXXI. 49–51].

When our will turns again to questioning, we can no longer receive enlightenment from the revelation of our personal experience of love. That experience reaches its full stature here in the eternal present and, having become one part of the total vision, it can no longer give us more than itself. It cannot take us to the comprehension of the whole. Therefore from the motherly care of our personal revelation—which was, after all, something given from without—we pass under the fatherly guidance of direct intuition [XXXI. 55–63].[7] The guide to the final union with being is therefore the authority that resides in our own heart; but to discover this authority we had to pass through the fearful way of self-knowledge (*Inferno*) and the painful path of purification (*Purgatorio*); we had to ascend the ladder of development led by a revelation given to us through another person. Yet now all that has come from without must take its place where it truly belongs [XXXI. 65–69]. However high above us she may be on the scale of closeness to being, we now see clearly the person through whom this revelation had come to us and turn to her for the last time with gratitude. Before we found the way that has led us so far, it was the thought of our experience of love which kept our hope alive and prevented us from becoming utterly enmeshed in the forest of confusion and ignorance. That spark of light burning in our darkness was a promise that we may yet come to stand in the light of what truly is. The greatness and excellence of the love kindled in us by another has enabled us to see with the inward eye of vision and recognize the nourishing and sustaining power in all that we saw on our journey [XXXI. 73–84]. Precisely because ours was a *personal* revelation, it could guide us into full

freedom from the bondage of illusion by ways and means most suited
to our individual needs [XXXI. 85–87]. Our guide has made our soul
whole and we ask her help now to preserve that wholeness in the
future [XXXI. 88–90].

Intuition urges us now to think of the short stretch of our path
[cammino, XXXI. 95] that still lies ahead. To ascend through the light
of being, our eye should first get accustomed to the eternal now [XXXI.
94–99]. In the voice of intuition we recognize the voice of the human
incarnation of being itself [XXXI. 103–108] and know that intuition
leads us both to active love and contemplative peace [XXXI. 109–111].

We also understand intuitively that we will not come to know fully
this joyous existence [XXXI. 112] if we restrict our vision to what is
on our own level. Spiritual reality must be explored fully, to the highest
reaches, where we discover what is closest to being. Where the light is
most intense, on the uppermost boundary of created reality, we see
the peaceful glow [XXXI. 127] of beauty itself [XXXI. 134], the
feminine principle, without whose help we can never attain the final
union with being [XXXI. 112–135]. We can unite with being only if we
become both active and peaceful, if we are in motion and in rest
simultaneously, in other words if we recognize and accept the feminine
part within us as well as the active, masculine tendency. By completing
our own being in this way we may become more like being itself and
advance to the final union.

Fully developed spirits serve beauty by creative activity that unites
the freedom of play with the harmony of music. As we look on the
beauty that is a source of heat as well as of light, of energy as well as
of understanding [XXXI. 140], our intuition infuses passionate love
into our gaze [XXXI. 130–142].

Canto XXXII

With our love fixed on the beauty of the Eternal Feminine, we take
in the vision of total reality. The first truth we understand here is the
role the principle of beauty played in our fall and redemption. As it
was the cause of our estrangement from being, it was also instrumental
in the closing of the wound of our separateness [XXXII. 1–6]. Without
her we could neither feel our separateness and estrangement in this
world nor could we find our way back, enriched by experience, to the
unity we have lost.

The ultimate reality of all Creation—the chalice of the rose—appears
to us in two equal halves. These show that one may reach union with

being by following the eternal law in hope or by living in the freedom of perfect love, according to one or the other aspect of the faith [XXXII. 38]. We also recognize the equality of the female and the male aspect of the total being; women who have followed the way of the law [XXXII. 7–18] take their places next to those whose life was love, whereas men who followed love are next to the people of the law [XXXII. 31–36]. Their position symbolizes the truth that although total reality is reached by individual paths, these paths have to unite somehow the two basic principles of love and the law as well as the male and female aspects of the soul [XXXII. 38–39].

We wonder next at the presence of beings who, though fallen, apparently had no opportunity to walk the paths that would lead them back to being. If they did not choose freely to return to eternity, how can they be part of it now? This seems far too difficult a question for our intellect [XXXII. 40–51]. But the infallible voice of intuition assures us that chance has no place to operate in ultimate reality. Perfect justice creates a perfect order within which all find their proper place, although we sometimes fail to understand how. The truth is that nothing happens without sufficient cause [XXXII. 52–60]. Here we behold the effect and this must suffice. For all beings fulfill the eternal plan in their diversity and all contribute to the love, the pleasure, and the peace that make ultimate reality into what it must be [XXXII. 61–66]. Those not elected to walk their own way toward being in a series of free choices will take their places (i.e., their appearance within ultimate reality is a direct manifestation of their being) according to their "primal keenness," i.e., the power of vision proper to them from the beginning [XXXII. 73–75]. (The allocation of "places" in the ultimate vision of *what is* remains a mystery; we can never fully understand why the reality of one person is different from that of another. We have touched here again [see XXI. 91–96] upon the mystery of individuality and thus upon the essence of being which we can never penetrate with our intellect, for the intellect itself is already a differentiated part of this essence and the part can never comprehend the whole. But one thing is certain: the real differences between beings are not measured in superiority and inferiority, strength and weakness. These measurements belong to the world of illusion, not to the full reality of the spirit.)

To achieve the final unification of our own divided being which is the end of life, men have to recognize and contemplate the feminine principle.[8] Only if our vision has wholly grasped the splendor of that aspect of being [XXXII. 93] of which women are the living representatives on earth, are we ready to look upon the perfect embodiment of being itself [XXXII. 85–87]. The feminine aspect of being is full of the vision-nourishing light which is the source of serenity. As we contemplate her we also understand the true relationship of the male principle to the female. We "see" how the male, driven by burning love [XXXII. 105], gazes with delight into the female mirror of being [XXXII. 94–105]. Intuition, which is directly connected with the feminine principle, drawing the beauty of its truths from her, also enlightens us about the characteristics of the male principle. It has vigor, energy above all, but manifested with gracefulness [leggiadria, XXXII. 109], not brute force [XXXII. 106–111]. Perfection of being—as exemplified by Christ—comes from the cooperation of these two principles without which no creation can take place [XXXII. 112–114].

Having understood these essential truths, we now turn to the contemplation of the individuals who make up total reality. Each of them is the type of a path to being. The man who fell, though he issued out into life with greater powers and greater freedom than any man after him, has finally come home and so has another who was born in infirmity, but enlightened and redeemed by the perfection of being in Christ. We have them both in ourselves; they are the beginnings of paradise [XXXII. 118–126]. The visionary poet belongs here, too, and also the leader of men who works for the realization of an eternal purpose in history. The world disregards the revelations of the first and is ungrateful to the second, but here they come into their own [XXXII. 127–132]. (If one of these paths is allotted to us we must remember their example and not seek the world's praise.)

Here is the woman who is so content to gaze at the perfect form of the feminine principle which she herself has brought into the world that she refuses any activity which might interrupt contemplation.[9] Another type of womanly perfection is she who brings illumination to men when they fix their eyes on the earth to avoid vision and rush into their destruction [XXXII. 133–138]. She has also saved us repeatedly when we have lost our way.

Now intuition urges us to enter the final stretch of our pilgrimage and approach with our visionary eye being itself. To penetrate as much as we can into the truth, into the unveiled reality of being,[10] we must here ask for more illuminative power. Without it all our efforts would only thrust us backward into ignorance instead of carrying us to the final union. It is from the Eternal Feminine, the most perfect mirror of being, that we receive the aid which increases our power of vision.[11]

To obtain this grace we must follow our intuition most scrupulously, not only with our mind but also with our heart [XXXII. 139–150].

Canto XXXIII

Our intuition now turns to the Eternal Feminine who unites in her relationship to being the three essential roles of woman, that of mother, wife, and daughter. She ennobles human nature so that the union of being and man can take place at last. Because in the perfection of womanhood the concern for the self ceases altogether (no man can be as self-forgetting as a mother) she is, in her humility, more exalted than any created being [XXXIII. 1–6]. In this total reality she is an ever-burning torch of love while in time-bound existence she is the source of man's hope. Through her the illuminative power comes to men; it is his love for woman that nourishes man's vision [XXXIII. 10–15]. Her kindness does not wait for men's asking; she takes them toward their fulfillment even before they pray. She overflows with compassion, piety, generosity, uniting all the goodness of created beings within herself [XXXIII. 19–21].

The inward eye of those who, like ourselves, have toiled upwards from the deepest abyss of self-knowledge, understanding all the states of the human being's development until they could behold the fullness of reality, must be strengthened by her for the last time. She has to remove the last veil of illusion and error from our eyes so that we may lift them to the saving and liberating truth as it unfolds itself to fill us with unsurpassable pleasure [XXXIII. 22–33]. We depend upon her even after our direct vision of being; she must then help us to keep our affections whole, our lives in harmony, for the overpowering experience might disrupt the balance of our weak humanity [XXXIII. 34–39].[12] Not only intuition prompts us to turn to the feminine principle for help but our revelation, too, [XXXIII. 38] though she no longer *guides* us here.

Now our vision is fully intent on the eyes of the Eternal Feminine which sink into the light of being more deeply and clearly than the eyes of any other creature. And, following her eyes, we arrive at the end of our journey: we gaze at the source of the light and approach union with being through direct vision. The burning intellectual desire for understanding that has brought us so far is now stilled [XXXIII. 40–48]. We not only follow intuition, but, as intuition would have us be, we become one with intuition as our completely cleansed sight penetrates into the full light of truth [XXXIII. 49–54]. The greatness of our vision then transcends absolutely the powers of speech and memory.[13] What remains is the sweetness of an emotion only, at the deepest core of the heart:

> Qual è colui che somniando vede,
> chè dopo il sogno il passione impressa
> rimane, e l' altro alla mente non riede;
>
> cotal son io, chè quasi tutta cessa
> mia visione, ed ancor mi distilla
> nel cor lo dolce che nacque da essa.[14]
>   [XXXIII. 58–63]

(Like him that sees in a dream and after the dream the passion wrought by it remains and the rest returns not to his mind, such am I; for my vision almost wholly fades, and still there drops within my heart the sweetness that was born of it.)

But while we are looking into the living light [XXXIII. 77] it holds our vision with such brilliance that we cannot turn away; if we did, we would be lost in dazed darkness. Immersed completely in the abounding stream of light, our sight attains at last the ultimate good, being itself, from which everything that *is* derives its worth [XXXIII. 76–84]. Here we find all the signatures of being collected in one, all that exists in separation throughout the universe fused together by the burning of infinite love into one simple flame [XXXIII. 85–90]. We arrive at an understanding of all that *is* by grasping the final principle or form, but when the vision leaves us no rational proof remains to testify to the truth of what we saw. All that is left is an emotion of joy [XXXIII. 91–93]. Even one single moment of *time* carries us almost infinitely far from this vision which can be attained only in timelessness. Yet we can recall how our mind, fixed in this intellectual vision of the truth, was totally absorbed in being, and our will would not turn away from all goodness gathered into unity.[15] For whatever the will desires can be found in its perfection only in being; if we seek it outside of being we will possess it only in imperfection [XXXIII. 94–105].

Strengthened by its immersion into the living light which is forever unchanging, our sight discerns the appearance of threefold nature within the "profound and shining being of the deep light." This being is forever itself but we cannot comprehend it as such. Only through appearances (which, however, do not obscure but reveal and manifest being) can we come closer to the ever unreachable core. And as our power of vision grows, as we change ourselves, so we discern new appearances changing in the living light of being. The three natures which we now behold are all perfect, all aspects of the same being and manifest by their continual interplay; they are the light of power, of wisdom, and of love [XXXIII. 109–120]. The eternal light which is being abides in itself alone; it understands itself, wills itself, and loves itself rejoicing. (Thus being manifests the supreme integration of those forces which we call reason, will, and emotion. The perfection of these is the unified, unceasing activity of being [XXXIII. 124–126].)

With a last effort at understanding we glimpse in the threefold appearance the unity of man with being [XXXIII. 127–131]. We *are* being; but we cannot grasp with the intellect this truth of the coincidence of a finite being with infinite Being ; it cannot be expressed in thought-symbols just as the circumference of the circle—an infinite number—cannot be given exactly in the terms of its radius that is finite. The wings of understanding that carried us through paradise were not made to lift us into this truth [XXXIII. 133–139]. But the vision's final purpose is—as always—by *understanding* to awaken the *will* to *love*. In a lightning flash we find our own will and find that our desire and will have entered the fullness of existence moved in perfect accord by the love that rules all that is [XXXIII. 140–145].

Images

vidi che s' interna,
legato con amore in un volume,
ciò che per l' universo si squaderna;
[XXXIII. 85–87]

(I saw that it contained, bound by love in one volume, that which is scattered in leaves through the universe.)

In the last three cantos the recurring images and image-themes of the *Paradiso* are all "gathered in one volume" and several of them come to a splendid climax in the great similes of the Empyrean. This integration of the imagery embodies the anagogical meaning of the highest heaven; humanity's latent powers which Dante saw gradually unfolding in heaven after heaven are all gathered together here in the fullness of existence given by the direct vision of being.

The diction also indicates the anagogical meaning at many points. I take only two outstanding examples. The threefold repetition of *vidi* in XXX. 95, 97, 99 marks the coming of the most penetrating sight to the pilgrim as the last symbol-veil of reality is withdrawn. In the same canto the words *riflesso, si specchia*, and *specchiarsi* occur in rhythmical repetition in lines 107, 110, and 113. This emphasis on reflection or mirroring warns the reader that the ultimate reality of Creation as it opens up in the white rose of the Empyrean is only the reflected light of being and not being itself. Even Beatrice, as she leaves Dante and takes her place in the rose, does not radiate light, only reflects the eternal beams:

> e vidi lei che si facea corona,
> riflettendo da sè gli eterni rai.
> [XXXI. 71–72]

(and saw her where she made for herself a crown, reflecting from her the eternal beams.)

What are the image-themes which have accompanied us through the *Paradiso* and are recapitulated here, as if the partial reality of all that we have seen in the individual heavens were now collected in the total reality of whatever truly is? Some of these themes have been leitmotifs of the whole *Comedy*: the theme of pilgrimage comes to a climax in the pilgrim's arrival to the shrine of his vow:

> E quasi peregrin, che si ricrea
> nel tempio del suo voto riguardando,
> e spera già ridir com' ello stea,
>
> sì per la viva luce passeggiando,
> menava io gli occhi per li gradi,
> mo su, mo giù, e mo ricirculando.
> [XXXI. 43–48]

(And like a pilgrim who is refreshed in the temple of his vow as he looks round it and hopes some time to tell of it again, so, taking my way up through the living light, I carried my eyes through the ranks, now up, now down, and now looking round again.)

In another simile the end of a concrete earthly pilgrimage is described [XXXI. 103–108].

The theme of dreaming, awaking, and recollecting the vanished vision is recapitulated in XXXIII. 58–63. Dante, as so often in the *Comedy*, again likens himself to a child in XXX. 82–85, 139–140, and XXXIII. 107–108. After seeing so many imprints of perfect forms in imperfect matter, the last imprint is finally blotted out by the sun of being as if it had been stamped on snow:

> Così la neve il sol si disigilla,
> [XXXIII. 64]

(Thus the snow loses its imprint in the sun).

From the city of Florence and the City of Dis the way was long to the eternal city [XXX. 130]. But Florence, though only in retrospect, haunts Dante even here [XXXI. 39]. And we remind ourselves that all the astronomy and star-imagery of the *Comedy* culminates in the last line, where love is said to move "the sun and the other stars."

Taking now certain recurrent images of the *Paradiso* only, we see how light and fire are everywhere in the last three cantos. The whole Empyrean is bathed in the "living light" which unites in itself heat and brilliance, love and intellect. The geography of the earth appears once more in XXXI. 31–36 and 103, the cloudy sky in XXXI. 73, the sea in XXXI. 75. A suggestion of the element of flight in XXXII. 146 and XXXIII. 139 brings to a close the imagery of air and of birds.

The eternal garden of the Empyrean [XXXI. 97; XXXII. 39] brings forth plants, flowers, and fruit.

All the circling harmonies of paradise point to the final vision of the three reflecting circles in XXXIII. 116. At the end of the poem Dante himself is caught up in the circular dance which he had observed in the lower heavens.

Similes taken from geometry culminate in the image of the insufficiency of the geometer to measure the final mystery of man's union with God [XXXIII. 133–135].

The theme of warfare against the "erring world" echoes again in the "soldiery of paradise" [XXX. 43–44] and in "holy soldiery" [XXXI. 2].

Even one of those similes Dante takes from the common life of trades appears in the highest heaven when St. Bernard says to him:

> Ma perchè il tempo fugge, che t' assonna,
> qui farem punto, come buon sartore
> che, com' egli ha del panno, fa la gonna;
> [XXXII. 139–140]

(But since the time flies that holds thee sleeping we shall stop here, like a good tailor that cuts his coat according to his cloth).

Heeding St. Bernard's words, I, too, feel that it is time to end the recapitulation of image themes and turn to the great images themselves that overarch, in these last cantos, the entire structure of the *Paradiso*. Here we see the imagery of paradise not only juxtaposed but organically integrated. Two of these complex images describe total reality. One shows the last symbolic disguise:

E vidi lume in forma di riviera
fulvido di fulgore, intra due rive
dipinte di mirabil primavera.

Di tal fiumana uscian faville vive,
e d' ogni parte si mettean nei fiori,
quasi rubin che oro circonscrive.

Poi, come inebriate dagli odori,
riprofondavan sè nel miro gurge,
e, s' una entrava, un' altra n' uscia fuori.
[XXX. 61–69]

(And I saw light in the form of a river pouring its splendour between two
banks painted with marvellous spring. From that torrent came forth living
sparks and they settled on the flowers on either side, like rubies set in gold;
then, as if intoxicated with the odours, they plunged again into the wondrous
flood, and as one entered another came forth.)

Light, fire, water, blossoming nature, gems, and the artefacts of
jewelry are the integral parts of this symbolic landscape. The other
complex image is, of course, the picture of undisguised eternity, the
rose of the redeemed which rises up in the shape of an immense
amphitheatre from the pool of reflected light on the top of the Primum
Mobile [XXX. 106–117]. The rose itself is the crowning image of all
the images that suggest perfection: of the garlands, reels, and circles
of paradise. It is also the emblem of emblems and sums up within itself
the triple ring of the Sun, the cross of Mars, the eagle of Jupiter, and
the ladder of Saturn.

The great simile of sunrise in XXXI. 118–129 fuses earth, sky, and
fire with the mythological allusion to Phaeton and with the oriflamme,
the battle standard of the ancient kings of France.

All three complex images span several terzinas like immense arches,
opening vistas into final reality. Then vision ceases while the pilgrim
gathers strength for the final plunge into the Source. Canto XXXII is
scarce of images and has no great similes to be compared to those we
have already mentioned or those that are to come. It is a final respite
for the reader before the last burst of a superhuman imagination.

From line 58 of Canto XXXIII to the end of the poem an uninter-
rupted flight of the highest poetry conveys something of the ecstasy
that the direct vision of being is. Images follow one another as in the
Greek choral odes, with a dithyrambic fervor. Like the Sybil's leaves,
they are carried higher and higher in the wind of inspiration which
invisibly links them together. They rise up rhythmically, as if the

feverish mind shot them out with volcanic violence, between two prayers.

The vision of the ineffable can be conveyed only gropingly: one dreams and wakes, the sun melts all shapes from the surface of the snow, the leaves of the Sybil—all fragmentary human wisdom—are lost in the wind. The interval of prayer is bridged by the memory of leaves flying in the storm—and of those human souls on the banks of Acheron falling like autumn leaves—leaves which are found again and bound into one volume where all may read them who come to look upon being. All that *is*, the entire complex, incomprehensible fabric of reality, fuses into one simple flame. And with this most daring exploit the boldest enterprise of the human intellect is over; Argo reaches the fabulous shore and Neptune, deep in his green water-world, gazes at man's triumph. The ship we have followed right through paradise has arrived at last. Another long-drawn breath follows, while imagination gathers strength to advance yet deeper into the center. But this interval is also spanned by a mysterious kinship between the image of a god looking on human handiwork and the second circle of the last vision where man's image is painted upon the Form of God. Then imagination falls back, as the geometrician draws circles and is vainly trying to measure them:

All' alta fantasia qui mancò possa;
[XXXIII. 142]

(Here power failed the high fantasy).

But with the last effort imagination has reached beyond itself: it has become a will and a desire, a *whole*. And now, after our ascent through mountain steeps and heavenly spheres, we, integrated into the whole human race as it existed from the beginning, are swept along by love in unimpeded movement with the sun and the stars.

XII.

Dante, Poet of the Future

The theological formulation of the truths and laws toward which the *Paradiso* is leading us is well documented but is in the deepest sense meaningless to many of us today. I have tried to give them another formulation in my interpretation of the poem and would now like to indicate, very sketchily and provisionally, some implications of this approach. For truth is like an object in space: one can walk around it and look at it from all angles, and the more one has seen of it the better one knows it.

The structure of meaning in the poem can be described in various ways; we talked of it as an approach to union with being, and, since this also means a union with our selves, as integration. Thus the gradual ascent through the heavens is also an inward journey from our periphery to our center.

If we think about the *Paradiso* as a "journey to the interior," a new light is thrown on those truths which we understand through the anagogical interpretation. In hell and purgatory Dante had to learn how to shed the many layers of illusion which covered his real personality. In hell he saw the reality of what had appeared desirable to his perverted will. In purgatory he understood how one suffers by having to follow the habits that slavery to illusion implants in the soul, long after one has recognized the original error, for purgatorial suffering lasts until the will is completely liberated from bondage to a self-centered view of reality. When on the top of Mount Purgatory Beatrice

191

calls the poet by his name [*Purg*. XXX. 55 and 62–63], the necessity
of registering the word *Dante* for the first and last time in the *Comedy*
is a deeper necessity than would first appear. For at this point he has
again become the *real* Dante whom Beatrice had known and is no
longer the man wandering lost in the forest of error. Thus here Dante
recovers his real personality which a life, in the world and of the world,
had covered over with layers of falsehood.

But the true journey to the interior starts only from this point.
Leaving the earth is the true beginning of the voyage of self-discovery,
for it represents the turning of attention from the outward to the
inward, from illusions and encrustations to the substance. Immersion
in the water-world of the moon sphere is the penetration into the secret
world of the self, the unconscious. What comes after the meeting with
one's "shadow"—which may perhaps be equated with the self-knowledge given by the *Inferno*—is, Jung says, "the world of water, where
all life floats in suspension; where the realm of the sympathetic system,
the soul of everything living, begins. . . . 'Lost in oneself' is a good
way of describing this state. But this self is the world if only consciousness could see it."[1] Whether we call this boundless and floating world
into which we have plunged here the collective unconscious as Jung
does, or an inner, spiritual reality where our psyches interconnect,
depends largely on our choice of terminology.

In the sphere of Venus inward progress is marked by the knowledge
of the real self in others and, consequently, an increased knowledge of
our own real self. In Mars, the meeting with Cacciaguida suggests the
finding within ourselves of a self deeper, nobler than we had hitherto
suspected. The ascent into the natal constellation in the Heaven of the
Fixed Stars marks the point in the inward journey where one begins to
feel one's identity with what one might call an eternal or higher self.
Yet development does not stop here; the meeting with Christ symbolizes the moment when the divine part begins to live and work within
us. The final union is the arrival at the center and true home, where
one always *is* but does not know it, where one is not separate and yet
is most one's self.

Thus, as we have said before, all the figures Dante meets in paradise
are but reflections of his own yet unrecognized potentialities, and in
seeing them he increases the knowledge of his own self.

Progress in paradise is not linear but has its own oscillating rhythm.
The diagram on the opposite page will illustrate what I mean. First of
all, the method of advance, as Dante outlines it, consists always of the

	Moon	Mercury	Venus	Sun	Mars	Jupiter	Saturn	Fixed Stars	Primum Mobile	Empyrean
HEAVEN										
FOCUS	self	the "world"	other selves	order of the universe	self-sacrifice	ideal state—justice	inner vision	community of eternal selves	pure energy	total reality *and* being
MODE	individual	social	personal	cosmic	personal	social	individual	communal	spiritual	total
FACULTY	seed of the self	will	emotion	mature reason	mature emotion	mature will	reason as imagination or "spiritual perception"	charity or spiritualized emotion	pure act or spiritualized will	integrated emotion will and imagination
DIMENSION	depth	breadth	depth	breadth	depth	breadth	depth	breadth	depth	breadth *and* depth

same steps, which are the application of spiritual understanding to the
proces of self-development:

(1) awareness of what one sees
(2) desire to understand it completely
(3) precise formulation of one's doubts
(4) enlightenment coming from revelation or intuition
(5) increased vision as a result of intellectual enlightenment

—and then the whole process is repeated on the next level. But in
addition to the rhythm of intellectual advance, the structure of the
successive states—or heavens—shows a larger and more complex
oscillation which one might call psychological.

The psychological law of progress in the *Paradiso* appears to be an
oscillation between introspection and outward turning, between a
penetration in depth—into another's self as well as into one's own—
and an expansion of energies on a wide surface. The expansion of
energies is at the same time a gathering of strength for the next thrust
into the unknown. The last advance into the source of eternal light
absolves Dante from this fluctuation; nourished by the final vision his
energies expand and, simultaneously, he gains ever-renewed insight
into the inexhaustible depths of the divine.

But would not such a psychologizing approach make the *Paradiso*
into an imitation of the *Poimandres* of Hermes Trismegistus? Would
this not be altogether false to the spirit of the poem? After all, the
Comedy is usually thought of as embodying Thomist philosophy, and
nothing can be further from Thomism than the doctrines of the
Poimandres. The point is worth examining.

Though Dante quotes freely from Aristotle and from St. Thomas
Aquinas, the philosophy embodied in the *Comedy* could not be called
either Thomist or Aristotelian. It has become almost a commonplace
to say that, in spite of his calling Aristotle *Il Filosofo*, Dante's way of
thinking has really much more in common with Plato. The work of
Bruno Nardi has made it abundantly clear that the *Paradiso* is thoroughly imbued not so much with the spirit of Plato as with Neoplatonism. The return of man to the One through intellectual knowledge in
which light and love are inseparably fused, is the way of the *Paradiso*,
and it is a distinctly Plotinian idea. The great passage on the creation
and emanation of all that exists by the divine *idea,* breathes the pure
spirit of Neoplatonism, in spite of the words being spoken by Aquinas.

> Ciò che non more e ciò che può morire
> non è se non splendor di quella idea
> che partorisce, amando, il nostro sire;

chè quella viva luce che sì mea
dal suo lucente, che non si disuna
da lui, nè dall' amor che a lor s' intrea,

per sua bontate il suo raggiare aduna,
quasi specchiato, in nove sussistenze,
eternalmente rimanendosi una.

Quindi discende all' ultime potenze
giù d' atto in atto tanto divenendo,
che più non fa che brevi contingenze;

e queste contingenze essere intendo
le cose generate, che produce
con seme e senza seme il ciel movendo.

La cera di costoro, e chi la duce,
non sta d' un modo, e però sotto il segno
ideale poi più e men traluce:

ond' egli avvien ch' un medesimo legno,
secondo specie, meglio e peggio frutta;
e voi nascete con diverso ingegno.

Se fosse a punto la cera dedutta,
e fosse il cielo in sua virtù suprema,
la luce del suggel parrebbe tutta;

ma la natura la dà sempre scema,
similemente operando all' artista,
ch' ha l' abito dell' arte e man che trema.

Però se il caldo amor, la chiara vista
della prima virtù dispone e segna,
tutta la perfezion quivi s' acquista.

[XIII. 52–81]

(That which does not die and that which is capable of dying is nothing else but the reflected splendor of the idea which our Father in loving begets, and this living light pours from its shining source so that it is not divided from him nor from the love that makes three-in-one of them, does out of its goodness unite its radiance in nine existences as if it were being mirrored back, while eternally abiding as one.

From thence it descends down to the lowest lying potencies becoming such from act to act so that it now makes only short-lived contingencies by which I mean the generated things produced by the moving heavens from seed and without seed.

The wax of these ephemeral beings and that which molds them do not always stay in the same condition and therefore the wax under the ideal stamp becomes now more, now less, transparent: from which it comes that the same tree bears better and worse fruit according to its kind, and that you are born with different talents.

If the wax were prepared perfectly for the stamping, and the heaven [that imprints the stamp] would be at the perfection of its power, the image of the signet would be all shining clear; but nature [the operation of the heavens] is always faulty in the execution like the artist who is well-versed in his art but has a trembling hand.[2]

Therefore, if the warm Love, the clear Vision of the Primal Power prepares and stamps [the wax] all perfection is acquired there.)

Before I would try to indicate in a few words the general tradition which I think includes the *Paradiso*, I wish to make one thing clear. I do not believe that a great poet has to take all his ideas from other thinkers; more often than not great poets find the truth in their own hearts. Therefore in what follows I do not wish to imply that Dante has actually read all the authors and consciously incorporated their ideas into his *opus*; but I would like to make the point that there is a religious and philosophical tradition which was partly known to Dante and to which the *Paradiso* naturally belongs.

First of all, the writings of Aristotle reached Dante not only through St. Thomas but also through Arab translators and commentators. Now the Arab philosophers and their translators in Spain who transmitted the writings of Aristotle to the Western world were often unable to distinguish the works of the Philosopher from the later works of neoplatonists. An instance of this is the *Liber de Causis* often quoted by Dante, which was for a time attributed to Aristotle, but was later discovered to have been largely the work of Proclus. Or, to take another instance of neoplatonic influence through the Arabs, we see Dante adopting the doctrine on the movement of the spheres from Alpetragius [*Conv.* III, Cap.2]. This theory, as Nardi has pointed out,[3] is of neoplatonic origin, deriving multiplicity from the One. The great Arab philosophers Alfarabi, Avicenna, Algazel and Averroes were all profoundly influenced by Neoplatonism. Ibn Arabi of Murcia, mystic and poet-philosopher, whether Dante had read him or not,[4] expressed this Arab Neoplatonism succinctly: "The aim of the soul, from the day on which the Creator unites it with the body, is to acquire the knowledge of its principle, God."

But apart from the influence of writings which Dante might have thought Aristotelian and which in reality were neoplatonic, many other links can be found between the *Paradiso* and what might loosely be called the neoplatonic tradition. The figure of Dante's last guide, St. Bernard of Clairvaux, is perhaps the strongest of these links. He knew and used the writings of Dionysius the Areopagite (or the unknown author whom the Middle Ages knew under this name) who, in turn, "often resorts to the terminology of Plotinus and Proclus."[5] One might almost say that it was the strong neoplatonic strain in his mystical theology that had made him fit to stand as the figure of intuition, Dante's guide to the direct vision of God. But Dante himself knew the *Corpus Dionysiacum* either directly or through the works of St. Thomas and Albertus Magnus. His doctrine of emanations [*Par.* XIII. 52–78] derives either from Dionysius himself or from his follower and translator, the Christian neoplatonist Johannes Scotus Erigena. Another link is Boethius, one of Dante's favorite authors, who believed in the platonic and neoplatonic doctrine of pre-existence. It was Boethius who inspired Dante with his first passion for philosophy. The abbot Joachim of Fiore ("*di spirito profetico dotato*" [*Par.* XII. 141]) has also held doctrines akin to those of Plotinus and Proclus, especially about the role of understanding (*intellectus*), which the neoplatonists would call νόησις.

The ascent toward union with God through the successive celestial spheres is used in the *Poimandres*. Macrobius in his commentary on the *Somnium Scipionis* applies the principle in the opposite direction. According to him souls who fall from the One into bodies acquire in each of the heavenly spheres the powers which they will exercise in their bodies. It is quite likely that Dante knew some of the Hermetic writings through Albertus Magnus who often quotes Hermes Trismegistus. Macrobius' commentary was also widely known in the Middle Ages. Some passages of the *Paradiso* recall another neoplatonic work, the commentary on Plato's *Timaeus* by Chalcidius. I am thinking here in particular of *Par.* XXIX. 22–36, especially in its treatment of matter as pure potentiality and of the corporeal heavens as the union of pure form to pure matter. Since the spirit of the *Timaeus* itself is Pythagorean, it might well be that through Chalcidius Dante obtained an indirect glimpse of Pythagoreanism which must have been quite congenial to his mind. A passage like *Par.* XV. 55–57 can certainly be clarified by remembering the Pythagorean concept of the monad.

I do not wish to insist that Dante drew on all these sources, though he almost certainly drew on some of them. Nor are all the similarities between some ideas in the *Paradiso* and the ideas of Plotinus and Proclus in any way conclusive. Yet the use of the circle as a symbol for God certainly occurs in Plotinus [*Enn.* VI. viii. 18] and Dante's constant use of the number three, his unceasing reminders of the doctrine of the Trinity recall Proclus' obsession with triads. Plotinus' νόησις which unites subject and object into one is the kind of knowledge which Dante teaches in the *Paradiso*, where the pilgrim has to be united to a sphere in order to comprehend it [*Par.* II. 29–30]. "I rejoice to hear that your soul has set sail, like the returning Ulysses, for its native land—that glorious, that only real country—the world of unseen truth," writes Plotinus to Flaccus. He uses the same metaphor to describe a spiritual voyage of discovery which Dante uses persistently in the *Paradiso*: the metaphor of the ship and the soul.

Later neoplatonists, especially those who gathered around Lorenzo de' Medici in what came to be known as the Medici circle, recognized in Dante a kindred spirit. Their master, Marsilio Ficino, born a little more than a century after Dante's death, attempted to bring together ancient Neoplatonism and the Christian religion in his *Theologia Platonica*, a philosophical work to which, in Ficino's opinion, the *Comedy* supplied the poetical equivalent. One of the members of this circle, Cristoforo Landino, wrote the most popular and extensive commentary on the *Comedy*, which set the direction for many commentaries in the sixteenth and seventeenth centuries.[6] Neoplatonist poets in the same circle, like Matteo Palmieri, Giovanni Nesi, and Ugolino Verino attempted to combine the manner of Dante with the exposition of neoplatonic doctrines.[7]

Insofar as Dante's way is intellectual and spiritual, a way of the understanding, he is in the neoplatonic tradition in the *Paradiso*, and, to a lesser degree, in the entire *Comedy*. This comes into particular focus when we follow the anagogy where the goal is to understand the Divine Principle which permeates the universe as the first terzina of the *Paradiso* clearly says. Plotinus called it the Good or the One; "It is by the One that all beings are beings," he said.

It has, I think, become evident to the reader in my explication of the anagogical sense of the third cantica that, in my opinion, Dante believes understanding—not merely rational but also spiritual—is the key to the soul's growth. Or, to put it differently, it is through the workings of the spiritual intellect that the divine aspect within the human being comes to fruition. This approach to God is Neoplatonism pure and simple. It resembles the Plotinian intellectual pilgrimage that ends in the flight of the alone to the Alone. Especially as the teacher of the way of understanding through an introspective approach that poses questions and then waits patiently for the moment of revelation when the knower and the known become one, Dante is Plotinus' pupil.

This "dialectic of the way" however, is only one half of his method. The other is his figural symbolism that presents the reader with flesh and blood characters, each of whom embodies a certain state of soul concretely. When he is more of a poet than a philosophic teacher, he is not looking for the universal vital principle as much as for the personal aspect of God, toward Whom all the people he encounters in paradise rise up on tier upon tier of the heavenly rose. The God of the Judeo-Christian religion to whom we relate personally as children to their father has an equally real existence for Dante as the Divine Principle. How God can be *both* principle and person as intimated in his final vision of a human face in the three interlocking circles throws him into the despair of the geometrician trying vainly to square the circle. But in that moment of perplexity Dante's mind is struck by a lightning-like illumination that persuades his desire and will to unite with the Love that moves the whole Creation.

His journey then should be looked upon not only as a philanthropic venture in understanding, but also as the path of one living in the world whose way of self-finding is through relationships with others, cooperating with and helping them as well as receiving from them support and enlightenment.

That the combination of these two approaches makes the *Comedy* particularly relevant to our time appears most clearly in the anagogy. More and more individuals who are relatively free of the pressure of material needs choose some form of self-actualizing, self-developing activity through which they hope to acquire an enlarged sense of self, first perhaps more on the material level and later psychologically and spiritually. Depth psychology and spirituality are not separate realms: they touch and intermingle. There is a steady movement away from some traditional attitudes and beliefs which are felt increasingly as constricting and limiting; much of this endeavor is about getting to know and fulfill one's potentials. When this movement becomes more balanced by a growth of interest in, and love and compassion for, fellow humans, it begins to resemble Dante's journey through paradise. Then will the *Paradiso* be seen for what Dante intended it to be: a prophetic book about the future of humanity.

Notes

Introduction

1. *Dantis Alighieri epistolae, The Letters of Dante,* trans. and ed. Paget Toynbee. Oxford, 1920. Ep. X, 7, 8. ll 134ff. contains the most important statement on his use of the allegorical method in the *Comedy*. For the English translation see Appendix I. Although some scholars have questioned Dante's authorship of Letter X to Can Grande, I am no more willing to accept their arguments than I would credit some more or less distinguished playwright or nobleman with the plays of Shakespeare.

2. *Il Convivio*, ed. G. Busnelli and G. Vandelli, Vol. I of Dante's complete works, Florence, 1934. II. i, contains the second most important statement by Dante on allegory. For the English translation by P. H. Wicksteed see Appendix II.

3. William Blake, "A Vision of the Last Judgment," p. 87, in *Poetry and Prose of William Blake,* ed. Geoffrey Keynes. London, 1956.

4. *Ep.* X, 15.

5. *Ibid.*, 11.

6. *Toward a Psychology of Being*. New York, 1962, p. 35.

7. *De Monarchia*, Bk 3, Ch. XVI. ll 48–53.

8. *La Vita Nuova*, II. 16–60.

9. For different views about the roles of both Pope Celestine and Cardinal Benedetto Gaetani in the drama of the "gran rifiuto" see a compilation of articles and views edited by Charles T. Wood, *Philip the Fair and Boniface VIII.*, New York, 1967, esp. pp. 9–12, 18–28, 42–46.

10. On the entire influence of Joachim on Dante and his contemporaries see Marjorie Reeves, *Joachim of Fiore and the Prophetic Future*, New York, 1977,

first three chapters. See also Leone Tondelli, *Da Gioachino a Dante. Novi studi. Consensi e contrasti*. Torino, 1944. Also by the same author, *Il libro delle figure dell Abate Gioachino da Fiore*. Torino, 1953.

11. See Robert Hollander, *Allegory in Dante's Commedia*. Princeton, 1969, p. 55, *note*.

12. Reeves, pp. 64–66.

13. See "Note on Dante's Hell" in Temple Classics *Inferno*, p. 393.

14. Reeves, p. 24.

15. *Ibid.*, p. 5.

16. Francis Fergusson, *Dante*, New York, 1966, pp. 37–69 sheds more light on Dante's state of mind between the death of Beatrice and the decision to begin to write the *Commedia*.

17. *Convivio*, I. ii, 111.

18. For Dante's confession of his discomfiture at the hands of Amor see his epistle to the Marquis Moruello Malaspina. Ep. III. 2. in Temple Classics' *Latin Works of Dante*. "It chanced, then, that when I parted from the threshold of that court [the Malaspinas'] (for which I was afterwards to sigh) wherein, as you have often marked with wonder, I had leave to follow the offices of liberty, no sooner had I set my feet by the streams of the Arno, in security and carelessness, than straightaway a woman appeared to me, descending like a lightning flash, strangely harmonious with my condition both in character and in person. Oh, how was I struck dumb at her apparition! But my stupor yielded to the terror of the thunder that followed. For like as thunders straightway follow flashes from heaven, so when the flame of this beauty had appeared Love laid hold of me, terrible and imperious; raging moreover, like a lord banished from his fatherland returning after long exile to what is all his own! For he slew or banished or enchained all opposition in me. He slew that praiseworthy determination in the strength of which I held aloof from women, those instruments of his enchantment; and the unbroken meditations wherein I was pondering on things both of heaven and on earth, he banished as things suspected; and finally, that my soul might never again rebel against him, he chained my free will; so that I needs must turn not whither I would, but whither he wills. Love, therefore, reigns within me, and there is no power to oppose him." (Trans. P. H. Wicksteed.)

19. *VN*, XLIII.

20. See Charles Singleton, "Dante's Allegory" in *Speculum* XXV (1950) *passim*. Although I like Professor's Singleton's ingenious solution of attributing a historical/factual truth to Dante's account of the state of souls after death, which, according to the letter to Can Grande, is the subject of the poem on the literal level, I cannot convince myself that Dante himself would agree with such a view. The solution can be found, I suspect, in recognizing that the inspired creations of the imagination can have a truth of their own which is not subject to material proof, but can serve as a key to unlock deeper meanings. Seen from the material level, the story still counts as a *bella menzogna*, but

for the *intellectus spiritualis* it has an equal value to historical truth which, after all, focuses more on the outward appearances than on the inner meanings of events. Contrary to it, poetic truth, which the imagination conceives, is deeper and appeals directly to the spirit. Therefore the literal level of Dante's allegory cannot be used to prove which souls are in heaven, in purgatory, or in hell. Dante would not arrogate such knowledge to himself. Also, he would have no way of defending himself against charges of heresy if he were to abandon the convention of the beautiful lie. My conclusion is that his allegory in the *Comedy* is a combination of the allegory of the poets and of the theologians, where he is enabled, through the story about the state of souls, to point out the higher spiritual truths he wanted to teach allegorically as he once promised in the *Convivio*.

21. Fra Dolcino. From the gory battlefield of the sowers of discord in *Inf.* XXVIII, Mohammed, whom the Middle Ages regarded as an arch-schismatic, sends a message through Dante to Fra Dolcino, fanatical leader of the Apostolic Brethren sect, to stack up provisions in the hills around Novara because when the snow comes they might be forced to surrender to their enemies. A crusade was preached against the sect which was fighting to overthrow the Church hierarchy and restore the apostolic brotherhood of the earliest Christian churches. They were accused of practicing the community of goods and women. Fra Dolcino and his mistress Margaret of Trent were captured and burnt at Vercelli in 1307.

22. *Ep.* X, 19.

23. Cf. *Inferno* XXVIII 139–142 where the word *contrapasso* is used by Bertrand de Born who had put a wedge between Henry II of England and his son and now must carry his brain like a lantern, separated from his body. *Contrapasso*, then, is the lawful working out of divine justice where the punishment exactly fits the crime. There is, at least in the *Inferno* where forgiveness and mercy do not exist, an automatic working out of cause-and-effect, somewhat like the law of Karma in Indian religion and philosophy.

24. See Reeves, p. 7, diagram illustrating the Relationships of the Three Persons and the Unity of the Godhead.

25. *Ibid.*, p. 6.

26. John I, 8.

Chapter I

1. Dante seeks liberty when he sets foot upon the island of Purgatory. "Libertà va cercando . . ." *Purg.* I. 71.

2. "ch l' alta terra senza seme gitta." *Purg.* XXVIII. 69.

3. *VN*, XI.

4. Charles Williams calls Beatrice Dante's *knowing* in the great act of understanding where Dante is the knower and God the known. I agree, but would insist on knowing as νόησις, i.e., threefold knowledge which comes only in the fullness of experience.

5. The sphere of fire in Aristotelian physics was held to be the place to which, in accordance with its proper nature, all fire tended to rise.

6. When I analyze the poetic imagery I use terms provided by the literal reading of the text, so that the reference should be immediately apparent to the reader. For example, in the section dealing with images I often refer to Dante, whereas in the intepretation of the anagogical meaning I talk about "us," because in the anagogy all readers share the same essential humanity and all travel, in their individual ways, on the path toward being.

Chapter II

1. As Dante put it in the *Vita Nuova*: "The vital spirit which dwells in the most secret chamber of the heart began to tremble so mightily that it was horribly apparent in the least of my pulses, and trembling, it said these words: *Ecce Deus fortior me, qui veniens dominabitur mihi.*" II, 20–25.

2. *Cf.* Milton's concept of the fall in *Paradise Lost*. Milton says that when Adam allowed himself to be persuaded by Eve and ate of the fruit, he was passive where he should have been active. He took inordinate pleasure in his dearest possession, Eve, who, after all, was only a part of himself, taken out of his side. In his anxiety not to lose this pleasure he fell from the state that was properly his.

3. Luke XIX, 26.

4. John VIII, 32.

Chapter III

1. Action is a means of self-expression and self-finding. Everything that is wants to be itself; action brings us closer to ourselves and therefore clears our vision and fills us with real pleasure.

2. *De Mon.* I. Ch. XII; I. Ch .IV; I. Ch. XI.

3. *Ibid.*, I. Ch. III-IV.

Chapter IV

1. Perhaps this is indicated by the fact that the spirits here see God in a mirror only [IX. 61–62].

2. *Cf.* Blake's *Vision of the Last Judgment*, pp. 69–70, where he contrasts the world of (sexual) generation with the infinite and eternal world of the imagination. "There exist in that Eternal World the Permanent Realities of Every Thing which we see reflected in this Vegetable Glass of Nature."

Chapter V

1. I take *scorge* here to mean *illuminate*.

2. As Dante says elsewhere: "The speculative intellect by extension becomes the practical intellect, the end of which is *doing* and *making*. And I draw this distinction because there are things to be *done* which are regulated by political wisdom and things to be *made* which are regulated by art. But

they are all alike handmaids of speculation, as the supreme function for which the Prime Excellence brought the human race into being." *De Mon.* I. Ch. III.

3. Siger the heretic and St. Thomas the official philosopher of the Church dance next to one another in the same circle, one turning clockwise, the other counterclockwise, sounding together the harmony that comes from the coincidence of opposites.

4. Joachim of Fiore, whom Dante puts among the spirits in this heaven, had prophesied the coming of a new dispensation which he called the Age of the Holy Spirit. In this age the clerical order of the visible Church was to be reabsorbed into the spiritual Church. The prophecies of Joachim were widely circulated during the thirteenth century and were prefaced by a bold introduction from one of the Joachimite Franciscans, Fra Gherardo da Borgo San Donnino. The book as a whole was popularly known as the *Vangelo Eterno*, or the *Everlasting Gospel*, and it unfolded a philosophy of history that was resurrected in a somewhat different form by romantics like Blake, Novalis, Shelley, and even by Hegel. Fra Gherardo was, incidentally, one of the favorite mask-personalities of the youthful Stephen Dedalus as he read forgotten medieval texts in a Paris library.

5. *Purg.* I. 107.

6. If, as Dr. Edward Moore suggests, the whole passage might derive from a passage in Albertus Magnus' *Physics*, lib. ii. Tr. i. ch. 5, where Albertus quotes the doctrine of Hermes Trismegistus, the Neoplatonism is by no means fortuitous. In nature as an artist with a trembling hand we can distinctly recognize Plato's Demiurge, adopted by the gnostics as the imperfect creator of the material world.

7. The triple crown—crown and mitre in one—can be regarded as the symbol of the Age of the Holy Spirit in the Joachimist interpretation of history. What Virgil does for Dante in purgatory as he "crowns and mitres" the poet [*Purg.* XXVII. 140–142], mankind as a whole may attain when a certain general level of intellectual maturity will be reached.

Chapter VI

1. For the use of the word *figure* here see E. Auerbach's "Figura" in *Scenes from the Drama of European Literature*, New York, 1959, *passim*. Figuring in this sense means symbolizing a larger truth by an actual event or person.

2. Though Dante does not reveal the name of Cacciaguida until the end of the Canto, his identity in the anagogical sense is made clear by the first lines he utters in response to Dante's question.

3. Cacciaguida here relates the history of ancient Florence and its families. The fact that Beatrice stands a little apart—*un poco scevra*—during this recitation is, to me, an indication that it would be hazardous to seek a spiritual meaning in this historical narrative beyond the very general considerations given above.

4. Blake's penultimate spiritual state in his fourfold vision is the state of Beulah (meaning "married land") which leads, in his hierarchy of states, to Eden or Eternity.

5. Cf. Blake's "Little Black Boy":

> "Look on the rising sun—there God does live,
> And gives His light and gives His heat away . . . ."

6. Cf. Macbeth's reference to his soul as "mine eternal jewel" [Act II. Sc. 1]. Dante himself contrasts the work of nature with the superior work of the artisan in *Par.* XXIV. 101–102:

> l'opere seguite, a che natura
> non scaldò ferro mai, nè battè incude.

(the works that followed, for which nature never heated iron nor smote anvil).

7. *Cf.* Yeats's "Sailing to Byzantium":

> Once out of nature I shall never take
> My bodily form from any natural thing,
> But such a form as Grecian goldsmiths make
> Of hammered gold and gold enamelling . . . .

8. *Cf.* "La Geometria si muove intra due repugnanti ad essa, sicome tra il punto e l' cerchio (e dico cerchio largamente ogni ritondo, o corpo o superficie); chè, siccome dice Euclide, il punto è principio di quella, e, secondo ch' e' dice, il cerchio è perfettissima figura in quella, che conviene però aver ragione di fine. Sicchè tra il punto e l' cerchio, siccome tra principio e fine, si muove la Geometria." Dante, *Convivio*, II. Cap. 14.

Chapter VII

1. "M is the *central* letter of the Latin and Italian alphabet." Note in Temple Classics ed. of *Paradiso*, p. 226.

2. A good example of such an abuse in our own day is the way in which the leading powers of the world try to make the concept and the power of freedom serve their own ends. On the one side we see it being used to increase and safeguard material gain and on the other to extend political tyranny over others. Dante chose the papacy for an illustration, but the principle can be applied everywhere.

3. "Poets, or those who imagine and express this indestructible order, are not only the authors of language and of music . . . they are the institutors of laws, and the founders of civil society, and the inventors of the arts of life, and the teachers who draw into a certain propinquity with the beautiful and the true that partial apprehension of the agencies of the invisible world which is called religion." Shelley, *A Defence of Poetry*.

4. "A man may prepare himself by what is contained in natural reason for receiving faith. Wherefore it is said that if anyone born in barbarous nations

do what lieth in him, God will reveal to him what is necessary for salvation, either by inspiration, or by sending a teacher." St. Thomas Aquinas, quoted in a note of the Temple Classics ed. of the *Paradiso*, p. 254.

5. *Cf.* "I am certain of nothing but of the holiness of the Heart's affections and the truth of the Imagination . . . . Imagination may be compared to Adam's dream—he awoke and found it truth. . . . Imagination and its empyreal reflection is the same as human Life and its Spiritual repetition." From Keats's letter to Benjamin Bailey, November 22, 1817.

6. *Cf.*

> The soul recovers radical innocence
> And learns at last that it is self-delighting,
> Self-appeasing, self-affrighting,
> And that its own sweet will is Heaven's will.
> W. B. Yeats, "A Prayer for My Daughter"

7. "It was the Sun, then, that I meant when I spoke of that offspring which the Good has created in the visible world, to stand there in the same relation to vision and visible things as that which the Good itself bears in the intelligible world to intelligence and to intelligible objects." Plato, *The Republic*, Bk. VI. 508. Cornford's translation.

8. Dante never turns to Beatrice in the Heaven of Jupiter. He evidently expressed here his belief in salvation through justice alone, for, to him at least, justice included the three theological virtues necessary for salvation. See the curious line 15 in Canto XX and especially XX. 127–129.

9. *Cf.*

> "astra tenent caeleste solum formaeque deorum,
> cesserunt nitidis habitandae piscibus undae,
> terra feras cepit, volucres agitabilis aer."
> Ovid, *Metamorphoses*, Lib. I. 73–75.

10. For the peculiar aptness of this metaphor see Vernon's *Readings on the Paradiso*, Vol. II. p. 112, note.

11. All these signs have a fairly obvious meaning on the level of political (or social) allegory in the *Comedy*, but with that level I am not concerned here.

Chapter VIII

1. As a great visionary had put it: "Everything that lives is holy." (Blake, "A Song of Liberty.")

2. Although the vision presented here is, quite naturally, the image of the spiritual state of contemplative or visionary existence, another meaning is discernible behind the figure of the ladder upon which contemplative spirits are seen descending. The ladder and the moving lights on it seem to present the contemplative's understanding of the universe of time and space. All things insofar as they *are* are good; they form a ladder of gold upon which beings of a higher order, endowed with free will (here likened to the creatures of the air)

descend and ascend as they move away from, and again toward, being. Such a vision of the world's spiritual purpose and thus of its essence is completely innocent: even those who descend farthest from being are seen here as splendors undimmed and undarkened by evil. If, as Aquinas asserts, evil is nothingness, i.e., the lack of something that should be present, then, indeed, evil cannot dim the fire of the inmost spirit in any created being, though for eyes that themselves have been veiled by the fall it may seem to obscure this light.

Such a conception of the universe is implied in St. Paul's saying, "All that is made manifest is light" [Ephes. V. 13]. It was elaborated by Johannes Scotus Erigena: "Hinc est quod universalis hujus mundi fabrica maximum lumen fit, ex multis rerum puras species revelandas et contuendas mentis acie, divina gratia et rationis ope in corde fidelium sapientium cooperantibus" [*Hier. Coel.* I. 1; 129 D].

On the title page of Blake's illustrations to the *Book of Job*, angels are seen descending on one side and ascending again on the other. This movement is interpreted by J. H. Wicksteed as "symbolical of Experience, the process of the casting out of evil." See Wicksteed, *Blake's Vision of the Book of Job*, London, 1910. p. 47.

Keats's famous letter on the "Vale of Soul Making" reflects a somewhat similar concept of the role of the created world in the universal scheme. "The common cognomen of this world among the misguided and superstitious is a 'vale of tears' from which we are to be redeemed by a certain arbitrary interposition of God and taken to Heaven—What a little circumscribed straightened notion! Call the world if you Please 'The vale of Soul-making.' Then you will find out the *use of the world* [italics mine]. . . . I say '*Soul making*' Soul as distinguished from an Intelligence—There may be intelligences or sparks of divinity in millions—but they are not Souls till they acquire identities, till each one is personally itself. Intelligences are atoms of perception—they know and they see and they are pure, in short they are God—How then are Souls to be made? How then are these parts which are God to have identity given them—so as ever to possess a bliss peculiar to each one's individual existence? How, but by the medium of a world like this? This point I sincerely wish to consider because I think it is a grander system of salvation than the chrystiain (*sic*) religion—or rather it is a system of Spirit-creation— This is effected by three grand materials acting the one upon the other for a series of years. These three materials are the *Intelligence*—the *human heart* (as distinguished from Intelligence or Mind) and the *World* or *Elemental space* suited for the proper action of *Mind* and *Heart* on each other for the purpose of forming the *Soul* or *Intelligence destined To possess the sense of Identity.* . . . I will call the *World* a School instituted for the purpose of teaching little children to read—I will call the *human heart* the *horn Book* used in that School and I will call *the Child able to read, the Soul* made from that *school* and its *hornbook*. Do you not see how necessary a World of Pains and troubles is to school an Intelligence and make it a soul? A Place where the heart must feel and suffer in a thousand diverse ways! Not merely is the Heart a Hornbook, It is the Mind's Bible, it is the Mind's experience, it is the teat from which the Mind or Intelligence sucks its identity—. As various as the Lives of Men are— so various become their souls, and thus does God make individual beings, Souls, Identical Souls of the sparks of his own essence—This appears to me a faint sketch of a system of Salvation which does not affront our reason and humanity. . . . Seriously I think it probable that this System of Soul-making— may have been the Parent of all the more palpable and personal Schemes of Redemption, among the Zoroastrians the Christians and the Hindoos." From a letter to George and Georgiana Keats, 14. February - 3. May, 1819.

Another somewhat similar vision is concerned directly with Jacob's Ladder. I am thinking of Arnold Schoenberg's oratorio fragment of the same title. Here the composer represents the ascending and descending figures on the ladder as the stream of reincarnation which he sees as the process of humankind's development toward spiritual perfection.

3. Dante's pessimistic view of monasticism as an institutionalized form of the contemplative life comes from a profound insight. Monasticism may have been the only possible way for many to contemplation at one stage of mankind's development, but it suppresses too many creative forces and could never open up a way for those who would be otherwise drawn to a life of contemplation.

4. Seen in the context of the interpretation of the movement of the contemplatives given in note 2 in this chapter, their upward rush and disappearance as the final revelation given to Dante in the Heaven of Saturn may have another significance. If the ladder represents the world of time and space and the spirits moving upon it represent the entities endowed with free will as they separate themselves from their source, this last action would symbolize the redemption of all creation, the return of all free creatures to their Creator.

5. See *Convivio*, II. Cap. 5.

6. "Ode on a Grecian Urn."

Chapter IX

1. Symbolized for Dante by the sign of Gemini, under which he was born.

2. This accords with the popular belief that the dying or the newly dead contemplate their past as if it were played to them on a film, but going backwards from the moment of death.

3. *Cf.* Blake:

> As the Pilgrim passes while the Country
> permanent remains,
> So Men pass on, but States remain
> permanent for ever.
> *Jerusalem*, p. 73, ll.42–3.

4. Latona, Maia, and Dione were all Titanidae and Hyperion a Titan, member of the race of gods which governed the world in the Golden Age,

under Saturn, "*sotto cui giacque ogni malizia morta.*" To connect the Moon with Latona, her mother, and the Sun with Hyperion, his father, shows an intention to associate these two deities with original innocence. But this intention is revealed even more clearly by the use of their mothers' names for Venus and Mercury; sexual passion and thieving were too closely associated with these deities for them to be mentioned at this point in paradise.

5. Trivia is another name of Diana, the moon, as goddess of crossroads, of ways. The simile emphasizes Christ's power of guiding us to the right way.

6. For a similar experience in a different context I quote these lines from Wordsworth's *Prelude*:

> Imagination—here the Power so called
> Through sad incompetence of human speech,
> That awful Power rose from the mind's abyss
> Like an unfathered vapour that enwraps,
> At once, some lonely traveller. I was lost;
> Halted without an effort to break through;
> But to my conscious soul I now can say—
> 'I recognize thy glory'; in such strength
> Of usurpation, when the light of sense
> Goes out, but with a flash that has revealed
> The invisible world, doth greatness make abode,
> There harbours; whether we be young or old,
> Our destiny, our being's heart and home,
> Is with infinitude, and only there;
> With hope it is, hope that can never die,
> Effort, and expectation, and desire,
> And something evermore about to be.
>   Bk. VI. 595–608; Text of 1850 ed.

However different roads Dante and Wordsworth may have travelled in their pilgrimage toward being, the recognition that man has his true home in eternity and that he has a true self which is "evermore about to be" within him brings them very close to one another at this point.

7. Milton, *Comus*, l. 263.

8. St. Peter is the typical everyman of the Gospels. He has all the common virtues as well as the human frailties. He is the rock upon which the Church is founded.

9. Peter would have sunk into the stormy Sea of Galilee had Jesus not caught him by the hand.

10. Though on the literal level of the poem this passage obviously refers to the Old and New Testament, on the anagogical level which deals with spiritual truth in the widest sense, it means any inspired communication, whether written or oral, Christian or pagan, that serves as a foundation of liberating faith.

11. "If any of you want wisdom, let him ask of God, who giveth to all men abundantly, and upbraideth not; and it shall be given him." James, I. 5.

12. *Cf. Convivio*, II. Cap. I. 57–65. Against the slavery of Egypt.

13. They that be wise shall shine as the brightness of the firmament; and they that turn many to righteousness, as the stars for ever and ever." Dan. XII. 3. I quote from W. W. Vernon's *Readings on the Paradiso*, p. 256, note.

14. Shelley came to a similar conclusion:

> Mind from its object differs most in this:
> Evil from good; misery from happiness;
> The baser from the nobler; the impure
> And frail, from what is clear and must endure.
> If you divide suffering and dross, you may
> Diminish till it is consumed away;
> If you divide pleasure and love and thought,
> Each part exceeds the whole; and we know not
> How much, while any yet remains unshared,
> Of pleasure may be gained, of sorrow spared:
> *This truth is that deep well, whence sages draw*
> *The unenvied light of hope.* . . . [Italics mine.]
> *Epipsychidion*, 174–185.

15. "Behold, the husbandman waiteth for the precious fruit of the earth: patiently bearing till he receive the early and the late rain." James V, 7.

16. Dante uses an *indirect* reference to the resurrection of the body when he talks about the "double vestments" of Isaiah which he identifies with the "white robes" in the Book of Revelation. I think he uses this image because it suggests more and is less defined than the direct statement about the resurrection of the body in I.Cor.XV. The two vestments may be variously interpreted on different allegorical levels, whereas St. Paul's calling the resurrected body not a natural but a spiritual body would restrict interpretation.

17. Or the Eros of Freud.

18. To lines 124–126 the following passage from the *Convivio* supplies a comment: "Di tutti questi Ordini [i.e., the angelic orders] si perdono alquanti tosto che furon creati, forse in numero della decima parte; alla quale restaurare fu l' umana nature poi create." Bk. II. Cap. VI. According to W. W. Vernon, "the elect were exactly to fill up the gap caused by the fall of the rebel angels, the number which, though not known to us, is known to God." *Par*. II. p. 266, note.

19. *Cf. VN*, XI.

20. "For where your treasure is there is your heart also." Matt. VI,21.

21. The reference to St. Paul's loss of sight and his recovery of it is something of a spiritual milestone on the journey through paradise. He, too, was blinded by perfect love on the road to Damascus and when he regained his vision he, too, was a changed man.

22. *Cf.* "The being which belongs to every essent whatsoever, and which is thus dispersed among all that is most current and familiar, is more unique than all else." M. Heidegger, *An Introduction to Metaphysics*. New Haven, 1959. p. 79.

23. Thus Socrates was right when he asserted that it was enough to know the good in order to follow it; this is true if by *knowing* we mean not mere awareness, or logical proof, but vision.

24. Adam. Both Blake and Joyce have conceived him as one giant form, the entire human race in One Man who has fallen asleep and all human history is his dream. We are his *disiecta membra*, each bound in his private dream and waiting, like Stephen Dedalus, to awake from the nightmare of our separateness.

25. *Cf.* Eve's adoration of the tree after tasting its fruit, in *Paradise Lost*:

> "O sovran, virtuous, precious of all trees
> In Paradise, of operation blest
> To sapience, hitherto obscured, infamed,
> And thy fair fruit let hang, as to no end
> Created; but henceforth my early care,
> Not without song, each morning, and due praise,
> Shall tend thee, and the fertile burden ease
> Of thy full branches offered free to all;
> Till dieted by thee I grow mature
> In knowledge as the gods who all things know;
> Though others envy what they cannot give;
> For had the gift been theirs, it had not here
> Thus grown."
>
> Bk. IX. 795–807.

Eve, misled by the pleasure of appearance, attributes to appearance the power of giving wisdom which belongs exclusively to being. She thinks the tree can "mature" her while in reality only the creator of the tree can do that. Thus she falls into the worship of appearance and declares that being is powerless: "Though others envy what they *cannot give*."

26. See the use of *spirare* and *sospirar* in a similar way to indicate spiritual birth in the *VN*.

27. *Cf.* "Men are admitted into Heaven not because they have curbed & govern'd their Passions or have No Passions, but because they have Cultivated their Understandings. The Treasures of Heaven are not Negations of Passion, but Realities of Intellect, from which all the Passions Emanate Uncurbed in their Eternal Glory." W. Blake, *A Vision of the Last Judgment*, p. 89. Also Blake's description of his "Eden, the land of life":

> Our wars are wars of life, & wounds of love
> With intellectual spears, & long winged arrows of
>   thought.
> Mutual in one another's love and wrath all renewing
> We live as One Man. . . .
>
> *Jerusalem*, p. 38, 14–17.

Chapter X

1. Between Dante's first backward glimpse [XXII. 124–154] and the second [XXVII. 79–87] the black shadow of night has crept over the face of the earth.

I take *"primo aspetto"* as referring to Dante's first glimpse of the earth in retrospect. The time that elapses between the first and the second earth-view is six hours, the same that Adam spent in paradise between his creation and expulsion. Thus if we take "the beautiful daughter of him who brings morning and leaves evening" [XXVII. 137–138] to be the earth on the literal level, she becomes humanity on the allegorical level [see *De Mon.* Bk. I. Ch. IX. 6–7], and human nature [as E. Moore says in his *Studies in Dante*, Vol. I. pp. 140–141] in the anagogical interpretation. But if we take the beautiful daughter of the sun to be the moon as some commentators suggest, the identification with human nature on the anagogical plane is again possible if we remember that in Canto II the spotted surface of the moon was taken to represent human nature as created in its original innocence.

2. In *Convivio* II. Cap. 15, the Primum Mobile is called the Heaven of Moral Philosophy, but here it is unmistakably the Heaven of Metaphysics. For it is Metaphysics, the science of pure being, that is expounded here.

3. *Sustanzie che t' appaion tonde* [75] i.e., perfect beings who have completely realized their innate potentialities and can therefore be called substances. See also *Purg.* XXX. 101.

4. An interesting application of the Gospel: "The first shall be the last and the last shall be first."

5. The following quotation might help to bring out the meaning of this passage: "*Doxa* means fame and glory. In Hellenistic theology and in the New Testament *doxa theou*, gloria Dei, is God's grandeur. To glorify, to attribute regard to, and to disclose regard means in Greek: to place in the light and thus endow with permanence, being. For the Greeks glory was not something additional which one might or might not obtain; it was the mode of the highest being." M. Heidegger, *An Introduction to Metaphysics*. New Haven, 1959. p. 103. Dante expresses the same sense of the identity of being and light—which Heidegger takes to be a characteristically Greek notion—in the opening lines of the *Paradiso*:

> La gloria di colui che tutto move
> per l' universo penetra, e risplende
> in una parte più, e meno altrove.

6. It might be interesting to consider that while Dante gives us an idea of the quality of the unfallen state by using the image of a transparent medium in which the light spreads instantaneously and without obstruction, Blake calls Satan, the epitome of fallen being, the "limit of opacity":

> There is a limit of Opakeness and a limit of
>   Contraction
> In every Individual Man, and the limit of Opakeness
> Is named Satan, and the limit of Contraction is named
> Adam.
>   *Jerusalem*, p. 42. 29–31.

7. *Turbò il suggetto dei vostri elementi* [51] reminds me of some gnostic speculations. According to Irenaeus [*Adv. Haer.* I. 29] the "gnostics" believed that Sophia had cast herself into the *primal substratum of matter*. In the Valentinian gnosis matter is not originally separated from the higher celestial world. The fall or *disturbance* is accomplished within the celestial world, and the material world first comes into existence through the fall. In this Canto lines 34–36 would suggest a similar idea: in the beginning were pure potentiality and pure act, but they were twisted together through some disturbance.

8. Though Dante condemns Parmenides, whom he had not read, in *Par.* XIII. 125 as a false reasoner, he does so only because he takes over Aristotle's opinion in the *De Sophisticis Elenchis* [see *De Mon.* Bk. III. Ch. IV]. It is therefore somewhat ironical that this terzina strangely echoes Parmenides' insistence that man should walk the path of being only and avoid the path of non-being ("for it is not possible for what is nothing, to be") and the path of appearance. On the path of appearance, as Heidegger says in his commentary on Parmenides' poem, "only opinions prevail. Men slide back and forth from one opinion to another. They mix being and appearance. This path is perpetually travelled and in it men lose themselves altogether." Heidegger, p. 112.

9. In scholastic angelology this truth was expressed by asserting that each angel was a separate species in itself. Since species are more different from one another than individuals, angels possessed a greater degree of uniqueness, being at the same time more universal in their nature, since the concept of species is more universal than that of the individual.

10. Though only three of them were mortal women; Leto was a goddess herself.

Chapter XI

1. Dante shared the medieval belief that all stars receive their light from the sun.

2. Though Dante does not interpret these images which he calls the "shadowy prefaces" of the truth, we can meditate upon their significance. They obviously represent life in ultimate reality and therefore I would suggest that the sparks arising from and plunging into the river of light are created entities who are absorbed in their contemplation of being itself and emerge from this state only to spend the love they gained through their vision upon other created beings. When they have expressed in loving acts the understanding which they gained in contemplation, they are absorbed once more in their vision. To suggest time sequence in this process is, of course, very much out of place; but our language to which we are necessarily restricted is itself only a very "shadowy preface" of the things of eternity.

3. *Cf.* "As newborn babes desire the rational milk without guile, that thereby you may grow unto salvation." I. Peter, II. 2. Dante's simile throws an interesting light upon this somewhat obscure passage.

4. δοχα θεου—Gloria Dei.

5. Dante, in accordance with the Ptolemaic system, saw the limit of the determinism, that is an aspect of matter, in the Primum Mobile, the widest outer sphere of a universe of concentric spheres. Beyond that fastest circling sphere nothing was determined; the Empyrean was itself the perfect freedom of the spirit. The free "order" of the Empyrean reflected most in the swiftest and largest physical sphere on which it bordered. Going downward from sphere to sphere freedom grew less and less, until we reached Lucifer in the center of the determined world, frozen in ice, *da tutti i pesi del mondo costretto*. Today, speculating along similar lines, we might see the limit of determinism not in the largest but in the smallest unit of the physical world, where Heisenberg's principle of indeterminacy begins to operate. There we seem to reach the realm of freedom which Dante and his contemporaries put beyond the most distant stars.

6. The use of the word *ritorno* is somewhat perplexing here if we recall the doctrine of the soul's creation in *Purg.* XXV. 67–75, which is in accordance with the teachings of the Church. The soul is created by God when the brain of the embryo is complete. Then:

> Lo motor primo a lui si volge lieto
> Sopra tanta arte di natura, e spira
> *Spirito nuovo* di virtù repleto [italics mine]
>
> Che ciò che trova attivo quivi tira
> in sua sustanzia, e fassi un alma sola,
> che vive e sente e sè in sè rigira.
>
> [70–75]

(The First Mover turns him to it, rejoicing over such handiwork of nature, and breathes into it a new spirit with virtue filled, which draws into its substance that which it finds active there, and becomes one single soul, that lives, and feels, and turns round upon itself.)

Dante here says that each individual's soul is created when he is born by a special act of God. In any case no soul can possibly *return* to heaven since it had never been there. We could, of course, say that when God creates the soul, the soul comes from Him and when it gains heaven it returns. But this is to equate God and heaven which Dante certainly does not do in his description of the Empyrean.

Though our main concern is not to find out what Dante's own beliefs were, we might remember Bruno Nardi's conclusion about the role of the Empyrean in the *Comedy*. "L'Empireo, in Dante, coincide coll' anima del mondo dei neo-platonici, ed è anello di congiunzione fra Dio e il mondo sensibile." *Saggi di filosofia dantesca*, Milano, 1930. p. 189.

How much we may accept the doctrine given in the *Purgatorio* as Dante's own belief is another question. The verses quoted above are spoken by Statius, newly liberated from purgatory (symbolizing perhaps Christian Reason against Virgil's unbaptized Reason) who has not yet reached paradise and obviously has much to learn.

A possible solution seems to be—if we must find a "source" or an "influence"—that we meet here a trace of the influence of Scotus Erigena, whose doctrine on the return of the soul to God might have made an impression on Dante.

7. St. Bernard of Clairvaux—the figure of intuition—was a speculative mystic who called God the *causal being* of all that is. He taught that man attains ultimate knowledge when in ecstasy his soul is united to God and enjoys deification. To reach this union man has to ascend the steps of humility and truth and unite his will with God's. See E. Gilson, *History of Christian Philosophy in the Middle Ages*. New York, 1955. pp. 164–167, and *The Mystical Theology of St. Bernard*, London, 1940.

8. *Cf.* these lines from the last scene of Goethe's *Faust*:

> Höchste Herrscherin der Welt,
> Lasse mich im blauen,
> Ausgespannten Himmelszelt
> Dein Geheimnis schauen!
> Billige, was des Mannes Brust
> Ernst und zart beweget
> Und mit heiliger Liebeslust
> Dir entgegenträget.

9. Rachel gazing into her mirror [*Purg.* XXVII. 104–108] typifies the same attitude beside representing allegorically the contemplative life. Though Dante does not describe the face of St. Anne, we know her expression from Leonardo's picture in the Louvre.

10. Truth in the literal sense of ἀλήθεια.

11. *Cf.* the last lines in Goethe's *Faust*:

> Alles Vergängliche
> Ist nur ein Gleichnis;
> Das Unzulängliche,
> Hier wirds Ereignis;
> Das Unbeschreibliche,
> Hier ists getan;
> Das Ewig-Weibliche
> Zieht uns hinan.

12. Hölderlin, who of all modern minds was perhaps closest to being, lacked the saving influence of the Eternal Feminine after he had lost his Diotima. Without her to anchor his affections, Hölderlin was completely overpowered by being and never found his way back to the human world.

13. Vision is the full perception of reality which we, in our limited condition, cannot retain. Speech and memory are merely imperfect channels for Platonic recollection. Dante says here that our closest approximation to the vision is not in speech or memory, both of which are under the control of reason, but in *feeling*. Proust, with his method of evoking the essence of the past by feeling linked to sense experience, might agree.

14. *Cf.*

> Was it vision, or a waking dream?
> Fled is that music:—Do I wake or sleep?
> Keats: "Ode to A Nightingale."

But where Keats is unsure of the reality of his vision, Dante is supremely certain of his.

15. *Cf.* Proclus' saying that the movement of life is toward the good, of thought toward being. Dante says here that the ultimate aims of intellect and will are reached together in the union with being.

Chapter XII

1. C. G. Jung, *The Archetypes and the Collective Unconscious*. Bollingen Series, New York, 1959. pp. 21–22.

2. Nature here means the operation of the moving heavens which stamp human lives with their influences.

3. See *Saggi di filosofia dantesca*. Milano, 1930. pp. 155–185.

4. As M. Asin tries to prove without much success in his *Islam and the Divine Comedy* (trans. by H. Sunderland). London, 1926.

5. E. Gilson, *History of Christian Philosophy in the Middle Ages*. New York, 1955. p. 84.

6. Nesca A. Robb, *Neoplatonism of the Italian Renaissance*. London, 1935. pp. 135–141.

7. Robb, pp. 136–161.

Appendix I

This is an earlier statement Dante makes in *Convivio* II. i. about the technique of allegory as he meant to use it in interpreting his Canzoni in the *Convivio*:

I say that, as was told in the first chapter, this exposition must be both literal and allegorical; and that this may be understood it should be known that writings may be taken and should be expounded chiefly in four senses. The first is called the literal, and the second is called the allegorical, and is the one that hides itself under the mantle of these tales, and is a truth hidden under beauteous fiction. As when Ovid says that Orpheus with his lyre made wild beasts tame and made trees and rocks approach him; which would say that the wise man with the instrument of his voice makes cruel hearts tender and humble; and moveth to his will such as have [not] the life of science and of art; for they that have not the rational life are as good as stones. And why this way of hiding was devised by the sages will be shown in the last treatise but one. It is true that the theologians take this sense otherwise than the poets do, but since it is my purpose here to follow the method of the poets I shall take the allegorical sense after the use of the poets.

The third sense is called moral, and this is the one that lecturers should go intently noting throughout the scriptures for their own behoof and that of their disciples. Thus we may note in the Gospel, when Christ ascended the mountain for the transfiguration, that of the twelve apostles he took with him but three; wherein the moral may be understood that in the most secret things we should have but few companions.

The fourth sense is called the anagogical, that is to say "above the sense": and this is when a scripture is spiritually expounded which even in the literal sense, by the very things it signifies, signifies again some portion of the supernal things of eternal glory; as may be seen in that song of the prophet which saith that when the people of Israel came out of Egypt, Judea was made holy and free. Which although it be manifestly true according to the letter is none the less true in its spiritual intention; to wit, that when the soul goeth forth out of sin, it is made holy and free in its power.

Appendix II

Dante is expounding to Can Grande how his poem should be understood:

> For elucidation, therefore, of what we have to say, it must be understood that the meaning of this work is not of one kind only; rather the work may be described as "polysemous," that is, having several meanings; for the first meaning is that which is conveyed by the letter, and the next is that which is conveyed by what the letter signifies; the former of which is called literal, while the latter is called allegorical, or mystical. And for the better illustration of this method of exposition we may apply it to the following verses: "When Israel went out of Egypt, the house of Jacob from a people of strange language; Judah was his sanctuary, and Israel his dominion." For if we consider the letter alone, the thing signified to us is the going out of the children of Israel from Egypt in the time of Moses; if the allegory, our redemption through Christ is signified; if the moral sense, the conversion of the soul from the sorrow and misery of sin to a state of grace is signified; and if the anagogical, the passing of the sanctified soul from the bondage of the corruption of this world to the liberty of everlasting glory is signified. And although these mystical meanings are called by various names, they may one and all in a general sense be termed allegorical, inasmuch as they are different (*diversi*) from the literal or historical; for the word "allegory" is so called from the Greek *alleon*, which in Latin is *alienum* (strange) or *diversum* (different).

> This being understood, it is clear that the subject, with regard to which the alternative meanings are brought into play, must be twofold. And therefore the subject of this work must be considered in the first place from the point

of view of the literal meaning, and next from that of the allegorical interpretation. The subject, then, of the whole work, taken in the literal sense only,
is the state of souls after death, pure and simple. For on and about that the
argument of the whole work turns. If, however, the work be regarded from
the allegorical point of view, the subject is man according as by his merits
or demerits in the exercise of his free will he is deserving of reward or
punishment by justice.

Select Bibliography

I. Works

The Vita Nuova and Canzoniere, Temple Classics. London, 1948.

The Inferno, Temple Classics. London, 1936.

The Purgatorio, Temple Classics, London, 1937.

The Paradiso, Temple Classics. London, 1954.

A Translation of the Latin Works of Dante, Temple Classics. London, 1904.

Il Convivio, ed. G. Busnelli and G. Vandelli. Florence, 1934.

Dantis Alighieri Epistolae, *The Letters of Dante*, trans. and ed. Paget Toynbee. Oxford, 1920.

The Paradiso, trans., with a Commentary, by Charles Singleton. Princeton, N.J., 1977.

Tutte le opere nuovamente rivedute del testo da Dr. E. Moore. Oxford, 1894.

La Divina Commedia di Dante Alighieri, ed. C. H. Grandgent. Boston and New York, 1933.

II. Historical and Critical Works

Auerbach, Erich. *Dante, Poet of the Secular World*, trans. Ralph Mannheim. Chicago, 1961.

―――. "Figura" in *Scenes from the Drama of European Literature*. New York, 1959.

223

224 BIBLIOGRAPHY

Barbi, Michele. *Life of Dante*, trans. P. G. Ruggiers. Berkeley and Los Angeles, 1954 and 1960.

Bergin, Thomas G. *Dante*: New York, 1965, Boston, 1965.

———. ed. *From Time to Eternity*: *Essays on Dante's Divine Comedy*. New Haven, 1967.

Boccaccio, Giovanni, and Leonardo Bruni Aretino. *The Earliest Lives of Dante* ("Milestones of Thought"). New York, 1963, 1965.

Brandeis, Irma. *The Ladder of Vision*: *A Study of Dante's Comedy*. London, 1960, New York, 1961.

———. ed. *Discussions of the "Divine Comedy."* Boston, 1961.

Carroll, J. S. *Exiles of Eternity*: *An Exposition of Dante's Inferno*. 2d ed., 1904; *Prisoners of Hope*: *An Exposition of Dante's Purgatorio*, 1906; and *In Patria*: *An Exposition of Dante's Paradiso*, 1911. London.

Cosmo, Umberto. "Rassegna dantesca," *Giornale storico della letteratura Italiana*, LXIII (1914) pp. 362 sq.: L'ultima ascesa, Chaps. 2, 19, 20, 21.

———. *A Handbook to Dante Studies*. New York, 1947.

Eliot, T. S. *Dante*. London, 1929. Also reprinted in his *Selected Essays*, New York, 1932.

Fergusson, Francis. *Dante's Drama of the Mind*: *A Modern Reading of the "Purgatorio."* Princeton, 1953.

———. *Dante*. New York, 1966.

Flamini, Francesco. *Introduction to the Study of the Divine Comedy*, trans. Freeman M. Josselyn. Boston, 1910.

Freccero, John, ed. Dante: *A Collection of Critical Essays*. Englewood Cliffs, 1965.

Gardner, E. G. *Dante's Ten Heavens*: *A Study of the Paradiso*. New York, 1900.

Gilson, Etienne. *Dante the Philosopher*, trans. David Moore. New York, 1949. Paperback reprint as *Dante and Philosophy,* New York, 1963.

———. *History of Christian Philosophy in the Middle Ages*. New York, 1955.

———. *The Mystical Theology of St. Bernard*. London, 1940.

Hollander, Robert. *Allegory in Dante's Commedia*. Princeton, 1969.

Mazzeo, Joseph Anthony. *Medieval Cultural Tradition in Dante's "Comedy."* Ithaca, 1960.

———. *Structure and Thought in the Paradiso*. New York, 1958.

Moore, E. *Studies in Dante*, Vol. I. pp. 140–141. Oxford, 1889.

Musa, Mark, ed. *Essays on Dante*. Bloomington, 1964.

Nardi, Bruno. *Saggi di filosofia dantesca*. Milano, 1930.

Passerin D'Entrèves, A. *Dante as a Political Thinker*. Oxford, 1962.

Reade, W. H. V. *The Moral System of Dante's Inferno*. Oxford, 1909.

Reeves, Marjorie. *Joachim of Fiore and the Prophetic Future*. New York, 1977.

Robb, Nesca A. *Neoplatonism of the Italian Renaissance*. London, 1935.

Santayana, George. *Three Philosophical Poets: Lucretius, Dante, Goethe*. Garden City, N.Y., 1953. Originally published in 1910 by Harvard University Press.

Sayers, Dorothy L. *Further Papers on Dante*. London, 1957. Also, New York, 1957.

―――. *Introductory Papers on Dante*. London, 1954. Also, New York, 1954.

Singleton, Charles. "Dante's Allegory." *Speculum* XXV (1950).

―――. "The Pattern of the Center" in *Dante Studies I—Commedia: Elements of Structure*. Cambridge, Mass., 1954.

Stambler, Bernard. *Dante's Other World: The Purgatorio as Guide to the "Divine Comedy."* New York, 1957.

Tondelli, Leone. *Da Gioachino a Dante*. Torino, 1944.

―――. *Il libro delle figure dell Abate Gioachino da Fiore*. Torino, 1953.

Toynbee, Paget. *Dante Alighieri: His Life and Works*. Edited, with an Introduction, Notes, and Bibliography by Charles Singleton. New York, 1965.

―――. *A Dictionary of Proper Names and Notable Matters in the Works of Dante*. Oxford, 1898.

Vernon, W. W. *Readings on the Paradiso*, Vols. I and II. London, 1900–1909.

Vossler, Karl. *Mediaeval Culture: An Introduction to Dante and His Times*. Trans. W. C. Lawton. New York, 1929 and 1958.

Whitfield, John H. *Dante and Virgil*. Oxford, 1949.

Wicksteed, P. H. *From Vita Nuova to Paradiso*. New York, 1922.

Williams, Charles. *The Figure of Beatrice*. New York, 1961.

Wood, Charles T. *Philip the Fair and Boniface VIII*. New York, 1967.

Index